UNTIL WE MEET AGAIN

UNTIL WE MEET AGAIN

A true story of love and war, separation and reunion

Michael Korenblit and Kathleen Janger

G. P. Putnam's Sons
New York

Library of Congress Cataloging in Publication Data

Korenblit, Michael.
    Until we meet again.
    1. Holocaust, Jewish (1939-1945)—Poland—Hrubieszów—
Biography. 2. Jews—Poland—Hrubieszów—Persecutions.
3. Korenblit, Meyer. 4. Korenblit, Manya. 5. Nagel-
sztajn, Chaim. 6. Hrubieszów (Poland)—Ethnic relations.
I. Janger, Kathleen. II. Title.
D810.J4K682 1983   940.53'15'0392404384   [B]   82-24148
ISBN 0-399-12776-3

Printed in the United States of America

Acknowledgments

The staff and associates of the Close Up Foundation, who put their energy and their hearts at our disposal—especially for Mike's pressure-free leave of absence; Joyce Golding, for being our friend; our editor, Chris Schillig, for being able to see through forests and around corners; our agent, Ann Buchwald, who took us on when we only had one miracle to write about, who celebrated the second, and whose humor and encouragement spurred us on; Chaim, for giving us all hope; Meyer and Manya, who did everything possible to help us write their story, especially for having the courage to relive it.

—Mike Korenblit and Kathie Janger

Shahnaz Mehta, whose support and enthusiasm are greatly appreciated; Vikki Bravo Brener, who gave me advice and encouragement when they were needed the most; my wife, Joan, who is as much a part of this book as I am, an inspiration who was always there for me.

—M.K.

My husband Steve; my children Jay and Andrea, for somehow metabolizing their mother's erratic attention and scantier meals; my daughter Margi, for doing without care packages from home and for being quick to help; my grandmother Sweet Pauli, for hurting when I hurt, and for all the days I was too busy to talk; my husband's parents, the champions of SOS; Joan Korenblit, for having the idea in the first place and for her constancy; and my mother, for reasons I am still discovering.

—K.J.

Dedication

To Adam, Andrea, Claire, Gemma, Jay, Jim, Joshua, Kimberly, Lianne, Luke, Margi, Michelle, Paul, Sarah, Todd, and children everywhere: May you make—and be—friends like Josef Wisniewski, John Salki, and Franiek Gorski.

The Nagelsztajn and Korenblit Families

The Nagelsztajns

Shlomo, 48*
Mincha, 44
    (Ely, killed in 1940 at age 21)
    Manya, 17
    Gittel, 16
    Chaim, 14
    Joshua, 12
    Letty, 10
    Pola, 8
    (Aunt Zlaty, killed in 1941 at age 57)

The Korenblits

Avrum, 43
Malka, 43
    Shuyl, 22
    Motl, 19
    Meyer, 17
    Toba, 14
    Minka, 11
    Cyvia, 8

*Age in 1942.

UNTIL WE MEET AGAIN

Prologue

January 25, 1982
British Embassy
Washington, D.C.

Mike Korenblit was holding the last Scottish telephone directory in his lap. He flipped through the pages as quickly as he could, looking for where the M's stopped and the N's started. Spread out all over the floor at his feet were another twenty directories. Some of them were open, others had paper sticking out of them, marking a place. He had carefully gone through page after page, his finger and eyes moving together slowly down each column. N-a-g-e-l, N-e-g-e-l, N-i-g-e-l, N-o-g-e-l. With every other directory came another lit cigarette. The ashtray next to his chair began to fill. He had come to the embassy so sure he'd be able to trace the name, but there had been nothing even similar to the correct spelling. Maybe he was hoping for too much; after all, each had thought the other dead for thirty-nine years. No, he thought, we're too close, it has to be here.

He fanned through the pages so quickly he was at the P's. He turned back. One more time his finger started down the page. There wasn't a single N-a-g in this directory. He tossed it down to the floor to join the others that had given him so much hope only an hour ago.

Why doesn't Neil call back? he thought. How long does it take to look up one name in just one city directory in England? Oh,

11

God, please let it be Newcastle. He didn't know where else to look.

Mike bent over and retrieved a few of the phone books. A third time couldn't hurt; maybe he had just missed it. He looked up from his lapful of telephone books to see Neil Matthews coming down the stairs. The embassy official was balancing an open directory across the palm of his left hand.

"You found it!" Mike shouted, startling the small group of security guards and visitors in the adjacent reception area of the embassy. The phone books cascaded to the floor as Mike leaped out of his chair and made his way to Neil's side. His eyes drank in the listing marked by Neil's pointing forefinger.

"That's it!" yelled Mike, squeezing Neil's arm. "That's it!"

"The spelling's a little different," cautioned Neil, "but it is the Newcastle telephone directory. Here, copy the listing down—"

"The phone number—all I need is the phone number," said Mike, his shaky hands fumbling for paper and pen.

"Now, calm down," said Neil, grinning. "Perhaps you should write down the address as well."

"Yes, yes—all right; here, I have my notebook—a table—I need a table to write on."

"Just over here, Mike, this will do," said Neil, guiding Mike to a stand near the pay telephone.

"I have to call him," said Mike, trying to make his fingers copy the address. "Can I call from here?"

"Yes, of course," Neil began.

"No! I can't call from here—if it doesn't go through right away, I'll have to wait here. I can't wait here. I'll go back to my office and call from there. Yes, that's what I'll do. My wife! I have to call my wife," Mike ranted.

"Yes, fine—the phone is just there."

"Thank you, Neil," said Mike, pumping the Englishman's hand, "thank you!"

"Not at all, Mike. Good luck. I'm very happy for you."

"Thank you for everything!" Mike bubbled, grabbing Neil's hand again. "Neil, the phone books . . ." said Mike, pointing at the mess near the chair.

"Never mind that, Mike," said Neil, holding up a hand to protest. "I'll take care of that later." Then he climbed the stairs to his office.

Mike reached into his pants pocket to find change for a phone call. But his nervousness sent the coins clattering across the floor. Stooping down, he quickly spotted a nickel and a dime, dropped them into the slot, misdialed, then dialed again. The phone rang twice.

"Hello?"

"Joan! I found him! I've got his phone number!"

"I *knew* you would," said Joan. "Where is he?"

"Newcastle—he lives in Newcastle, England."

"Well, call him!"

"I will, I will, but I'll do it from the office. It's going to be a shock, Joan, maybe I should wait and get my thoughts together. I feel kind of tingly all over—excited, but scared. Maybe he has a bad heart or something."

"Mike, you have to call him right away!"

"Okay, you're right. I'll go back to the office and call him from there—sometimes you can't get a connection immediately."

"But call me back as soon as you've spoken with him—as soon as you hang up."

"I will, I promise. Joan, I found him!"

"I love you, Mike."

"I love you, too."

Mike replaced the receiver and bent over to gather the coins on the floor. He dropped the notebook into his knapsack and hurried to the door, calling out more thank-yous to the amused guards. His cheeks hurt from the wide grin frozen on his face. He exited the stately building and headed across icy mounds of packed snow toward his car. The next thing he knew, his feet flew out from under him and down he went on the cold ground.

"Goddammit!" he yelled to no one.

He climbed into his car and drove as quickly as he could to his office at the Close Up Foundation in Arlington, Virginia, encountering every possible red light and casual driver en route. It seemed like half a lifetime before he reached the Foundation's fifteenth-floor headquarters, where for almost nine years he had participated in Close Up's government studies program by working with high school students and teachers from all over the country. He threw off his coat, fumbled for his notebook in the knapsack, and walked down the hall to find Kathie Janger. He had to share this with Kathie, too—they had been working on the book, living and reliving the story for a year and a half; he wanted her with him when he made the call.

Mike walked around a partition. Damn, wouldn't you know it, she was on the phone. He paced back and forth in front of her, clutching the notebook and making little "Hang up!" gestures. Come on, Kathie, hang that thing up before I rip it out of the wall! Why was she taking so long? He walked away, back up the hall. Finally she appeared and followed him into his office.

He showed her the notebook where he had written: Nagelsztajn, C. She looked at him and put one hand over her mouth.

"I'm going to call him right now," said Mike, closing the door.

"Oh, Mike," said Kathie. "Oh, my God!" She reached for one of his cigarettes and lit it with shaking hands.

"Operator, I would like to place an international-credit-card call, please."

"For what country?" came the response.

"England, I'm calling Newcastle, England," said Mike, giving the number.

"I can do that for you," said the operator. "One moment, please."

"It's ringing," Mike said to Kathie, and crossed his fingers.

"Hello?" A woman's voice. Mike froze. How could it go through so quickly? Why didn't the operator say something? Was it Newcastle? What the hell was happening? He had expected an exasperating delay—at least a couple of hours or more. Surely it couldn't happen this fast. But he had to say something; they might hang up.

"Uh, hello?" he stammered, "is this Newcastle?"

"Yes," said the woman.

His carefully constructed thoughts of how to ease into the conversation came apart. Better to plunge right in.

"Is this the residence of C. Nagelsztajn?" asked Mike.

"Yes, it is," said the woman.

"Does the C stand for Chaim?" asked Mike.

"Yes," she said.

Kathie's face was intense. She couldn't hear the answers, but she hung on each new question, each inflection, and her mind raced ahead, conjuring up the next dialogue, linking the slim possibility of a miraculous discovery to reality. Her shiny eyes turned from anxiety to hope.

"Is Chaim Nagelsztajn from Hrubieszow, Poland?" asked Mike.

"Yes, he is," said the woman, only now there was a slight question, a hint of uncertainty in her voice. "He is right here, let me call him to the phone."

Mike heard the woman call out, "Harry, Harry!" Harry! Had he heard that right? Not Harry, Chaim! I want Chaim! Nothing to do but wait a few more moments. My God, she knew Hrubieszow—that can't be coincidence. What the hell is she saying to him? Did I sound like some kind of a nut? Come on, Harry—be Chaim!

"Hello?"

"Is this Chaim Nagelsztajn?" asked Mike.

"Yes, yes, what is it?"

"I think you had better sit down, because what I'm going to say will shock you."

Slowly the tears made their way down Kathie's cheeks.

"My name is Mike Korenblit. My mother is Manya."

"Who? I don't understand," said Chaim.

"My mother is Manya."

"I'm sorry, but I don't know what you mean."

Oh, God, there couldn't be a mistake—it wouldn't be fair. Got to keep talking.

"Was your father's name Shlomo?"

A noticeable pause was followed by: "Yes, my father was Shlomo."

"And your mother was Mincha?"

"Mincha? Yes, my mother was Mincha."

"And you had a sister, Manya."

"Manya? No, I had a brother Ely, another brother Joshua, a sister Gittel, a sister Matl—"

"Matl! Yes, that's her Polish name—in America we call her Manya!"

"But no, she's . . . That's not possible."

"Chaim, listen to me, do you remember Meyer Korenblit?"

"Korenblit?"

"Yes, Meyer Korenblit—as a boy he came to your house to see your sister before the war, Chaim."

"Meyer—you mean Mayorek?"

"Mayorek! Yes! Mayorek is my father. He's alive—"

"Mayorek's alive?"

"Yes, he's alive. He and Matl are married. They live in Oklahoma!"

"Matl? She's alive?"

"Yes, Chaim, my mother is your sister!"

1

Hrubieszow, Poland
October 27, 1942

It was half-past five in the morning when Avrum Korenblit quietly awakened his son.

"Meyer," he whispered, shaking the youthful form, "Meyer, wake up."

The young man quickly arose from the bed, pulled on his trousers, and grabbed his boots. He followed his father into the kitchen, trying to button his pants and hold on to his boots as he walked. Avrum turned to his son, now seated on a wooden chair sliding his cold feet into the boots. The two had been up late the night before. They had needed to discuss what was happening in Hrubieszow, but had waited until everyone else was in bed so as not to alarm them. The older man's face was gaunt and lined with too little sleep and too many worries.

"How long have you been up?" asked Meyer. "Why didn't you wake me sooner?"

"Sh-h-h, you'll wake the others. Now, listen carefully. There are some things you must do. It's important that you find out what's happening, but first you must go to Josef's to make sure everything is prepared."

"Yes, Papa, I'll run there as fast as I can."

"No! You must not appear to be in a hurry. They would surely stop you. Walk calmly. If you're stopped, tell them you're going to the bakery for your mother. On your way back from Josef's, go to Salki. He'll tell you everything we should know."

Meyer saw the concern on his father's face, and knew that Avrum would have preferred checking on everything himself. But sometimes older people went out and never came back. It was up to Meyer to make the rounds.

"Don't worry, Papa, I'll be fine."

"I know, Meyer, I know. But remember, come straight back here. Do not stop anywhere else, do you hear me? Don't go anywhere else."

Meyer put on his jacket and ripped off the armband. He went to the door, opened it as quietly as possible, and slipped out into the cold Polish dawn. Avrum watched through the window as his son casually walked down the street, kicking a loose stone here and there to perfect his role of innocence. A half-smile crossed Avrum's face as he thought: He'll go to Manya's—no matter what I say, he'll go to Manya's anyway.

Avrum sat down at the small kitchen table and put his hands to his head. He was weary, and anxious to act. But he'd have to wait for Meyer's return, and that might take some time. He reached for his prayerbook and fingered the worn pages, forcing himself to follow the lines of Hebrew—to control his thoughts with prayer. But his eyes skimmed the page without reading, and finally gazed on the tattered armband with its Star of David lying on the table. His vision clouded as relentless, haunting thoughts won their battle against calm at last.

They should have left Poland and gone to Russia! He knew that now—had known it for months. After all, it was only three miles to the border. Perhaps, somehow from Russia they could have made their way to Palestine. He looked at the photographs on the wall, sent by relatives who had journeyed to that distant land years ago. The smiling faces in the pictures provided only an instant of comfort before his mind surged again with recriminations, envy, and anger.

He had settled into the alien routine established by the Germans more than two years before, sustained by his religion and the conviction that this hardship was God's will—indeed, His commandment—to atone for the inadequacies and indiscretions of others. If this was his test, he would strive to be equal to it. He had chosen to suffer the indignities and injustices inflicted on the Jews of Hrubieszow: armbands, curfew, minimal food rationing, thievery of property and assets, suspension of religious services, and desecration of synagogues. His acceptance stemmed not so much from fear as it did from devotion to his God. This was the one thing the Nazis could never take from him—to believe in God as a Jew. He was not yielding to terror; he was surrendering himself to God's justice.

Avrum supposed that Meyer should have reached Josef Wisniewski's house by now. He and Meyer had met Josef years ago when Josef would bring wheat from his farm on the edge of town to Avrum Korenblit's flour mill. Avrum had been awed by the man's strength. Josef would pick up two hundred-pound sacks of flour at once and toss them about with ease. Standing six-feet-two and weighing about two hundred pounds, Josef was powerfully built, with not an ounce of fat on him. He was a good-natured man with smiling dark eyes, who had a reverence for life and a zest for living it. He wouldn't harm the smallest of living things, nor would he run from a good fight, as the scar on his left cheek attested. He had spent untold hours at his favorite tavern in town, and it wasn't unusual for him, his ego swollen with drink, to issue or accept challenges from fellow patrons. What had begun as a flirtation with alcohol soon grew into a serious dependence, so that now, at twenty-eight, Josef was never without a cork-topped pint of vodka in his hip pocket.

But Avrum had seen another side of Josef Wisniewski. The farmer had always taken time to play and joke with Meyer during his visits to the flour mill, and before long, Meyer cautiously ventured over to Josef's farm to help him with the chores: milking cows, pitching hay, or threshing wheat. Although Avrum needed Meyer's assistance at the mill, he encouraged the friendship, and, as it developed, found himself surprisingly at ease in business dealings with the farmer. Over the years, Avrum's respect and affection for Josef grew into a bond of trust. But whatever the past had been, the same chilling question gnawed tenaciously at his very soul: Could he trust their *lives* to Josef? This man was not a Jew, but had agreed to help them. Avrum could no longer understand why. Too many Poles had indifferently redeemed a Jew for the bounty offered by the Germans—a pound of sugar. No, he'd have to rely on Josef, even though trusting a Pole made him fearful and uncertain.

Avrum brought himself up short. He felt ashamed as he thought of the Catholic Poles who had offered assistance to his family. He was grateful that the Polish foreman at the brick factory had succumbed to Meyer's urgings by falsifying his manpower requests to the Germans, sometimes doubling the number of people he actually needed to complete the available work. Avrum might long ago have been taken away by the Germans had it not been for the foreman's cooperation.

Franiek Gorski, the chief of police, had hidden Avrum's family in the attic of his house a few months before. Antonio Tomitzki and Isaac Achler in Mislavitch, a small town eleven miles away, had recently offered them a place to stay if they needed it. John Salki, the commissioner of roads in Hrubieszow, provided them with information, assistance, and, once, a place to hide. They were all Poles, but more than that, they were human beings who were risking their own safety and that of their families by protecting Jews.

He considered the possibility of going to Mislavitch, but it was too late for that now. The arrival of massive numbers of SS reinforcements, now encamped around the town, had eliminated that option. They couldn't go back to Gorski; enough had been asked of him already. John Salki had no room to hide eight people. They'd have to place their brittle trust with Josef Wisniewski.

Avrum and Meyer had visited Josef to seek his help. Without reluctance, he had agreed to devise a plan. Avrum even remembered Josef's exact words: "Not to worry, my friends, I will take care of you," uttered with that big, warm smile on his face. In the weeks that followed, Meyer and his father knew little of their benefactor's activities, for their involvement with him might have aroused suspicion. When Josef was finally satisfied that all the preparations were complete, he revealed his idea. Only the three of them knew of its existence—that is, Avrum thought wryly, unless Josef had blurted it out in a fit of revelry; or, worse, made up a song about it and bellowed it at the top of his voice as he lurched home from an evening's boozing. "My mouth has a lock on it," Josef had assured Avrum and Meyer soberly; but a drunken Josef might be their downfall. Even John Salki, who knew Josef was helping them, had warned: "Josef's a good man, but what if he goes on a binge?" Avrum had replied with a shrug, "It's already arranged."

That was yesterday. Today they were told there would be no work. Today the turmoil and rumors would intensify. Today the Hrubieszow Jews would mill dazedly about, reaching out to each other for direction, their instincts dulled and confused, their spirits shattered, their resolve undermined. Today something was going to happen. And so today Avrum's plan for freedom and escape would be put to the test.

2

On the other side of town, Shlomo Nagelsztajn stood silently in the sparsely furnished main hall of Hrubieszow's Jewish Center. The room was crowded, more populated than it had been on either of his two previous trips that day, and the mood was decidedly tense. What had once been the center of a thriving network of Jewish social and religious activities had been transformed by German occupation into the dreary depository of mandated work orders and SS dictates. Shlomo had little faith in the ability of the Jewish Center to provide direction or shelter for the town's desperate Jews, managed as it was by men no less trapped than he. But on this day he'd been driven to its doors by a compulsion to confirm or deny the rampant rumors that had engulfed the community since daybreak. This was his third visit, and like the others it was made with a sense of both hope and despair.

Even as he stood brushing shoulders with the unsettled crowd, Shlomo wasn't sure what he expected to learn. It had been years since he'd seen Jews clustered together on the streets, but today they were everywhere, nervously sharing tidbits of information. There was more noise than usual in Hrubieszow's Jewish area. In the turmoil, scattered individuals could be seen running about begging for answers. Some were crying; others walked silently, locked in their own thoughts. The dreaded SS troops were conspicuously absent, and open shops stood empty in mute testimony to the omnipresent danger. No Jews had been indifferent to the mounting German reinforcements that had begun to arrive in the area earlier in the week. Now the enemy encircled the town, choking its inhabitants in confusion and indecision.

Behind a cluttered desk, the Jewish Center's chief spoke quietly, his voice taut and laced with uncertainty, as he patiently addressed the endless questions of the crowd. Listening to the rote responses given helplessly by the Jewish leader, Shlomo realized that this man could offer little more than fragile comfort and empty words. The real truth was written on the faces of those around him. Shlomo could see his own growing fear in their eyes, hear his own uneasiness in their voices as they posed identical queries over and over. What does this troop buildup mean? What will happen to us? Why do they hate us so? Where can we hide? Throughout the day he had seen hundreds of people looking for answers to the same frantic questions, yet finding none.

Shlomo left the Jewish Center, stepping out into the sunshine without feeling its warmth. There was nothing more he could learn here. Two men stood talking outside the door of the Center. They looked up expectantly as he passed. Shlomo smiled grimly and shook his head. Much to his relief, the men returned to their whispering. Shlomo suddenly felt the need to be alone with his thoughts.

He thought of his family waiting at home, and knew they'd be concerned if he was gone too long. He wondered if his daughter Manya had seen Meyer Korenblit in the last few hours and if Meyer had brought any new information. He knew that when all this was over and if they all survived, he'd be giving his daughter's hand in marriage to this young, sometimes brash, but always thoughtful boy.

A soft breeze caught his brown hair, sending a few strands across his forehead. He pulled his light coat around him and concentrated on the secret hiding place he had built with his own hands. It was a consoling mental exercise, bringing relief to his pounding head as he traced the steps he'd taken to provide safety for the ones he loved.

Shlomo had realized early that the only way he could protect his family from the unpredictable horror of the German raids was to build a hideout. A bricklayer all his life, he turned to the craft he performed so grudgingly for the Germans to provide protection for his family. Shlomo constructed a concealed room in his own home. He had chosen the basement, laboriously creating a brick partition that would stretch its length and serve as a false wall, leaving an opening just large enough for an adult to crawl through.

For weeks after making the decision, Shlomo had searched for the exact bricks to fit his needs. They would have to be the right size and color, worn and aged to the same degree as the other bricks in the underground room. He knew a single mismatched piece could cost his family their lives. These stolen bricks, at first hidden under his masonry tools, would later be stuffed in the waistband of his trousers for the journey home. He could still feel the rough texture of the bricks chafing at his skin as day after day he smuggled them, camouflaged by his coat, from work to the relative safety of his basement.

Shlomo had risen early on the day he had selected to build the wall. He knew that he'd only have the daylight hours to complete his task, for the glow of a candle in the basement window would surely have brought a suspicious German sentry to investigate. The job would have to be accomplished in one day. Shlomo couldn't risk a half-finished wall being discovered during a raid. With clay and straw that had been carefully collected and hidden for weeks, he mixed a sturdy mortar to weave the rows of bricks into a solid fortress behind which his beloved family could hide. When he finished, he propped an old mattress and carefully positioned potatoes and other vegetables in front of the opening to complete the deception. At dusk, the exhausted craftsman stepped back to survey his handiwork. It was a masterful job.

Thinking back on it as he walked along, Shlomo could almost recall the sense of accomplishment he felt when the wall was completed. His real triumph, however, came a few months later when he and his family used the hideout successfully during a German raid. But months of harassment and stress had taken their toll, tearing away at his confidence. Although Shlomo still felt that his hiding place was a good one, disquieting pictures formed in his mind. The hideout *was* in the center of town. That was a risk in itself. And there was the question of food and water. Their stockpile of vegetables would sustain them for a while, but water would have to be replenished often. How was he to manage that? This proud but simple bricklayer, who usually walked with an air of assurance, was now slouched, his hands thrust deep into the pockets of his coat, the burden of decision on his shoulders. How safe or long-term could any hideout be? Shlomo shivered with the sudden thought that instead of walling the Germans out, he might have walled his family in.

Shlomo crossed the road and turned into a street dotted with familiar sights. He passed in front of the bakery and the tailor shop, both previously owned by Jews who were forced out of business at the start of the war. He recalled the hours spent in discussion of business and politics with these merchants. Scenes from the past raced through his mind, taunting him with pleasure and pain. He remembered many occasions in the synagogue with these people. Weddings, bar mitzvahs, and holidays celebrated with vodka, cake, and wine.

He'd seen some of them today at the Jewish Center. They had nodded recognition to each other, of course, but they hadn't come to talk. A few men had asked him what he was planning to do, where he would hide his family. Shlomo hadn't told them about the basement hideout, mentioning instead that he would travel with his family to the nearby towns of Zamosz or Kreliv to stay with relatives. He couldn't tell them the truth. Despite his longing to band together with his friends, he couldn't weaken. Many cleverly disguised hideouts had been revealed to the Germans, who relied on informers and followed up every insidious rumor. Even the most trustworthy had broken under the brutal beatings of the SS troops, forced to disclose the whereabouts of friends—even family. It wasn't something that Shlomo could understand. He just knew it to be true.

He fought off the nagging sadness that the lies to his friends had caused. He hated the Nazis most for bringing him to the point where, in order to survive, he'd have to deceive the very people who made up the fabric of his life.

His steps brought him to the edge of an empty soccer field in the park. He stopped, and for a moment recalled the spirited contests of happier days. The bricklayer had been to this field many times to watch Ely play. In his imagination, he heard the cheers of a long-ago crowd, their voices building to a reckless crescendo. "Ely! Ely!" Shlomo remembered how his eldest son was always careful not to give the spectators too much attention, concentrating instead on the black-checkered ball as he kicked it confidently to the goal. But once home, there were hugs and warm praise for the young man with the talent to become a professional player. How proud Shlomo had been of his son. Especially for overcoming his handicap of being born without a right hand or forearm. What a fine handsome face, and how bright the boy had been. But that was over now. Ely had been killed over a year ago in Russia, where he'd gone to escape the Germans; 1941—it was a year Shlomo would never forget. Shlomo turned his back on the field in a futile effort to shut out the past, and let the tears make their way down his face unchecked.

His thoughts drifted to Aunt Zlaty. Shlomo could see her as clearly as he had seen her on the night that she disappeared, her face almost serene in the decision to stay upstairs while the rest of the family retreated to safety in the hideout. It must have been hard for her to say good-bye to them, especially to the children, and yet Zlaty had shown no fear.

Shlomo liked to imagine that she'd worn the same expression when the Germans found her that night. He wasn't sure why. Like so many of his friends, the only steps he'd taken to fight back were defensive ones—building the basement hideout, for example—yet his own sense of himself and that of those he loved begged for the image of dignity if their worst fears were realized.

As he approached his block, Shlomo wondered what had brought him to this point; why hadn't he listened to Ely's pleas for them to leave Poland? How many times since Ely's departure had he been forced to compromise? He'd exhausted his limited realm of influence to buy freedom for his family. Had he really believed even then that it would mean survival? In some ways, Shlomo realized that he had decided his own fate by denying his apprehension and dread for so long. It was in his nature to abhor violence and all its consequences. But this enemy was relying on his pacifism to destroy him. Still he wouldn't make it easy for them. He'd put his trust in the only weapon at his disposal: a stubborn will to live. Contemplative but undefeated, he reached his home.

Slowly, Shlomo climbed the many steps that led above the shops. He was a small man, but he put his shoulders back to give his countenance the sturdy, assured look that he hoped would disguise his mood when he faced his family. They'd need his strength. Crossing over the threshold, Shlomo touched his fingers to his lips and placed them on the mezuzah nailed to the right side of the doorpost. Despite his agony, Shlomo still believed in the words written on parchment inside the tiny religious symbol:

שְׁמַע יִשְׂרָאֵל יְיָ אֱלֹהֵינוּ

Hear, O Israel: the Lord our God . . .

3

Avrum Korenblit shifted in the hard wooden chair, as he read:

יְיָ אֶחָד:

. . . the Lord is One.

He felt the sting of restored circulation as he lowered his stiff arms and closed his prayerbook. For the first time in hours, he focused on the room. Avrum looked at his wife Malka and his three daughters. The girls were pressing themselves to their mother, occasionally moving back and forth, bumping against her. Malka hardly noticed either the irritating thumps or the hunger-induced whines coming from her daughters.

He turned slightly, peered into the living room, and looked with admiration at Moniek Pulaski's impassive face. This talented artist, who delighted the children with his quick sketches, had been brought with his wife, Rela, from Lodz to Hrubieszow and lodged with Avrum and his family. They arrived not long after Shuyl and Motl Korenblits' departure for Russia three years ago. Their presence seemed to ease the emptiness created by the absence of the two older sons. Moniek and Rela were sitting on the threadbare couch, their arms entwined, her head on his shoulder, waiting. That was the irony of it all: so much to do, so much to think about, so little time, and yét they were paralyzed with indecision—their senses numbed and spent. Avrum wanted to offer some hope of deliverance by telling them of the hiding place, but he couldn't. He must be sure that this was the time. He must wait for Meyer to return. He couldn't take a chance by telling them prematurely, for he wanted no one else to find out.

Avrum felt powerless to protect his family. Not long ago his anxiety would have been quelled by prayer, but for more than a year he had battled a growing sense of God's abandonment. How could God allow this to happen? his brain screamed, echoing the question that Meyer often posed to him. His veined hands clenched the edge of the table. He wanted to shake his fists and roar his anguish. He wanted to—

The sound of footsteps climbing the outside stairs caused the huddled figures to stiffen, their eyes riveted to the door. There was a brief fumbling with the latch, and then the door swung open. Meyer burst into the room, his shirt dark with sweat, his chest heaving. So intent was he on reporting to his father that he didn't see the terror in the faces before him.

"Papa, it's true—it's all true!" gasped Meyer. "I've just talked to Salki, and he confirms it. He says we must go away or hide. The Germans are going to take all the Jews away this time. I've been to Manya's house—they're ready to hide. It's all so terrible—the Jews are wandering around, talking and crying . . . there aren't any soldiers in town, Salki says they're all at the encampment. No one knows what to do, they kept asking me what we were going to do—"

"You didn't tell them—" began Avrum.

"No, Papa, no—I said only that we might try to go to Mislavitch," Meyer reassured him.

"Tell them what, Avrum?" asked Malka, trying to comprehend the flurry of words.

Meyer acknowledged his mother's question with a glance, then shifted his gaze to his father. Avrum rose heavily from the table.

"Moniek, Rela," he called to the next room, "come in here. I have something to tell you." The couple made their way timidly into the kitchen. Avrum looked at his wife Malka and nodded a promise to explain.

"We have a hideout," he began, weighing every word carefully as he searched each anxious face, trying to measure the reaction. Avrum kept his voice low and even as he continued.

"Meyer and I made all the arrangements with Josef Wisniewski long ago, but we wanted to keep it secret. Meyer spoke with him again this afternoon. Josef is expecting us."

"Wisniewski!" exploded Malka. "Wisniewski! You went to a drunk for help? You told a drunk where we would hide and kept it secret from your own family? That's crazy. We can't trust him— what can you be thinking? It's no good, I tell you—we're doomed. . . ." Unable to continue with words, she flailed at the air in her frustration and torment.

Avrum was shocked. He'd meant for this announcement to soothe their fears and give them confidence in the hours ahead. But he'd forgotten his own struggle with the decision to trust Josef. Avrum was able to summon no verbal comfort; instead he simply reached out and caught one of Malka's hands and grasped it in his, seeking to transfuse his flagging strength. She drew his hand to her cheek, grateful and apologetic, her face contorted with the shame of weakness and the pain of useless accusation.

Eleven-year-old Minka and fourteen-year-old Toba approached their mother shyly, reaching out to her. Before long the small hands that bestowed pats of consolation were gripping the folds of Malka's skirt, demanding caresses in return. Meyer saw his youngest sister look away from the doll that had held her attention up to now. At eight, Cyvia could hardly be expected to understand what had caused her mother's outburst. But Meyer could see her usually bright round face cloud with tears. She scrambled off the floor to hold on to Malka. Meyer didn't know who needed comforting more.

Moniek and Rela turned away from the emotional scene, as if their backs could shield them from painful memories and lend some sense of privacy to the Korenblit family. Meyer wondered what they were thinking as they stood near the black-shrouded window. They looked so alone, so isolated. He thought they might not understand that any plan for the Korenblits was a plan for them, too. Time was slipping away, and he wanted to urge them all to action. Then his father spoke.

"I know I always said we would go to Mislavitch, but it's too late for that now. If we were going to Mislavitch, we should have gone six months ago . . . or to Russia—we could have gone to Russia."

Almost as if Avrum realized that his rambling confession was alarming them, he turned imploring eyes to his son.

Meyer's words came without hesitation. "There's no time to look back—there's no time for more talk. We have to go!"

"We're going to a hideout where we'll be safe." The renewed authority in Avrum's voice bespoke his agreement with Meyer. "No one will ever find us in this hideout, I promise you. Then maybe in a few days we will go to Mislavitch. Malka, have the girls put on extra socks and underwear—we mustn't carry too much, it would look suspicious. We'll take a little food—no need to carry water, we can get that from Josef."

Malka stood transfixed.

Avrum sharpened his tone. "Malka! Quick! We're leaving now!"

Meyer saw his mother's trancelike gaze snap into focus. She released her steadying hold on her daughters and spun around. For a moment her eyes darted about, her hands reaching uncertainly. Finally she swooped up two straw baskets, and with Rela's help, packed what little food they had. She instructed Toba, Minka, and Cyvia to fetch some extra clothes for themselves, and denied their request to take dolls and other playthings. She looked at their drawn faces and fought down the impulse to relent.

"No, my little ones, we'll take only what we need," she said gently but firmly, "and we don't need dolls. Get your clothes as Papa asked. Toba, help your sisters—be sure to put on jackets, too." Toba ushered the two upstairs; Rela joined Moniek in choosing from their meager array of belongings, and soon Malka herself was running up to the bedrooms, calling to Meyer over her shoulder to change his shirt.

Meyer stood back as the preparations for departure swirled around him. The time had come. He'd rehearsed it in his mind so often, and now he stood watching, almost as if it were happening to someone else. He knew what was causing his sense of distance. He was thinking about Manya. Meyer was sure he couldn't go to Josef's without her, but how was he to tell his father? The older man picked up his prayerbook and tucked it safely in his pocket.

Meyer knew he couldn't delay any longer. "Papa . . ." he started. "I have to see Manya."

Avrum turned to him. "Manya! Why? You've seen her already today. Besides, they're probably closed up in their hideout by now—you could cause them trouble by going over there again. Someone may follow you."

"Papa, I can't leave without letting her know that we have a place to hide, that we'll be safe. She'll worry about me. I don't even know if I can leave her. Maybe I'll hide at her house."

"No!" said Avrum. "That's no good. It's in town—you won't be safe there. No, you'll come with us. You'll be able to check on her later. She'll understand, Meyer."

"I'm going to Manya, Papa, I have to see her," Meyer repeated. "I have to be with her—I want her to be with me. There's room in our hideout. I'll go get her and bring her to Wisniewski's."

"We have enough to worry about with our own family," Avrum retorted, annoyed. "There might not be enough room at Wisniewski's for anyone extra. Please, Meyer, be sensible. Help me get the flashlights. Just stay here and go with us."

It was difficult for Meyer to argue with his father, but he persisted. "I'm going to Manya's; I can make it—I've sneaked over there after curfew hundreds of times—I'll be all right. I'll come back to the house, and if you're gone, I'll meet you at Wisniewski's barn."

"Even if you'd gone a thousand times, it wouldn't matter," begged Avrum. "It's too dangerous to go to town now—and your clothes, you'll need something!"

"Tell Mama to bring something for me," came the reply. Meyer turned to the door, then saw his mother standing on the stairs, one arm laden with a tangle of clothing, the other slipped inside one sleeve of a light coat. Their eyes met and he could read the message, but before she could lend her objections to those of his father, Meyer started for the door. He knew she deserved an explanation, but he couldn't spare any more time.

"I'll be back, Mama, don't worry," was all he could offer as he closed the door behind him. He hoped she'd understand.

Malka and Avrum stared at the emptiness where their son had been.

"They'll catch him this time, I just know it," she said. "He's the only son we have left, and they'll catch him."

"He said he'd be back, Malka, and he will be."

Meyer stood holding the latch, relieved to be out of the house, where he'd begun to feel trapped and closed in. The darkness held more threats, and yet over the months he'd become accustomed to it. Despite its dangers, the night with all its challenges allowed him to be a man. He turned and surveyed his route. Everything seemed to be quiet. He went down the steps by twos, landing hard in the dirt at the bottom, adding yet another layer of dust to his damp skin. After all the times he'd traveled this route, he'd have to be more careful than ever now. He must not allow familiarity to trip him up. He couldn't tell whether he felt fear or elation—perhaps a mixture, he decided—but he had to remain calm, to reach his destination quickly, to make no movement that would betray either his family or himself.

He knew his father was right; he was taking a big chance, but logic and reason were impotent adversaries against the urgings of his heart. He smiled to himself when he thought of the rather offhand way he had treated Manya only a few years before. His young manhood had been boosted by Manya's instant warmth at his briefest look or word. He'd even been pleased by the hint of jealousy she showed when he was attentive to other girls. Only since he returned from Russia had he found himself anxious to be with her all the time, to share the stories of his trip with her. And so, night after night, he risked the unthinkable to make his way stealthily to her house after curfew. He was proud that he'd never been caught; the sense of daring satisfied his starved ego, and each successful journey represented a small rebellion against the Germans.

He had always known that he would never leave without Manya. He hadn't told her about their hideout, but kept the pledge of secrecy to his father. For two years he had ached to tell her, to smooth away the worried lines on her face with this comforting antidote. He'd come so close to blurting it out—but his father had sworn his own silence, and Meyer could do no less.

Instead, he held Manya, murmuring again and again, "I'll take care of you." He turned his energy to sharpening his every sense, drinking in and storing away every bit of information, everything he saw, knowing that the time would come when he'd need it. He picked up his pace and hurried to Manya's.

4

Avrum descended the stairs from the second floor. The beds were stripped, contents of the drawers scattered about. He paused halfway down to use the slight elevation as a vantage point. He was quite calm now, confident of his ability to win out, to survive this crushing enemy. He scanned the lower floor with an objective eye. They'd done a good job here, too—no pictures on the walls, a rolled-up carpet that looked as if it had been abandoned in a hasty departure. In a few minutes they'd be gone. As the group reassembled in the kitchen, it was very quiet. Malka checked each of the little girls over carefully, then looked down at her own body—almost as if she could step out of herself. She was ready. Avrum sensed the bubble of fear that expanded with each second's inactivity.

"We go," he announced. He opened the door and motioned them out. As they crossed the porch, he looked over the room. He was glad there had been no cooking that day—there would be no stale odors or warm stove. He was satisfied that the house would appear to have been deserted for some time. His eyes moved to the kitchen table. His armband! No, he thought, he didn't need that anymore, and he stepped quickly outside and closed the door.

They made their way as casually as possible across the fields in the direction of Josef Wisniewski's farm. The determined rhythm of movement seemed to accentuate a grim silence. They didn't look back, but proceeded intently toward their destination. Avrum led the way, constantly glancing over his shoulder to make sure everyone was staying close to him, and taking special care to caution his young daughters to move along quietly.

Josef Wisniewski was in his barn, tending his horses and waiting. His talk with Meyer only hours before had set their plan into motion. Josef wasn't concerned about his personal safety, but he didn't want to endanger his mother and sister. For this reason, he and Avrum had agreed that if the Korenblits were discovered in the hideout, Josef would deny any knowledge of their presence.

He hadn't told his mother about the hideout for the Korenblits; he knew she'd be upset, not because he was aiding Jews but because she would fear for her own family. Everyone knew what happened to Poles who helped Jews—the Germans had made it very clear. But Josef feared his mother's wrath almost as much as he hated the Germans, and he'd have to be resourceful in unveiling the secret in just the right way. After all, he had planned for her to prepare food for the hiding family.

Keeping his eyes on the path to the barn, Josef continued to watch for the Korenblits. He hadn't intended to be here when they arrived. The plan was for the Korenblits to enter the barn and climb into the loft on their own. But it was taking longer than usual for his mother and sister to milk the cows. Tonight of all nights, the cows were uncooperative—stupid animals! he thought to himself. Even though the stalls were on the other side of the barn, he had to wait and warn the Korenblits to be careful.

For the fiftieth time Josef looked through the barn door into the fields. There they were at last: two, four, six, seven. Seven! There should be eight! Meyer wasn't with them! Josef leaned outside and motioned them in, holding his finger to his lips and gesturing toward the cows. He pointed to the ladder leaning against the loft, and shooed them in its direction.

As Avrum came close, Josef whispered, "Where's Meyer?"

"He'll be coming soon," Avrum replied.

Moniek and Rela climbed up first, then reached down to assist Toba, Minka, and Cyvia. Malka struggled her way up, and finally Avrum scaled the ladder and pulled it into the loft behind him. They settled in with as little movement as possible.

After a moment Malka leaned over to Avrum. "So this is the wonderful hiding place where no one will find us?" she hissed. "Right by the fort, with hundreds of German soldiers! There couldn't be a more obvious place for Jews to hide!"

"Hush, Malka," he whispered, "rest a bit. This is temporary. We must wait until it's late. Then you'll see how safe we'll be." He turned away from her to show the finality of his words.

Soon he could hear the sound of deep breathing around him, but he couldn't sleep. To him this was the most perilous stage of the plan: Malka was right. They were vulnerable in a barn, subject to routine searches by the Nazis, for barns were common hiding places for Jews. But if this was a weak link in their escape, it was necessary to safeguard the location of their final destination. No, Avrum couldn't rest. First he'd listen for Meyer's arrival; then he'd listen for the Germans.

5

It was a little more than a mile from his house to Manya's, and Meyer was making better time than expected. He was close now, only a few more blocks, straight ahead, turn left, through the al-

ley, cross over, past the baker, turn right, past the shoemaker, the
tailor, the dressmaker, through the narrow doorway, and up the
steps.

The building was quiet, with no sign of activity, as he proceeded down the hallway to the sliding doors of the small bedroom adjacent to the kitchen. He threw the doors open and
peered in.

Manya's family, frozen with alarm, stared at the intruder.

"Meyer!" Manya exclaimed in a tone of disbelief. She thought
he would be hiding with his family and had resigned herself to
the fact that she wouldn't see him soon. Standing next to her
mother, Manya could only stare at him.

"Meyer," said Shlomo, "what is it? Why have you come? Do you
want to hide with us? Has something happened to your family?"

Meyer shook his head, gasping for air. "I've come because I
want Manya and me to be together. My family is going away to
hide, but I had to see Manya."

"We were just going down to the basement hideout," Shlomo
told him. "Come with us; stay with us; we'll be safe."

Delaying for breath and time, Meyer leaned against the wall.
He was strangely comforted by Shlomo's confident tone, and considered the man's offer. It was true that the basement hideout
had been tested, Meyer thought. Perhaps he _would_ be better off to
stay here. He wiped the sweat from his face with the back of his
arm, grateful to shield his eyes from the penetrating stares for
even a second, and wished that his resolve was as firm as it had
been when he left his father's house. He remembered his final
promise to his mother. He'd have to go to Wisniewski's. Meyer
couldn't live with the knowledge that his parents would think he'd
been caught. He shifted his weight back onto legs still shaky from
running. Meeting Shlomo's gaze, he groped for the strength to
make himself understood.

"No, I don't want to be in town; too many people have been
caught. I don't think it's the best thing. I want Manya to come with
me—you can all come with me—we have a good hiding place."

Manya looked away from Meyer and sought her father's strong
face. The expression alone was enough to tell her that he
wouldn't accept Meyer's offer. She saw Shlomo's lips part, and
then heard the reply she dreaded: "No, we can't leave; we'll be
safe here."

She squeezed her eyes shut and shook her head as if to throw off the burden of Meyer's suggestion and her father's answer. She'd have to choose between staying with her family and going with Meyer. Manya could feel them all looking at her. She wanted to run and shut herself away. Instinctively she drew closer to her mother, her already small stature shrinking further still.

She hadn't expected this. Everything was happening so quickly, she didn't know what to do. A few minutes earlier she'd been wishing for Meyer's presence, aching for the comfort that only his touch could provide. Now her wish had come true: Meyer was standing a few feet away from her, but the distance to his side could be bridged only by choosing one love over another.

"Will you come with me, Manya?" Meyer's voice was pleading and tense as he called her name. Only then did she look up. His eyes beseeched her for a response. His hand reached out to her urgently, his look loving and vulnerable, his attitude annoyed and impatient. He loved her so, and yet couldn't indulge this delay, this reluctance. He felt threatened by her dilemma, but his unwavering confidence in her eclipsed the doubt that fought to take hold. What was the matter with Manya? There was no time for debating, no time for more tears—NO TIME!

Helplessly Shlomo watched his daughter's struggle. There was a time when seventeen-year-old Manya would have looked to him for guidance and permission. But now that instinct was remote; he could offer no paternal order to ease her quandary. He wanted to ask Meyer where they would hide, to demand some sort of assurance that Manya would be safe, but he knew it was useless. If she went with Meyer, she might be safe or she might be caught; if she stayed with them, the same was true. In these days when one came to expect nothing and everything, even the smallest chance was worth the risk. But the pain was in the choosing.

Mincha's look begged him to speak.

"It's all right, Manya," he offered.

Manya turned to face her mother.

"Manya, if you're coming, we must leave immediately!" Meyer demanded.

"You go ahead, Manya," Mincha whispered, holding her arms out to her eldest daughter. "I know Meyer will take good care of you. If you go, maybe one of us will survive." The word rang in Mincha's head, and the dark memory of Ely's departure came on her in a rush. She tasted bile, and fought to stay the surge of it, swallowing air in great gulps as her throat battled her will for control. She had given her blessing to her eldest son to leave; she could do no less for her daughter. But Ely was dead. . . . No! She wouldn't think terrible thoughts. It was the right decision. She knew it.

Manya tried to form words with her lips, but her constricted throat allowed only wails to emerge. She and her mother clutched each other and sobbed their grief. Manya finally pulled herself away and knelt to embrace her younger brothers and sisters, then stood before her father.

"We'll be safe, Manya, don't worry about us. This will be over soon. We'll see each other again, I'm sure of it," he said, clinging to her. Manya nodded hopefully, her fist stifling the scream of desolation she felt building within her. She turned to Meyer. The tears running from his eyes made small rivulets in the dust on his face. He understood; he felt her pain, and the hand he held out to her now was gentle and promised comfort.

"Come," he said quietly.

Manya moved toward him and grasped his outstretched hand tightly. She reached up and tenderly touched his tears. Manya looked at each person again. Her eyes met her younger brother Chaim's and held. She turned her back and they started out of the room.

"I want to come too," said Chaim. Manya spun around and looked at her brother, then at Meyer.

"You're welcome to come—you're all welcome to come," said Meyer. "But let's go!"

Mincha couldn't believe her ears. She wanted to scream out: No, Chaim! Her world revolved around her family, and it was splintering away. Though she accepted losing Manya to Meyer and believed they'd be safe, she could never have prepared herself for this announcement from Chaim. She wanted him with her, but she was no longer able to make decisions for her family. She let him go. Her knees buckled, she gagged, retching the emptiness inside her.

Shlomo moved to brace his wife. "It will be good for Manya to have him with her," he choked.

Manya stared dumbstruck as Chaim said his good-byes. Somehow this usually quiet and malleable fourteen-year-old had made his own decision while she was going through her personal hell. Then her father spoke.

"Go with God, Chaim, but know we will feel your absence." Pair by pair the hands released Chaim and formed a new chain among those who would stay—except for twelve-year-old Joshua. The young boy gripped his only brother fiercely, his dry eyes wild, his fingers clawing for a new hold as Shlomo gently pulled him away.

Chaim turned to go, then felt a feathery touch on his shoulder. With growing force, Mincha pulled him to her once more, her arms encircling his body, her fingers digging into his flesh. Manya saw Chaim wince, and couldn't believe that the older woman still had such strength within her. Mincha finally loosened her grip, taking his face in her trembling hands.

"Be strong, Chaim, and care for your sister. I love you." Then she reverently kissed his forehead and let her fingers trace the outline of his face as if she would burn it into her memory. Manya turned to Meyer, desperate to escape. Without a word, Meyer guided the two through the doorway.

6

Night had fallen during the fifteen minutes Meyer had been in the Nagelsztajn house. He had been so conscious of the minutes ticking away, for he had hoped they would have the light of dusk for their journey. But now he was glad for the safety of the darkness. He knew it was unlikely that the Germans would launch the final phase of their evacuation of Jews at night—night raids were used more as terror tactics and to keep the Jews off balance. The first two cleansing operations had taken place in the daytime, and tomorrow, October 28, the last third of Hrubieszow's ten thousand Jews would simply be herded out.

Meyer spent his whole day gathering information. Like everyone else, he knew that the regular SS sentries were no longer posted in town—they'd been pulled back to the encampments around the city. His visit with John Salki that morning reconfirmed that fact and more. Salki outlined the German plan in detail, giving the location of the encampments as well as the specific circuit of the German patrols. He recommended a safe route for the Korenblits to take once they were out of the city.

After leaving Salki's house, Meyer tracked down Gorski, hoping that the chief of police might offer further help. Finding him at last, Meyer sought to corroborate Salki's description of the Nazi offensive.

"What more can you tell me? What about the fort?" Meyer urged.

"Stay away from the fort—there aren't many soldiers, but the SS could make reassignments." Gorski sensed the plea for more information on Meyer's face.

"Polish informers are dispersed throughout the city. Their orders are to report any Jews attempting escape. These places must be avoided as you leave town," Gorski said, giving Meyer the locations of the Polish lookouts. Only Gorski, who had chosen and positioned them, had this vital information.

Meyer shook his head in an effort to make himself alert. He and Manya and Chaim were nearing the tavern where German enlisted men sneaked drinks. He mustn't let down his guard—he had to concentrate on getting through the maze of streets undetected.

Manya strained to see over her shoulder as they proceeded down the street. She couldn't remember the last time she'd been outside under the light of the stars. For nearly three years her home had become a prison at six o'clock each evening. She yearned to go back, but her legs defiantly carried her forward. She stared at her house as long as it was in sight, took a deep breath, and reached for Chaim's hand. They moved along, blindly following Meyer's whispered instructions and wordless signals.

Suddenly she was aware that she had no idea where they were going.

"Where is the hideout?"

"Trust me, Manya. I can't explain now."

No, of course he couldn't, Manya realized, watching his head turn left, right, then to the rear, his practiced eyes checking again and again that their route was clear; pausing to listen, then striking out once more in the darkness; freezing in mid-stride: Hush! What was that? Whirling around as a leaf was scrunched underfoot; flattening themselves against a wall, then darting for the next alley. On and on they sneaked, out the opposite end of town, crashing through marsh grass and a frenzy of chirping crickets, which, by their abrupt silence as the trio passed, seemed to report the escape. Then, as they entered open fields, Manya heard Meyer curse the moonlight as it flooded the pastures and exposed them.

Wait! That was Meyer's house just ahead! She felt Chaim break stride as he, too, recognized their location, but she tightened her grasp on his hand and firmly pulled him along. They wouldn't question Meyer's plan again.

As they reached the Korenblit house, Meyer motioned them to stay put while he crawled up the stairs. He lay across the top steps and part of the porch, getting as close to the door as possible, then cupped his hands and called very softly, "Papa?" He listened a moment, poised to flee, then eased himself down backward and knelt with Manya and Chaim.

"They've gone," he whispered to their puzzled faces, adding, "Come, follow me."

He paused, looked across the landscape, then steered his companions toward the fields. They had almost three miles to go. He had traveled this route many times, but at night it looked so different, and he knew it offered no shelter. They'd have to pass painfully close to the German-occupied fort, again a practiced exercise for Meyer, but now there would be three figures scurrying through the night. Even though he knew there was only a skeleton crew left in the building, Gorski's warning rang in his ears. With the fort dead ahead of them, Meyer pulled Manya and Chaim into a crouched position and signaled them to wait. He crawled a few yards to the left, then past them again and to the right, trying to see around both sides of the structure. He saw only two guards, and they were taking their duty lightly, standing in a relaxed pose facing the building. There was a brief flare as one of them lit a cigarette. Meyer scooted quickly back to Manya and Chaim.

"Keep low," he breathed, drawing them half-erect and on their way again. The German guards didn't turn around.

As they approached Wisniewski's barn, Meyer drew Manya and Chaim close.

"Be very quiet now," he whispered, "we're going into Josef's barn and up into the loft. My family is there already."

"Is that the hiding place?" cried Manya, anxious for familiar surroundings and her mother's comforting arms.

"We'll stay in the loft for a few hours," came the reply, "and then we'll go to the hideout."

"But where is the hideout?" she demanded.

"It's very close by. You can almost see it from here," assured Meyer. "Come, we must get inside!"

Manya looked out into the night, trying to pick up a clue, but all she saw was emptiness. She didn't understand why Meyer wouldn't share the secret of the hideout with her, but she had no strength to argue. He was right. They must not delay any longer out in the open. They entered the barn, and once again Meyer called to his father. As if by magic, the ladder appeared from the loft and was slipped silently to the floor.

"Up you go," said Meyer to Manya and Chaim, giving them a boost.

At the top, Manya collapsed in the hay. Too weak to crawl, she rolled her leaden body aside to make room for Meyer and Chaim. Her head pounded and her eyes burned. Without the moonlight she had difficulty seeing, but soon she could make out other forms lying in the hay. Meyer pulled the ladder up and fell into the hay alongside her, Chaim on the other side.

As they lay so close to each other, their heartbeats seemed to settle into a common cadence. Then the rhythmic beats slowed. The darkness, the cradling hay, warm bodies, and exhaustion spun a cocoon and lulled her into the escape of sleep. She dreamed.

Her subconscious spewed pictures, traveling backward in time: she was working at the brick factory; the heat of the ovens made her sweat; the bricks she carried were heavy, but she was strong. Her father's bruised and bleeding face appeared; the Nazis had beaten him up at work. There were scores of people being pushed through the streets; they were so tired, so frightened, so thirsty; she tried to give them some water; the Gestapo shoved her away, she fell down, scraping her hand on the bricks. Then there were no more soldiers. She was a little girl at school; the teacher was scolding her, telling her to hold out her hand; she didn't want to be hit with the ruler; she wanted to go home. And then it was market day in Hrubieszow.

Her mother and she were going together, and nine-year-old Manya was thrilled. The noisy, redolent streets were choked with people, loaded wagons, and animals; the stalls brimming with succulent fruits and shiny vegetables; vats of pickles; warm, frothy milk; pungent cheeses; plucked chickens, ducks, and geese hanging like clothes on a line. There were mountains of crusty loaves of bread and delicate sweet pastries, crockery, scrub brushes, soap, harnesses and horse blinders.

Mincha Nagelsztajn assumed a vacant stare, ignoring the urgings of the vendors, but her practiced eye belied her unimpressed demeanor. Manya knew better than to touch or admire anything. Nothing would be purchased on impulse, for Mincha knew exactly what she wanted and wouldn't be swayed by either the loud hawking of the merchants or the wistful fancies of her eldest daughter.

They would buy half a chicken, three or four eggs—broken ones would save a few pennies—a few ounces of tea and sugar, a half-jar of milk, flour, oil, and if she could manage it, fruit. Later, at home, Mincha would go about her routine of stretching the food items to feed her family of nine, while Manya minded the new baby.

The milk would be diluted three-to-one with water. The clusters of fat and bits of fatty skin would be removed from the chicken, cut into small pieces, and heated slowly. When they melted, she would add sliced onions, cooking them until they were brown. Then she strained the liquid from the solids, or grebenes. The whole house was full of the aroma, tantalizing the family and causing Manya unnecessary trips to the kitchen to snitch a flavorful morsel or two. Manya would pop one in her mouth and suck on it, reveling in the taste, somehow keeping herself from chomping it to nothingness. "Make it last," she told herself over and over, "savor the taste."

The precious cracklings and liquid fat were reserved to lend their potent flavor to baked noodles, thick kasha melanges, soups, and vegetables for their numerous meatless meals. Mincha would make bread: rye for every day, and white for the Sabbath. The chicken itself would also be reserved for the Sabbath meal. Manya's father often said, "Even a poor family is rich on the Sabbath." One or two of the precious eggs would be mixed with rye flour to make dark, rich noodles—a family favorite, eaten in a bowl with a splash of milk.

As Manya and her mother proceeded through the narrow streets, each purchase was carefully placed in their straw shopping basket. Mincha had bargained well—there was enough money left to stop at the fruit stand. Mincha guided her daughter firmly past the Polish merchant with his strings of spicy sausages, slabs of bacon, and rosy hams, for somehow even pausing to take in the aroma of these forbidden foods was an indiscretion.

Manya obediently skipped along, hardly noticing her confined toes which threatened to burst through the front of her tight shoes; but her eyes stole a curious glance at the pork vendor. She felt the pressure of her mother's grasp on her arm, and made an effort to pull back, to delay—she wanted to watch the merchant cut the thick slices of ham and chunks of ribboned bacon for his Polish customers. She wasn't ready to leave yet— just a little while longer—there was so much to see, and her mother said they might stop at the shoemaker's to arrange for a new pair of shoes. But the pulling on her arm was more insistent now, and she couldn't ignore it.

7

Manya opened her eyes. Where was she? Meyer's face was next to hers. He had awakened her as he softly released their entwined arms, rousing her from her dreamy refuge.

She finally responded, "What is it?"

Meyer lifted his finger to his mouth. "Shh! It's almost time to go. I'll be right back."

"Where are you going?" Her eyes followed him as he slowly stood up and moved away. She watched him pick his way around the others, trying not to awaken them. He stopped short of a dark figure, standing at the edge of the loft. As her eyes adjusted to the darkness, she recognized Avrum's silhouette.

Rustling sounds from below diverted her attention. Who could that be? The Germans? she wondered as her eyes darted back to Avrum and Meyer, who were quietly making their way down the ladder. Unable to see them, she rolled over onto her stomach, crawling to the side, being careful not to push hay over the edge.

She watched intently as Avrum and Meyer joined a third man, who towered over them.

"Josef," she heard amid the muffled words.

So that's Josef. That's the man Meyer has told me so much about. She nodded to herself, remembering pieces of the many stories he had shared with her about his Polish friend.

The whispering stopped. Josef turned and walked out the door.

Meyer and Avrum moved toward the ladder and climbed up. Manya's mind raced. Do we have to leave? Are the Germans coming? Meyer did say that this isn't the hiding place. She had to see what was happening. She got up and inched her way to the ladder. Her eyes met Meyer's as he stepped from the last wooden rung.

"What's going on?"

"Josef says that it's time for us to leave for the hideout. We must awaken everyone."

Avrum gently nudged Malka. "We must go now."

Meyer shook Moniek and Rela.

"What's the matter?" Moniek asked.

"It's time."

Meyer quickly turned when he heard Cyvia whine, "I don't want to get up now, I'm sleepy!"

"I know, my little darling, but we must go now. You'll have time to sleep later."

"Chaim, Chaim, it's time to get up," Manya said, shaking him gently. Chaim jumped to his feet. All eyes turned toward Avrum.

"Josef has been keeping watch for the past two hours. He says there has been no activity nearby; everything is quiet. He's sure it's safe for us to go to the hideout. We'll be walking across a large open field, so we must go very quickly and stay close together. Nobody, *nobody*, should utter a sound."

"Where are we going?" Minka demanded.

"We're going to a place where we'll be safe. Malka, follow me down with the girls."

In a few minutes Manya found herself carefully edging down the ladder, then joining Malka and the little girls in a corner of the barn. As they waited, Manya watched Malka's lips move silently. She knew Malka was asking God to see them safely to their hideout.

Meyer used his hands to sweep stray bits of straw away from the edge of the loft and did his best to fluff the flattened areas where they had slept. He joined Moniek at the ladder, and then the two half-slid to the barn floor.

Avrum inhaled deeply, then sighed. Only one mile between us and safety, he thought, just one mile. In God's name, let us make it. In a hushed voice he spoke. "Josef is outside. We should hear his signal any moment." Again he emphasized, "Quiet! Nobody should speak!" Even the cows and horses in the barn followed Avrum's command and were silent.

Manya whispered to Meyer, "Where are we going?"

He held her tight against his body. "Shh, it's very close and it's safe. Nobody will find us."

Avrum whipped around and snapped, "I said *nobody* talks!"

They waited tensely for the signal from Josef, and then picked up faint noises. It sounded like a tiny squeaky hinge, then a pop, then the squeak again. Meyer knew immediately what it was. He'd heard it many times. He smiled to himself, and Manya looked at him. He pressed his mouth to her ear and breathed, "It's the cork in Josef's vodka bottle."

Avrum shot him a look, then returned his gaze to the barn door. There came a hoarse, muffled, "Avrum! Avrum!"

Avrum leaned down to grab Cyvia's hand, then motioned for the others to follow him outside.

Keeping pace with Josef's long strides, Avrum turned his head only long enough to assure himself that the others were following. He was oblivious of Cyvia's struggle to keep up with him, her short legs taking three steps to each of his.

They had walked some two hundred yards when Josef stopped. Confident that Avrum had his bearings, Wisniewski moved aside and held out his hand to him. The older man gripped the outstretched hand, then looked squarely at Josef's face. Wisniewski swung his free arm around his friend's shoulders in a powerful, bracing hug. Cyvia, still clinging to Avrum's hand, stared at the two men standing together. Then, following her father's example, she moved close and gave Josef a shy pat. He smiled down at her and stepped back, dropping a massive hand to stroke her hair. Avrum nodded, turned, and led his family on into the darkness.

Malka and Minka passed Josef. Malka looked at him hard, determined to find a crack in his facade that would confirm her doubt of him. He returned her gaze steadily, his eyes bright with honesty. Ashamed, she turned away and solicitously beckoned to Moniek and Rela to move along quickly.

By twos the procession continued to file past Josef. When Meyer stopped in front of him, the Pole reached in his back pocket, extracted the half-pint bottle, and held it toward Meyer in a salute. The characteristic gesture made Meyer grin and warmed him as if he had taken a jolt of the raw-tasting liquor. Josef popped the cork, leaned back, and drew a long, healthy swig. As he did, his half-buttoned shirt allowed the moonlight to flash on the crucifix hanging from his neck.

"Dziekuje, Josef."

"We will drink together again in happier times, my friend."

Meyer turned away, pulling Manya along in a half-run to catch up with the others. Within seconds they had closed the gap and assumed their place just behind Toba and Chaim. Meyer watched the two moving along obediently. He liked Manya's brother and knew Chaim would be safer here than at home. But he felt responsible for the fourteen-year-old's decision, and hoped that Chaim was not regretting it. He could sense Manya's silent suffering, and knew that there was similar anguish in the Nagelsztajns' basement. He could only hope and pray that their clever hideout would once again outwit the Germans. He still wished they had decided to come with him, but, he thought, maybe in a day or two I can sneak back and persuade them to join us. He looked up. The moon beamed its soft yellow light, and thousands of stars sparkled in the black velvet sky. How could the beauty of this night be party to such impending evil and destruction?

He tightened his viselike grip on Manya's hand, but she was too distracted by fear and confusion to notice the pressure on her numbing fingers. Should I have come with Meyer? Why didn't I stay with my family? Oh, I wish Papa had decided to come along! I should have stayed at home—I am the oldest—I could be helping with the little ones. Oh, God, please watch over my family and keep them safe!

Keeping pace with Meyer's quick steps, she searched for a clue to their destination—Meyer had said it was only a short distance from the barn, but where? There was nothing. The flat landscape stretched on and on, with not even a tree to interrupt the monotony. Just as she thought she could go no further, Meyer pointed straight ahead.

"There's the hiding place," he whispered, giving her a congratulatory squeeze.

Manya blinked her eyes, trying to focus on the looming, shadowy object of his triumph. What was it? It couldn't be a house—that would be too obvious a place to hide. She squinted in an effort to concentrate. "Where?" she asked.

"Right in front of us," he said, pointing once more.

The dark shape got bigger and bigger until she could see nothing else. Suddenly she knew what it was. She'd never seen one this large before. It was taller than her house. They stopped in front of it. She put her arm around Chaim automatically and looked at Meyer. "This is where we are going to hide? Behind this . . . this mountain of hay?"

"Not behind it," came the exultant reply, "*in* it!"

8

"What do you mean, in it? A haystack is a haystack; there's no 'in,' there's just hay. What are you talking about?" asked Manya, unable to comprehend what was happening. She kept her voice very low, but she was excited and mad. She tried to set her face disapprovingly, to show Meyer that if he was joking, she didn't find it very amusing. Her thoughts flashed to her parents at home. She should have stayed with them in the basement. It was a safe hideout. Now she had put Chaim in danger as well as herself. Why hadn't she talked Meyer into staying with her family? Then they'd all be safe.

Meyer moved to face her, enveloping her in his arms.

"Manya, Manya, Josef has dug out the inside. The Germans will never think to look for Jews in a haystack! Look at my father—he's trying to find the small wire that marks the entrance."

As they stood in the damp predawn cold, Avrum whispered instructions to Malka that everyone should go quietly to the nearby cornfield, for that would be their bathroom. There were more whispers and several reluctant looks, but soon they stumbled in pairs into the furrowed area with its dry stalks of camouflage.

But Manya stood rooted to the ground, watching Avrum as he crawled around the base of the haystack. She saw him draw his hands slowly along the circumference, pausing here and there to refeel, retrace. His searching fingers beat out a faint rhythm—pat, pat, pat, brush, pat, pat, pat. She could tell Avrum was getting frustrated at not being able to find the opening. Even though they had flashlights with them, he wouldn't dare use them.

Where was it? Why couldn't he find it? Hurry, Avrum! Soon it would be dawn; they'd be standing in the middle of the field with nowhere to go.

Then she heard a break in the pattern of sound; Avrum stiffened, and with great effort she saw him tug at the base of the haystack—once, and again, and then very slowly a chunk of hay slid ponderously away from the monstrous pile. Manya caught her breath, expecting the mountain to topple, burying them in its avalanche, but it held.

The group came back from the cornfield. Meyer went to Manya and propelled her toward the haven's gate, but Avrum thrust out his hand to stop Meyer.

"You go in first, Meyer, and make sure it's safe. It may have caved in. Be careful, but go quickly. We've been out in the open too long."

All eyes were focused on Meyer as he dropped to the ground and crawled into the entrance. In an instant he was out of sight, swallowed up by the haystack.

As Meyer pulled himself along the ground, he reached out to feel the sides of the narrow passage, testing to make sure the walls of hay would hold steady. Then he felt nothing. He scooted in a little farther and turned 360 degrees on his hands and knees to make sure the area was cleared out. Slowly he stood up, finally reaching full height. His head didn't touch the top, so he raised his arms, and his fingers met the sturdy ceiling of hay. He wanted to yell out: Hurray, Josef, you did it! Instead, he quickly scurried back through the passage to tell the others.

Nobody had moved. All eyes were still fixed on the opening as Meyer came popping out of the mouth of the haystack, grinning from ear to ear. Avrum helped Meyer up.

"Papa, Josef did it! There's plenty of room for all of us. We can even stand up."

With a deep sigh of relief, Avrum said, "Good, let's go in."

Led by Meyer, one by one they lay on the ground and crawled through the tunnel of hay, clawing the ground for traction, so afraid were they of pulling the straw down on top of them. Avrum slid in last, backward, stopping to sprinkle bits of hay and smooth the ground to camouflage their tracks, then yanking the "door" of hay along with him. In the narrow passageway he strained to reposition the bale that sealed them in their hideout. Again and again he adjusted it, pulled on it, making certain that it fit so well as to be unobtrusive from the outside. Satisfied at last, he rolled over on his back and lay still, breathing hard.

"It smells in here," came Cyvia's tired croaking voice in the darkness.

"Shh, now, darling, you'll get used to it. See how cozy we are?" Malka soothed. "We're all going to sleep—we're so weary. Come, let's snuggle and think about a nice dream to have."

"I want my doll to cuddle," Cyvia cried. "Why couldn't I have my doll?"

"Tch, sleep, darling Cyvia, sleep, now; you'll feel better when you wake up."

Recovered, Avrum felt his way along the straw-covered floor, repeatedly bumping into one set of legs and then another. It occurred to him that it might be difficult to find a spot for himself in the crowded space, but the others moved closer together, reaching out in the darkness, prodding him to a slot on the floor. Gingerly he eased himself against the wall of the haystack. He desperately wanted to flick on one of the flashlights, but resisted the temptation. He didn't know if the light would be visible from the outside. They'd have to experiment with that tomorrow night.

Manya pressed herself as close to Meyer as she could. She was trembling with cold and the stark realization that it would take all her strength to keep from screaming in this cramped, pitch-black, smelly enclosure. Yet, in another way, the darkness was rather nice, she thought. Here she was, in Meyer's arms, with his parents no more than a few inches from her feet. Think of it! It was quite daring, but she didn't care. She nuzzled closer, and placed her hand on Meyer's cheek. She felt him smile, and stifled her own giggle of delight. Nothing mattered; she could lose herself in his closeness, in his warmth. She leaned her head against his, and felt his lips on her hair and on her cheek, settling hard on her mouth. She shivered with delight, and pressed the length of her body against his.

9

Meyer awoke with a start. How long had he slept? It was so dark in the haystack, there was no way of knowing. Nor did it matter—he had no place to go. Trying to get comfortable, he reached into the wall of hay behind his head to pull some loose to fashion a pillow. "That's better," he sighed as his arm gathered Manya closer to him. Then he heard something. His eyes shot open and he sat up abruptly. Manya stirred but didn't awaken, and he closed his eyes against the darkness and tried to concentrate on the muffled noises from the outside. He wished everyone would stop breathing for just a moment so that he could sort out the sounds he wanted to hear.

He pictured the fields as he'd seen them the day before: the corn furrows, the wheat fields, sugarcane, Josef's house, the barn, more open fields, the fort . . . THE FORT! Soldiers, guns, horses, and trucks. Suddenly he knew what it was. He lay back against the hay, his eyes glazed, his body prickly all over.

"It has begun," Avrum stated quietly, startling Meyer again.

"It sounds like it, Papa," he answered, trying to regulate his voice to the same even, matter-of-fact frequency as his father's.

"Today will be very difficult, Meyer. The little ones especially will be frightened and bored. We must fill the time with talk—it will help us pass the hours. We must try not to think about what is going on in town. Remember, too, for Manya every sound will mean tragedy for her family. We must help her to think of other things."

"I know, Papa, I know," Meyer replied. "It must be daylight by now—do you think we can turn on a flashlight?"

"Soon, but not now—I think the others should sleep as long as possible. No more talking now, Meyer."

Meyer let his thoughts carry him away. There were many good times to remember, and he knew the children would like hearing some of the old stories again. He decided he would talk about his adventure in Russia—it hadn't been exactly a "good time," but it was exciting and might take the edge off the fear that promised to grow in the hours ahead.

He wondered how long the day would seem. He didn't like waiting, but they would have to—for days, even weeks. It didn't seem possible that they could hide here indefinitely. Now that he thought about it, he didn't think his father had ever considered the "other end" of hiding. All their energy had been devoted to getting into the hideout, and they'd never really considered a plan for leaving it. Meyer had thought that the Germans' hammerlock on the Jews would loosen as it had before; now he wasn't so sure.

He sat up suddenly, grabbing at his neck and rubbing his face and arms. It seemed as if something was creeping along his skin. Realizing it was only stray bits of hay, he explained to his newly awakened family, "I'm itchy all over. It reminds me of Russia, but not so bad as it was there."

"But why were you itchy when you were in Russia, Meyer?" asked Toba.

"The lice—don't you remember, Toba? I told you—"

"Tell it again," piped Cyvia. "What are lice?"

"Lice are tiny little bugs, and they get in your hair and crawl around. Then they lay eggs that are glued to each of your hairs, and when the eggs hatch there are more bugs crawling around. You scratch and scratch so much that your head bleeds, but still you have to scratch some more. They hop around and get in your clothes, and they keep laying more eggs. It's terrible, Cyvia, terrible! You think you'll go crazy!" Meyer looked around at the nine people facing him and saw them each scratch imaginary itches.

"But the lice didn't come first. It all started not long after Motl and Shuyl went to Russia. Things were difficult in Hrubieszow, with lots of talk about the Germans and the Russians invading Poland. Many people went to Russia. Quite a few came back, telling about bad conditions, no work, no food. That was when Manya's brother Ely went, too. Anyway, Motl and Shuyl left and crossed the border. I was almost fourteen, but Papa wouldn't let me go because he said I was too young."

"Papa was right, Meyer," said Malka. "Look at everything you did; you grew up very fast after Motl and Shuyl went away." Her eyes glistened as she added, "God watch over them wherever they are; I pray no harm has come to them, but it's been almost three years since we had any word. . . ."

"If Motl and Shuyl had stayed at home," said Moniek, "we might never have been quartered in your house, Meyer. We might be in the camps or dead right now."

"I want to hear more," said Minka. "When did you go to Russia, then? Who did you go with? What happened?"

"It was about a month after Motl and Shuyl left—November of 1939. The rumors of what was going on in Warsaw and Krakow got worse and worse. Finally three of my friends—Wolf, Dudie, and Buzi—and I decided we'd leave. Papa told me I should try to find Motl and Shuyl.

"So, off we went. The border was open and we crossed into

Russia. A Pole rowed us across the river in his boat. Wolf's father arranged it all. I remember I had a cloth bag with a little food—bread, apples, pears, and some pressed white cheese. The Russians didn't want a lot of people near the border, so they loaded us on trains and took us to Grodno. We stayed there a few weeks but we couldn't find work, so we went wandering around from place to place—I remember we stayed in Minsk for a long time, with no money, no ideas about what to do, and no success in finding my brothers.

"Life was very bad. We slept wherever we could find a place, sometimes in the park, often on the floor in people's houses. We could take only cold baths—icy cold. The people who tried to help us did all they could, but they hardly had enough for themselves, so we kept moving on. We got very discouraged and homesick and started thinking that things in Hrubieszow looked pretty good compared to Russia. Soon the lice were all over us. We went to a river and soaked in the cold, cold water and washed our hair and combed and brushed it until our scalps were raw, trying to get the lice out. I shiver to think of it even now, but it worked and we got rid of those awful bugs. We sold whatever we had to get money so we could buy other pants, shirts, and jackets, and then threw our old clothes away. We continued to move around and look for work to get a little money to buy food, sometimes loading trains in exchange for a free meal. But even with money we had to stand in line, and sometimes after waiting for hours, we still didn't get a turn. We waited all night in line once, and I was about twenty-fifth to the window of the store when it was announced that there was no more food to buy. They just closed the window."

"But what did you do? How did you get something to eat?" asked Toba.

"We didn't. We just stayed another night and waited. We decided then that we were probably going to die in Russia so we may as well go home—it couldn't be any worse."

"How could you get back home? Did you walk? What about food?" asked Minka.

"It wasn't easy, and we got very hungry. But we walked along the roads and hoped that a truck or a wagon or a cart would pass by and give us a lift. We heard that the border guards were becoming more strict and that you needed money to pay off the guards to get across. Everybody told us to stay in Russia. They said, 'You might starve in Russia, but you won't get shot.' I met a man who knew where we could cross; he had a friend who would let us through if we would give him money or valuables. Buzi had a pair of real nice boots that he could offer the man, and I had a pocket watch. Dudie surprised us all by pulling out a gold coin. He said his mother had given it to him for emergencies."

"But why didn't he use it before, when you were so hungry? That was an emergency, wasn't it?" asked Toba.

"My stomach thought it was an emergency, Toba," said Meyer, shaking his head, "but it's a good thing he didn't. Anyway, the guard, a Pole on the Ukrainian side, was very nice. He saw how bad we wanted to go home, and he refused to accept anything for helping us. We stayed near the border for five nights and waited for a good wind or snow."

"Why would you want wind or snow?" asked Toba.

"Because the river was frozen, and a strong wind would blow snow over our footprints after we walked across. Anyway, on the fifth night it was safe for us to go. Wolf decided he would stay in Russia—he thought it was safer. So the three of us sneaked over the river. We reached the German side, but didn't know what to do from there to get home. There was a Jewish community nearby, and the people raised a little money for us and we went to Warsaw. Buzi and Dudie decided they liked Warsaw and felt they had a better chance there. I spent a few days looking around and trying to decide how to get home. When I couldn't stand being homesick any longer, I started walking. A truck driver finally gave me a lift and took me about thirty-five miles. I got a ride on a couple of wagons after that, and then walked the rest of the way. I remember when I came into the house, the first thing Mama asked was about Motl and Shuyl. I had to tell her that I never found them. Papa was upset with me. He told me I shouldn't have come back home, that things were getting very bad. All the Jews had to wear armbands with the Jewish star on them, we weren't allowed to walk on the sidewalk when the Germans were present, and there was a curfew."

"Did you go to see Manya?" asked Minka.

"Oh, yes, as soon as I got back. I remember Mama was crying and telling me I'd better be home by six o'clock. I didn't think I'd be later than that, but when I got to Manya's we talked and talked, and the next thing I knew, it was after curfew." He turned to Manya. "Remember that, Manya? Remember how we sat in your little room?"

"I remember, Meyer," she said, reaching for his hand. "I remember how you used to pretend to pay attention to the other girls before you went to Russia. I remember going to your house day after day while you were gone to see if your family had any news about you."

Meyer turned and looked toward his three little sisters and Chaim.

"I'll tell you something I have only told Manya. When I was in Russia, I thought about Manya constantly, and all the wonderful times we had together—especially whenever things got really bad. It made it easier to get by. Although life was very difficult, that isn't the reason I came back. It was Manya that brought me back. I missed her so much. I didn't realize how much I loved her until I was away from her. I want you to remember what I've told you always. Whenever you're sad or things are very bad, you must make yourself think of happy thoughts and how much you love Papa and Mama and each other. This won't make the bad or the sadness go away, but it will make it easier and you'll have something to fight back with that nobody can take from you. Do you understand what I'm saying?"

For the first time, Chaim spoke up. "Meyer, I've been doing just that all these hours." Chaim had listened to Meyer's words carefully. He had always looked up to the older boy. "Memories are painful, but it does help to think of things as they used to be. I remember following you everywhere you went and being so glad when you came to our house to see Manya or play dominoes with my father . . ." His voice cracked, and Manya quickly finished his thought.

"Ah, yes, Chaim, I know, I know." She paused, then went on. "Meyer, the night that you returned from Russia—I remember you got to my house and you weren't wearing an armband. I told you that people were beaten or killed for that. But you said you wouldn't wear it, it was degrading and you wouldn't abide by the Nazis' dirty rules."

"I changed my mind about that pretty quick," said Meyer. "I learned what I had to do to stay alive."

"Didn't anybody fight back?" asked Cyvia.

"Yes, Cyvia, but not in the way you're thinking," said Avrum. "People did many things they weren't supposed to, like holding secret religious services, smuggling food and medicine into the ghetto, listening to radios, or hiding out like we're doing. You see, if people had fought back with fists or guns, the Nazis would have punished other Jews. Do you understand, Cyvia?"

"I'm not sure."

"Think of it like this, Cyvia," inserted Meyer. "Minka does something wrong, but not only does Minka get punished, so do you and Toba and Mama. Minka feels so bad that everyone else is getting punished for what she did that either she confesses to what she did or she promises herself she'll never do it again. After all, she doesn't want harm to come to others."

"People had to be very careful about what they did," added Manya. "Remember the time with your hat, Meyer?"

"Ooooh, yes," said Meyer with a wince. "I was feeling good that day, on my way to Manya's. About four blocks from her house, I was walking on the sidewalk and I saw two Germans coming toward me. I remember noticing that they were SS officers, but I didn't pay too much attention. Maybe I didn't see them soon enough, or maybe I just wanted to show them I wasn't going to obey the rules. I should have stepped off the sidewalk and tipped my hat, but I didn't. They called me dirty names and pushed me off the walk, beating me on the face with their fists. I wanted to hit them back so bad, but I knew they would shoot me if I did. I finally fell on the ground, so they kicked me and walked off. I was in a lot of pain, but finally I got up and dragged myself to Manya's house."

"You were lucky that time, Meyer. I saw many people killed for less than what you did," interjected Avrum.

"I know. After that, I did as I was told—followed all the rules . . . all but one," said Meyer, grinning.

"Which one was that?" asked Cyvia.

"The curfew," he replied. "I never observed the curfew. I wasn't stupid about it, but when I wanted to go to Manya's, I went—almost every night for three years. We all learned how to do what we wanted and still give the Germans the idea that we were obeying them. It was the only way to survive. We fought back, but in small ways, smart ways—ways that gave us satisfaction, but also allowed us to live. That was the most important thing: to keep hope for tomorrow. . . ."

Manya's thoughts wandered. She could hear spurts of gunfire in the distance, and she knew what it meant—had seen it with her own eyes. Once she and Meyer and a few others had followed a German-led march of elderly Jews to the edge of town. As they watched, the Jews were lined up in front of foxholes dug by the Polish Army in its early attempts to defend the city against invasion. The noise was deafening: shrieking, praying, pleading, gunfire, and more gunfire. Manya opened her mouth to scream, but no sound emerged. The bodies crumpled into the gash in the ground. She stood paralyzed, while dirt was pushed into the hole over the bodies. Then the Germans departed. But the horror intensified as the mound of earth undulated with the efforts of the half-dead to claw their escape from the grisly grave.

Manya and Meyer and the others crept away from the scene silently, for there were no words—nothing to say. The teenagers stumbled along together numbly, dropping away one by one to take individual routes home. Manya tried to shake off the specter, to pay attention to Meyer's words, but she couldn't stop the pictures in her mind—pictures of her own family being led out and slaughtered.

10

Josef Wisniewski heaved his body out of the chair and walked to his front door. He stared into the distance at the town he had grown up in. It was quiet now, its citizens making ready for bed even though it was still fairly early. They'll go to bed to forget what they have seen today, he thought, to forget what they have allowed to happen. He listened to his mother and sister in the kitchen, clearing away the supper dishes. Very soon it would be time to take the food to the Korenblits, but tonight he wished there were someone else to do it. He didn't want to face them, to answer their questions. He felt somehow responsible for the horror he'd witnessed today, and he was ashamed. The full impact of what had happened was taking hold.

As much as he believed there were many good Poles, they hadn't been in evidence this morning. No, they sat inside their homes and let the Nazis get on with their massacre. Just as he had sat in the otherwise deserted tavern dulling his raw nerves with vodka. For some reason he thought that helping the Korenblits would assuage his guilt, make it easier for him to observe the expulsion, but he was wrong. He felt as guilty as if he himself had held one of the Nazi guns.

Josef shook his head and sighed. Pulling on his jacket, he strode into the kitchen for the food he would carry to the haystack. Without a word he left the house and was on his way. Last night he had thought his mood would be jovial and victorious. Last night he was looking forward to tricking the Germans by hiding a Jewish family. But tonight he was very, very weary, and dreaded meeting the searching faces of his charges. What could he say? How could he describe the scene?

He had seen a deportation before—the violence and death— but not like this. He had seen hope flicker in the victims' eyes when selections were made and some were chosen to stay and some to leave. But there were no selections today; everyone was going. He watched the captives try to gather some composure, even some dignity, just to survive the expulsion.

He had gone into town that morning; why, he wasn't exactly sure. It had taken only a short time for the well-organized Nazi brigade to storm the town. The trucks and cars appeared as if from nowhere, belching loads of soldiers and shutting off all access to escape. He heard sharp orders barked on the streets of the Jewish section for Jews to vacate immediately and line up in rows. Rifle butts pounded on doors, punctuating the guttural commands, as troops burst into homes and dragged out dazed mothers, fathers, and children.

A few doors were opened cautiously by the residents, then roughly thrown wide by passing corporals and privates whose faces were twisted with loathing as they shoved families to the ground outside. As the street filled, odd figures here and there streaked for the alleyways, but were shot down by staccato bursts from machine guns. Some watched terror-stricken, holding their children close, while others ran mindlessly, abandoning their sons and daughters. The captives' eyes searched for sanity among their aggressors, but even their Polish neighbors watching through shuttered windows turned away from the stares. Instead they found only more horror as they watched infants tossed in the air and blown apart by rifle shots.

The screams dulled as the first group was herded by engine-revving trucks and gun-wielding Nazis, pressing the captives on top of each other. Some tripped, and were shot as they fell out of line; others stumbled, and were trampled, then kicked aside. Big hands gripped little hands, half-carrying the little ones lest they fall and be lost. Other hands reached ahead to hasten those in front, pitching them off balance; some used a free hand to steady a partner.

Behind them came cries of more frenzied victims and unceasing German orders. The train depot was just ahead; a thick column of steam rose from the locomotive. There was no time to look back—the past was gone forever.

11

For seven nights the routine had been the same. Josef came to the haystack around ten o'clock bringing food and other necessities. He would signal; then Avrum and Meyer would crawl out. It was always good to see Josef—their only contact with the outside—because he passed on information about happenings in the city that day. But it wasn't only the food and information that provided relief to the hiding family, it was also the knowledge that the outside world still existed, even though they were isolated from it.

He was always the same Josef, with the smell of liquor on his breath. But as each day came and went, Josef's face grew more somber. The Germans were intensifying their search for Jews, putting immense pressure on Poles to aid in this hunt. While there was no doubt that Josef would continue to help them, he was now gravely concerned with the increased danger to his mother and sister.

Each night Josef stayed for about ten minutes. He always said the same thing before he left: "Everything will be fine. Don't worry. Nobody has any idea that you're here. I'll see you tomorrow." Then he would turn and amble off in the direction of the barn. After that, Meyer and Avrum would crawl back into the haystack. It was time for a visit to the cornfield. Manya and Meyer let the others go first so they could have the haystack to themselves for their only moments of total privacy. They looked forward to this time, cherishing each brief moment.

The group would file back into the enclosure, eat, discuss Josef's report, tell stories, and drift off to sleep, usually at dawn. By early afternoon they were awake. Avrum would open his prayerbook and read out loud. He would tell a story from the Torah; then someone else would tell a story or recall an incident—anything at all that was amusing or adventuresome or interesting. Then the pattern was repeated for the next twenty-four hours, and the next.

It seemed later than usual to Meyer, and Josef had not yet arrived. He looked around the small enclosure. Josef had mentioned again last night that Poles were looking in every conceivable place for hidden Jews, in order to claim the bounty offered by the Germans. There were ten of them in the haystack. Ten people: ten pounds of sugar—a virtual gold mine. A Polish family could live very well with that on the black market, trading a few ounces of sugar for the necessities and luxuries of life. It was a tempting notion, Meyer had to admit.

"Daddy, I can't wait any longer. When can I go to the bathroom?" Cyvia whined.

"Josef's a little later than usual," Malka said uneasily to Avrum. "Do you think something has happened?"

"You know how careful Josef has been. He probably just wants to make sure everything is safe."

"He'll be here soon. We don't have to worry about Josef. He hasn't failed us yet, and he won't now," Meyer added with assurance.

"If need be, we have enough food to make it through tomorrow," said Avrum.

Meyer sensed the tension building. He knew they should talk to take their minds off Josef. Suddenly he thought of something, and began laughing out loud.

"What is it, Meyer? What's so funny?" Moniek asked.

"I was just thinking back," Meyer explained, with a snicker still on his lips. "We used to do some pretty funny things. I'll never forget the times when my friends and I figured out a way to play a joke on that farmer on the other side of town, the one who was always so grouchy with everyone. Remember, Chaim? I told you about it. We'd sneak into the man's barn very early and milk his cow. I can still taste that warm, bubbly milk—it was so good! Then we would hide when we heard him coming. He just couldn't figure out what was wrong with the cow when he didn't get any milk. We'd listen to him cursing at it; then we'd run away. We did it several times."

The laughter became contagious as one by one they joined in. Cyvia held her stomach with her hands as her merry giggle rang out in the enclosure.

"Wait!" Chaim pleaded over the gaiety. "I remember something else you told me, Meyer—the Russian soldier who tied an alarm clock around his neck! I still don't believe it!"

"It's true, I swear! He'd never seen a wristwatch before and I guess he thought that a clock would be just as good! We'd see him coming down the street with that thing bouncing against his chest—it was all we could do to keep quiet until he passed by!"

Cyvia squirmed, waving her hands, warning of her loss of control.

"Meyer, please, no more," said Toba. "Poor Cyvia, she's going to wet her pants!" Her plea only sent them into another helpless outburst.

When the laughter died down, Avrum made a decision. "Since we don't know when Josef will get here, we'd better go to the cornfield. But we'll go together. Wait here while I check to see that it's safe."

Avrum inched his way to the opening. He listened for a few moments before he cautiously slid the bale of hay from its slot. He peeked around the entrance, then pulled himself out and stood up. He pushed the bale back into place and slowly walked around the haystack. Confident that there was no one around, Avrum went back to the opening and signaled the others to join him.

"Now, stay together, be as quiet as possible, and hurry."

Moniek led the group to the cornfield.

Avrum pulled Meyer aside. "Meyer, I'm worried. We must find

out what has happened to Josef. If he's been caught, it might be too dangerous for us to stay here."

"I'll go over to his house and talk to his mother."

"But that could be far more dangerous."

"I can go, Papa, and not be caught."

"I don't know. Someone could be watching the house."

"It's all right, Papa, I can make it—we have to find out what's going on."

"But you must return here immediately."

"Papa, I'll come right back."

"Nothing more. You promise?"

"Yes! Yes! I'll go straight to the farmhouse and back."

"Go quickly, then. And return as soon as possible. I'll tell the others where you've gone." Then, anticipating Meyer's request: "Yes, I'll talk to Manya and tell her not to worry."

"Thank you, Papa. I don't want her to think I've left her alone."

Meyer turned from his father and disappeared into the shadows of the night. Maybe one of the animals is sick and Josef is still in the barn, he thought. He'd better check there first.

The night was chilly, but the humid air felt wonderful on his face. Meyer always liked this kind of night. Before the war he and Manya would go walking through the park in the evening. He'd wrap his arm loosely around her, but as the night air got colder, he'd pull her tightly to him to combine the warmth of their bodies. Someday they'd share that closeness again. He could feel an old exhilaration returning and knew that he wasn't one to be satisfied with waiting or inactivity.

It wasn't long before the shape of the barn loomed into view. He couldn't see a light inside, so he doubted that Josef was there, but he had to make sure. Meyer pushed the barn door open just a crack and looked in. It was dark inside, but he could see the silhouettes of some of the animals. Except for an occasional snort from one of the horses, it was quiet. He opened the door a little farther, causing it to creak, stirring the animals from their sleep. He could see better now as a splinter of moonlight shone in over his shoulder. In a raspy voice he called out, "Josef, Josef. Are you here?"

There was no response. He walked back into the night air, closing the door behind him. He'd have to go to the house. It was very early in the morning, and he'd probably scare Mrs. Wisniewski and Josef's sister half to death by knocking at their door.

The house was just across the yard from the barn. He scurried in its direction and stepped up onto the porch. All the shades were drawn, so he couldn't see in, but he could detect a dim light escaping from a gap in the window covering. He raised his shaking hand and tapped gently on the door. There was no response. He rapped again and waited.

He heard some movement inside, then a woman's voice: "Who's there?"

Meyer hesitated, then summoned the courage to speak. "It's Meyer Korenblit."

The door opened and Mrs. Wisniewski stood there in her robe with a look of panic on her face. He was putting her in tremendous danger by being here. If anyone saw him, it would mean death for all of them.

"Come in quickly before someone sees you." She shut the door and led him into the living room. Her hands fingered her rosary as she asked, "What is it? Why are you here?"

"I'm looking for Josef. He didn't come with the food tonight." Meyer saw the dread on her face soften as he spoke, and then realized that she feared he had come with bad news. "It must be one o'clock in the morning by now. We were afraid something happened."

"No, it's way past one o'clock. And that's why I'm worried, too. I was hoping that you'd come to tell me where he is. He left the house this morning as usual at six-thirty, and I haven't seen him since. He didn't come home for dinner. He always tells me if he won't be home to eat."

"Where do you think he could be?" asked Meyer.

"Maybe the Germans . . . No. Why should they take him? He has done nothing to them," she choked, almost breaking down. Suddenly her expression changed.

"If they did, maybe they just wanted to question him, or perhaps they know he's hiding us," Meyer blurted out.

Mrs. Wisniewski crossed herself, and resumed her rhythm with the beads, her eyes pleading for Meyer to deny his words.

"No, that can't be so, or they would have come here for you and your daughter. They would have searched the whole area," he said, trying to calm her.

"You're probably right. Yes, that would be true."

Meyer groped for more words of consolation, but could find none. He'd better leave the old woman to her thoughts and not endanger her further with his presence.

"I must go now. I have to get back to my family," he said, heading for the door.

Mrs. Wisniewski grabbed Meyer's arm. "Wait! Let me give you the food that I prepared." She moved into the kitchen and returned lugging a deep pot and some heavy loaves of crusty bread.

"Thank you, Mrs. Wisniewski, everything will be all right," Meyer said reassuringly.

The woman brushed Meyer's words aside, peeked outside, and opened the door.

"You mustn't come back here. It's too dangerous for all of us."

Meyer nodded, turned, and left. Juggling a loaf of bread tucked under each arm and holding the pot with both hands, he trudged off in the direction of the haystack, disappointed. He'd have to report to his father that there was no news of Josef. If only there was a way . . . Suddenly he stopped. Of course! There was someone who'd know if something had happened to Josef. But Meyer had promised his father to come right back. No, they had to get the information. Meyer turned 180 degrees and started walking as fast as he could toward John Salki's house.

12

Meyer realized he was taking a big chance by going to Salki's. Salki lived on the main road outside the city, between the fort and the brick factory—both Nazi strongholds. There was always some type of movement on the road—from the fort to the brick factory, from the brick factory to the city, and from the city to the fort. It was a dangerous cycle to intrude upon. Meyer had about two miles to cover, and he was already having trouble with the cumbersome pot, and the loaves of bread kept sliding out of his grasp. The food was slowing him down.

Every second was precious. He would have to allow two hours for travel time, and that would leave only about an hour before daybreak. He would need at least that long at Salki's. His approach to the house would have to be guarded and gradual, for even though John Salki's door was always open to people in need, his official status as commissioner of roads required that it also be open to the Nazis.

Meyer was sure that Salki wouldn't be upset with him for arriving at this late hour. He had gone there at strange times before, and further, Salki was a close friend. While many of the Poles of Hrubieszow had turned on their Jewish friends when the Nazis took control of the city, and helped in the persecution and suffering, not so with Gorski, or Salki, or Wisniewski.

Even though he knew the way, he looked for familiar sights to gauge how far he still had to walk. He struggled along, trying not to spill the contents of the pot. Damn this food! He should have left it; he was *never* going to get there. What a relief it would be to see Salki's house!

Meyer knew the house well. Once when the Germans had come to take the Jews away, Salki had hidden the Korenblits for several days under a false floor in the attic. Salki had even warned them that trouble was coming. He told them that the Germans were planning to take away only a certain number of Jews then, not everyone. Although the haystack hideout on Wisniewski's farm had been ready, Avrum decided to save it for when there would be no next time.

John Salki wasn't overly impressive at first glance. He was in his mid-thirties, about five-feet-six, a little on the heavy side, with a small bald spot on his head. He always wore his uniform and tall black boots, his pants tucked neatly into them, an ever-present cigarette burning between his fingers. But his proper appearance and rigid habits paled when you looked at his face and saw his warm, friendly hazel eyes. Salki was married and had four children, the eldest a thirteen-year-old boy, Janek.

The commissioner had always been nice to the Korenblit family because of a favor Avrum had done for him years ago. Even before the war, the Korenblits and the Salkis had been good friends. For the past three years, since the Nazi invasion, Salki had given his help whenever necessary, asking nothing in return. There was never a moment's hesitation on his part. Once again they were calling on this relationship for assistance. Meyer had learned the true meaning of friendship.

His fingers were numb now as he skirted the tree-lined road into the city. Stumbling into the brush across from Salki's house, he gratefully set down the pot and let the bread fall from under his arms. As he watched the house and the street, the sound of his own heavy breathing filled his ears. His practiced eyes panned the area meticulously. Even when he was satisfied that he had a clear path to the house, he forced himself to scan it again. There was nothing. He half-crawled into the open, and then raced toward the door, keeping his body hunched over and using it to increase his forward momentum. Diving for a shadow by the door and crouching in its safety, he held his breath to listen. He reached up and knocked.

Meyer listened for footsteps from inside the house, but all he heard was the wind blowing softly through the trees. For the first time since he had left the haystack, he felt the cold of the November morning. Maybe he should knock again.

He raised his hand, then heard a weary voice: "Is somebody there?"

"Salki! It's me, Meyer Korenblit. I need to talk to you."

The door opened and Meyer hurried inside.

"Meyer, what are you doing here? You know how dangerous it is for you to be out. The Nazis would shoot you on sight!"

"I know, I know. But something has happened to Josef."

"What?"

"I have no idea. He didn't arrive with the food tonight. He's never failed to show up before. Do you think the Germans got him?"

"I don't know, Meyer. I haven't heard. I told Avrum it wasn't good to trust Wisniewski—that drunk." His voice rose in anger, the words hissing through his teeth. "I warned him something like this could happen. You'd better stay here until tonight, when it will be safer to go back to the hideout. Since this last deportation, the Nazis have been sending out patrols at all hours to catch any Jew who may have escaped. They don't want to miss even one. The dark hours are no longer safe the way they used to be."

"I understand, but I can't stay here. My family would worry and wouldn't know what to do. I told Papa I'd be back soon."

"Do as you must, but remember, it's risky. As for Josef, I'll check around town later today. Gorski might know something. I'll go see him. Now, listen to me, Meyer, if I find out anything, I'll send Janek to the hideout. The Germans know he is my son,

and they won't bother him. If you don't hear from me by night-
fall, tell your father to leave the hideout and come here. We'll put
you up until I can find a safer place. Do you understand?"

"Yes, Salki."

"Good. Now, go quickly, and be careful."

"Thank you for everything—"

"Don't thank me yet, it's not over." Salki peeked out the door,
checking to see that no one was in sight, and waved Meyer on his
way.

With two steps and a single bound Meyer was off the porch and
racing across the clearing to the bushes where he had left the
food. He crouched down and patted the ground, searching for
the bread. As he placed the loaves back under his arms, he felt
the dull ache of a cramp begin in his shoulder. He had to think of
another way to carry it. He buttoned the bottom of his jacket and
stuffed the bread inside, high enough for him to brace the pot on
his belt buckle. It seemed secure, and if it wasn't, he'd heave the
whole mess into the river and be done with it.

He pictured Manya curled up and waiting for him in the haystack, and he struck out into the fields once more.

13

"Shouldn't Meyer be back by now? He's been gone a long time,"
asked Manya.

"There's nothing to worry about, Manya, he'll be all right. You
should know better than anyone," Avrum responded. "Knowing
Meyer, he probably went to all of Josef's favorite places to find
him," Avrum joked, trying to ease everyone's fear. But he, too,
was worried. Meyer had been gone nearly four hours, and Avrum
had spent that time encouraging the others to talk, even allowing
them to switch on the flashlights for a short time. He suggested
that they divide the sparse leftovers and stale bread for a snack,
but no one seemed to be hungry. Finally Cyvia prevailed upon
him to braid some straws of hay into a doll, which she then
wrapped in a handkerchief and serenaded in a squeaky voice.
The older girls, anxious to find amusement, settled on sticking

straws of hay in their noses and ears, making faces, and giggling.

Manya watched the merriment wistfully, wishing Meyer were present, then thinking of her own family. Malka leaned down to her, reached out and put an arm around Manya, brushing the dark blond hair away from her face in a gentle, loving gesture. The tears that Manya had held back so bravely for seven days spilled down her cheeks as she pulled Malka's arm tighter around her. Meyer's mother held her until she felt Manya's shaking stop, then whispered to her, "They'll be all right, Manya, they'll be all right." She crawled to the opposite side of the hideout, quietly ministering to her sleepy daughters.

Manya watched the older woman with renewed respect and deepening affection. She wasn't an outsider any longer. She had been accepted by Meyer's family. She couldn't wait to tell Meyer. She must have dozed off, for the next thing she heard was Malka speaking to Avrum.

"Avrum, there's something terribly wrong. First Josef disappears, and now Meyer. He's been gone too long—at least three hours. Aren't you going to do something?"

Avrum didn't want to tell her that it had been longer than three hours. He was concerned himself. Why couldn't Meyer ever do just as he was told? he thought. It never occurred to him that Meyer might have been caught—he had too much faith in his son and his God to believe that. He had to believe it. The alternative was unthinkable.

"Now, listen," he began. "For three years we've seen the horrors of this tragedy all around us, yet somehow we've made it this far. There is a reason: God is watching over us and He will bring Meyer back here safely. Meyer is just being careful to make sure nobody will find us."

"Avrum, I've been thinking," said Moniek. "We should be considering what we'll do if Meyer doesn't—"

"No! There is no 'if,' Moniek, Meyer will be here soon, I'm sure of it. We need no plan, we'll go nowhere—we'll wait for Meyer."

"Avrum, please, I had no intention of suggesting that Meyer wouldn't return. I'd never think such a thing, let alone say it after all you've done for Rela and me. I was going to say if Meyer doesn't find Josef or learn of his whereabouts, we'll need to make some decisions for all of us—including Meyer. I've been giving some thought to the underground. Do you think there is a chance that we could—?"

Avrum waved him silent. He thought he heard something. Yes, there it was again. Could it be Josef?

"Papa, Papa, it's me," came the voice from outside.

It was Meyer. Avrum heard a relieved sigh come from Malka. "Oh, thank God."

"Yes, thank you, God," Manya heard Avrum say in a half-whisper. He moved swiftly to the opening, and within seconds was outside with his son. They were hugging as though they hadn't seen each other for days.

"Where have you been? You've been gone for so long—it's nearly dawn. Did you have a problem? Did you find Josef?"

"Papa, we must get inside. I want to see Manya."

"Yes, of course. Go ahead."

Manya grabbed Meyer as soon as his head cleared the tunnel, and hugged him with all her strength. He squeezed back and then kissed her on the lips.

"Tell us, son, what did you find out?"

Meyer explained about going to the barn and Wisniewski's house. "After that, I went to Salki's, and he—"

"Salki's! Why did you go there?" demanded Malka.

"I figured if anyone would know what happened to Josef, it would be Salki."

"And what news did he have?" asked Avrum.

"He doesn't know anything either. But he's going to try to find out, and then he'll send word with Janek."

"Janek is coming here?" Avrum gasped. "That's crazy. It's far too dangerous. How could Salki put his son in such danger?"

"It's all right, Papa, the Germans know Janek, so they won't be suspicious."

"I hope you're right, son."

"But wait, if Janek doesn't come, it will mean there is no news of Josef, and then we are to go to Salki's house to hide. We're to stay there until a safer place can be found."

Avrum looked at Malka, then around the room at the rest of the group. They were all waiting for his response.

"I don't know if that's the best thing to do. I've been thinking—maybe it would be better if we went to Mislavitch. I know that

Tomitzki or Achler would help find a place for us to stay. Or Moniek was just mentioning the possibility of escaping through the underground. Salki and Gorski could help us with that, but the arrangements might take too long—there are so many of us. That would make it difficult for them. What do you think, Meyer?"

"I would rather go to Salki's and then see if he can smuggle us out a few at a time through the underground. That sounds good to me; then, when we're safe, we could help others escape, too. I like that idea."

"I think they need men without the responsibilities of a family, who are willing to take great risks," Rela interrupted. "I don't think that women and children are taken into the underground. That means we'd probably have to wait a long time. I don't want Moniek to do it—I don't want to be left alone. Moniek, please, you can't do this!" she sobbed.

"Now, Rela, we haven't made a decision yet. We're simply discussing choices that we can make," soothed Avrum. "I, for one, don't want to leave my family behind. We've been lucky so far, and the only way I'll leave my little girls is if I'm taken away by force. Perhaps Mislavitch would be the best choice, although Salki and Gorski are of great help to us here, and there is no one in Mislavitch who can get the kind of information they can."

"Avrum, that will be a long walk for the girls," said Malka.

"That's true, Avrum," echoed Moniek, "and we won't be able to walk along the main road, which means it's even a harder and longer distance to travel."

"I know, but I feel it's very dangerous right now in Hrubieszow."

"Can we make it all that way in one night?" asked Rela.

"We have to; we have no choice," responded Avrum.

The decision was made. They would leave for Mislavitch as soon as it turned dark again.

Meyer leaned heavily against the hay. "Ooooh, I'm tired," he murmured to Manya.

"Do you want something to eat? I think there's enough for a few bites, anyway; maybe you'd feel better—"

"My God, the food!" Meyer yelled. "I brought food from Mrs. Wisniewski! I put it down outside. Wait." He scrambled back outside and retrieved his bounty.

"We've gone a long way together," he said to the pot as he slithered it along the tunnel floor and pitched the bread inside. "Now we'll see if it was worth it."

14

Meyer had eaten his fill of Mrs. Wisniewski's stew, using his bread to soak up every glutinous drop. Sleep came easily and was deep, and he awakened to the glow of a flashlight and a clatter of dishes.

"Sorry," Malka said, regretting the noise.

Meyer watched his mother making order in the enclosure, wrapping dishes and utensils in clothes to soften their rattle on the long walk ahead. As she filled the baskets, she tested the weight of each so that even Cyvia could carry her share, for a time at least. As the group stirred to life, Malka's activities became less hushed. They all stared at her dreamily.

Picking up a loaf of bread, she tore chunks from it, tossing them to her family.

"Dip it in the stew," she ordered, nudging the pot and its congealed leftovers to the center of the group.

"Come, come," she insisted when no one moved. "It may not look so good, but we need to eat. We can't take it with us, and we will *not* waste it. There may be a time when we'll be grateful for even a smell of such food."

Manya obediently reached over to the pot, scooping a healthy smear onto her bread. One by one the rest complied, and before too many minutes, the pot was scraped clean. They settled back, feeling the heaviness of the food and the journey they were about to undertake.

Avrum figured they should wait one more hour before leaving for Mislavitch. They had to go as soon as night fell, to make sure there was enough darkness to complete the journey. It was eleven miles to Mislavitch. Normally he could travel that distance in two to three hours. But not tonight. They'd have to make their way through the fields, and then, there were the children. There was no way they could travel that distance quickly.

"What more must we do to be ready?" Avrum asked.

"Everything is packed," replied Malka. "There's a bundle for everyone to carry, but I think the little ones may get tired before we go too far."

"Meyer, Moniek, and I can carry them if need be; we'll manage. Now, girls," Avrum addressed his daughters, "you understand that we have a long walk, and we must go as quickly and quietly as possible if we are to arrive at the flour mill before dawn. Do you remember the flour mill, Cyvia, where Papa used to have a business?"

"Of course she doesn't remember, Avrum," Malka broke in. "She was too young. It's Minka you used to take on the wagon."

"Ah, yes, that's right, isn't it, my little Minka? You liked to watch the big stone wheels grinding the grain, didn't you? And you, Toba, I remember how you helped me with the sacks. You used to tell me the flour mill needed dusting, right?" He chuckled as his eldest daughter beamed at him.

"We'll tell stories and talk of old times when we get to Mislavitch. Who knows? Perhaps we can all help Mr. Tomitzki in the mill. But first we must get there, and the journey is very dangerous. You must promise me to do exactly as I say and make no noise outside. We don't want the soldiers to catch us, now, do we? You understand: there will be no chance to talk outside."

The little girls nodded their solemn promise.

"Very good. I think we're ready. We'll wait a few moments to be sure it's good and dark."

"I was just thinking, Papa," said Meyer. "Why do you suppose Janek didn't come today, as Salki said he would?"

"It's just as well, son," Avrum answered. "As much as I would like to know some news of Josef, we've made our plans. Salki knows enough to guess where we are. He's been very good to us, but we can't expect too much. We should recognize those times when we must do for ourselves. God helps those who help themselves, Meyer."

"Why do you say that?" flashed Meyer's anger. "Is God helping us to run like rats through the night? Is God watching as our friends are shot down, their children beaten against brick buildings until their heads crack open? Papa, can't you see? God has abandoned the Jews!"

"No more, Meyer! I will not hear any more. This is no time for such talk, do you hear?"

Silence engulfed the group. Meyer was infuriated with his father's unyielding religious beliefs and tried to gather an effective response.

Then Avrum spoke again. "Shh, what's that?"

"It's a dog," Meyer announced.

"A dog, yes, but there's something else. Shh!"

Oh, God, not dogs, thought Moniek. The Germans are using dogs to track Jews. They were lost. It was over. But he could hear no sharp commands, no shouted instructions. Instead, a singsong chant penetrated the walls of hay.

A grin crept across Meyer's face as the sound became intelligible.

"It's Josef," he cried. "I know it. Listen, Papa, listen—can't you hear what he's saying?"

Avrum pressed his ear to the hay as the words wafted through the haystack: ". . . wheat and flour; flour and wheat. My life is dry—do you hear me, dog? A little vodka makes it easy to swallow the flour and wheat. . . ."

Avrum scrambled for the tunnel and the outside. Malka tried to hold him back, but he shook her off. Meyer was right on his heels. With a certain lack of caution they shoved the bale of hay outward. They were startled at the darkness outside—where had the time gone? But Josef's big hand reached down to pull them out of the haystack. They leaped to pound each other in greeting, fairly dancing about the hard ground.

"Josef, for God's sake, where were you?" Avrum cried.

"Why didn't you come last night?" Meyer chimed in. "I went looking for you!"

"Yes, my mother told me," said Josef sheepishly. "I went to town last night, I'm afraid," he explained. "It wasn't too late when I came home, and I remember unhitching my horse and putting him in the stall, but I can't recall anything else. I woke up this morning in the barn."

"The barn?" shouted Meyer. "That's impossible. You couldn't have been in the barn. I looked for you there!"

"Well, maybe you were looking for a Josef who was standing up, Meyer. This Josef was passed out on the ground."

The three stared at one another, then laughed, savoring the moment of friendship.

"Then everything is all right?" said Avrum.

Josef faced him, his look serious and dark. "I don't feel so confident, Avrum," came the heavy reply. "The situation is worse than ever before. The Germans haven't let up the pressure—they're like madmen, obsessed that our city be 'Judenrein.' That's all you hear; there are notices posted everywhere. But there's more: they're hounding the Poles, too, shooting anyone who is even suspected of helping Jews. I fear for my mother and sister, Avrum. I can't ask them to sacrifice their lives. I never thought it would get so bad. I don't want to turn you away . . ."

Avrum threw an arm around Josef's brawny shoulders. "It's all right, my friend. You've already done more than any man could ask of another. God grant me the time to do the same for you. We've done some planning and are thinking of going to Mislavitch. Also, Meyer saw Salki last night—we can go there for a time anyway. What do you think?"

"Avrum, I feel I have failed you. We thought this would work, but I have the feeling I'm being watched . . . no one can be trusted . . ."

"Enough, Josef. Put it out of your mind. Salki will take over now; then we shall see," Avrum consoled.

"Stay at Salki's a few days. You could come back to the haystack; maybe things will improve."

"Thank you, Josef, it helps to know that you'll take us back when the tension eases. You're a good friend and a decent man, Josef. We'll always be in your debt."

"Do milego zobaczania," Josef said in a husky voice.

Meyer grabbed the man's outstretched hand in both his own. "Yes, Josef, until we meet again."

Meyer saw the tears in Josef's eyes. He moved close to Avrum, and the two watched as Josef summoned his dog and walked ponderously toward the farmhouse.

15

"Josef has lifted the burden of his family's danger from his shoulders, Meyer, but he looks as if he is bearing a bigger one: his conscience. He should think about how much he's already done to help." Shaking his head, Avrum added, "Come, let's get back inside; we must decide what to do."

"Do you think we'll see Josef again, Papa?"

"I hope so, son, but I'm afraid it'll be a long time."

"So many people, Papa, all our friends. The kids I grew up with and went to school with. Where are they now? Do you think any of them are still alive?"

"We can only pray that some are."

"What about the Nagelsztajns? How can we find out if they're all right? Maybe in a few days I can sneak into town."

"No! I know Manya and Chaim are very concerned, but you'd be endangering us and them if you went. Besides," Avrum added, moving to the entrance of the haystack, "we may not be here in a few days."

The wind whisked through the open field. Meyer narrowed his eyes against the cold of its gust and stared after Josef. When will this be over? he thought. He wanted to walk down the street in the daytime with his head held high. He wanted to be with Manya without worrying that someone was watching or would turn them in because they were Jews. He wanted to be with Manya anytime he wanted, wherever he wanted. We are human beings, he thought. They have no right to do this to us or to anyone.

Avrum turned and looked at his son. He'd grown up a lot in these three years, he thought. We could never have made it this far without him. Thank God for Manya. If not for Meyer's love of her, he might still be in Russia searching for his brothers. The two of us have shared fear and sadness, exchanged worries and hopes, and all of it has made us close and trusting of one another. Had our lives been normal, we might never have achieved such a bond. All the harder to lose each other, he thought, opening the entrance of the haystack. No, Avrum resolved, such weak thoughts will betray the Jews. The Nazis may kill me with bullets, but I'll never allow my own thoughts to defeat me.

"Meyer," he called, "we must go inside."

The young man nodded, moving to join his father. He motioned Avrum to go first, then slid inside himself.

As soon as Cyvia saw Meyer, she blurted out, "What did he say? What did Josef say?"

"Things aren't good," Avrum began. "Josef can't bring us food anymore. He says the Nazis are arresting Poles they suspect of helping Jews. He isn't scared for himself, but he doesn't want his mother and sister hurt. Poor Josef, the man feels he has failed us. The entire Jewish population of Hrubieszow has been killed or deported. Yet here we are, alive and together because he was willing to risk his own life rather than turn his back on a friend. He did say we can stay here as long as we want and that maybe later when things calm down he'll be able to help again. If there were more people like Josef, maybe more Jews would be hiding out safely."

"So, last night he didn't come because he was afraid of being watched?" asked Moniek. The dim glow from the flashlight gave off just enough light for everyone's face to be seen. For the first time in many days, Moniek saw Avrum break into a smile.

"No, that isn't why Josef didn't show up last night. He didn't come because he got drunk, fell asleep in the stall of the barn, and didn't wake up until noon today," answered Avrum.

There was total silence in the haystack, and then, as if they'd been given a cue, everyone burst out laughing. It was a moment of relief that they all needed.

"Now we must decide what we'll do," said Avrum. "It's too late to leave for Mislavitch. Salki said he would continue to help us, and we still have Gorski. Remember, Josef feels we're safe here. He was just afraid of being seen when he visits us. I think we should have Meyer go back to Salki and find out what he thinks would be the best thing for us to do."

"I should go immediately, Papa, before Janek gets here," Meyer said, motioning Manya to follow him outside.

As they crawled through the tunnel, Meyer heard his mother call out: "Be careful, Meyer, and please don't take any chances."

Manya pulled herself through the tunnel on wooden legs. She didn't want Meyer to leave again. Why must it always be his job to take the risks? she wondered. Why was he so quick to say yes? She decided to assure him that he didn't need to prove anything; he was already a hero in her eyes. She saw him scramble to the side, then felt his strong arms grip hers, drawing her the rest of the way out and capturing her to him in one fluid motion. Falling back against the haystack, they clung to each other, their embrace hungry and wild one moment, tender and reverent the next. I must tell him now, Manya thought, but when she drew back to speak, he crushed her to him again, touching her everywhere and moaning softly. He knows, she realized. I need only translate the message his touch delivers. She sighed deeply and answered his every caress with one of her own. Then, without a word, he was gone. Manya inched her way into the haystack and to her place beside Chaim. She grabbed one of his hands and gave it a sweet kiss and a warm pat.

"He's on his way," she told everyone.

There was no pot to slow him down this time, and he was able to run as fast as he could on the way to Salki's and back. Meyer was glad he had arrived before Janek left. There was no need for the young boy to endanger himself when it wasn't necessary. Since Salki would once again be making the arrangements for their safety, Meyer was sure Janek would be taking enough risks in the weeks ahead.

Meyer also knew that tonight of all nights he shouldn't delay. With the news Josef had brought, his mother and Manya would be that much more worried with each minute that passed. Too often he'd made a decision to do something without telling anyone, causing him to be late and others to worry. He promised himself there would be no delay this time.

As he went racing past the barn toward the haystack, Meyer couldn't help but think of Josef. It seemed appropriate to send him a wordless message: Don't worry, my friend, we'll drink together again.

True to his promise, Meyer had taken less than four hours to return. He was still breathing heavily when he made his way into the haystack.

"What did he say?" asked Avrum.

"Let him catch his breath, for God's sake," shot Malka, passing Meyer a cup of water.

Meyer swallowed the water in one gulp, regained his breath, and began. "Salki thinks the best thing for us to do at this time is to stay here. He feels it's the safest place. He's been checking around town along with Gorski, but nobody has even a clue that we're here. The Germans have already searched out this area. That doesn't mean they won't come back, but for the time being he and Gorski feel this is the safest place."

"What about food, Meyer?" asked Rela.

"For the next few nights I'll go to Salki's house and get it. Then maybe they can work something else out."

That wasn't the answer Avrum wanted to hear. But what else could they do?

"Maybe we can get by with what we have for a few days," said Avrum. "Until they decide what's best. I don't think I want you to run over there so much."

"Don't worry, Papa. I can do it. I know I can do it."

16

"A machine gun, that's what I'd like to have," said Meyer three days later. "I'm tired of all this. All I'd have to do is set it up and mow down the Nazis. That would make them leave us alone!"

"Meyer!" cried Malka. "How can you say such a thing! Avrum, tell him that's crazy. You know what's happened in other cities. Remember what Moniek said about Lodz? The Nazis don't wait for a reason to kill a Jew, but when they have an excuse, it gives them even more pleasure. When a German is killed, it's always Jews who pay, usually with their lives. What's the matter with you? We've seen it ourselves right here in Hrubieszow! And now you want—"

"Mama, don't cry," said Meyer. "I only mean that I think about it sometimes. After what we've been through, anyone would want some power over them—to make them fear for their lives every time they walk down the street or go to sleep at night. I know it wouldn't really do any good. Besides, about the only way I could get a machine gun would be from the underground—"

"Don't start with that, Meyer. We've been over it again and again. It only upsets everyone," said Avrum. "We must remind ourselves that we're safe here. Everything is working out."

"Yes, it's working out," said Meyer, "but for how long? I . . . we have to sit in here hour after hour, day after day—who knows? Weeks? Months? I'll go crazy, you hear? I can't stand it!"

"Control yourself, Meyer!" Avrum commanded. "We're *all* cooped up, we're *all* bored and tired of waiting, we *all* want to get out! We must reach for patience and continue to believe that we'll be all right."

The musty air in the haystack crackled with tension. Even Avrum had to fight for clarity of mind in countering his son's frustration. Two weeks ago he had turned their despair into hope and triumph. Now it fell to him to maintain the momentum of success. Doubt was unacceptable. They had to believe they would win, and not allow tedium to destroy them.

Then they heard sounds from the outside. Ten figures jumped to their knees; sixteen days of isolation and immobility flooded through Avrum's dam of willpower. Wild eyes searched calmer ones for direction, scoured the enclosure for avenues of escape, then glazed with the uselessness of it. Avrum waved his arm in a demand for control. The group splintered into twos and threes, heads drawn together, arms woven protectively around each other. It was silent inside. But outside, the voices continued to shout, sounding close one second, farther away the next, then closer still. But the words were muffled, indistinguishable to those who lay listening in the house of hay. They lapsed into concentrating on what they *didn't* hear. There was no gunfire and no noise from engines. No barking, therefore no dogs. No familiar chant, so no Josef. But what? Now it came from one side, then another. Sometimes they heard bursts of chatter; once in a while a yell, and a few times, laughter. If you're going to get us, get it over with! thought Moniek. But his plea was ignored, for the voices continued most of the afternoon. Then they faded away completely. It was a long time before anyone spoke inside the haystack.

"Do you think it's time to check?" Meyer finally asked.

"I'm not sure we should go out tonight after what we heard today. Someone may be waiting outside," Avrum responded.

"I agree with Avrum," said Moniek. "We have no idea what was happening out there."

"I know," Meyer retorted, "but if Janek and Henrik brought the food, and someone else finds it, that could really give us away."

"I think you're right, son, but let's wait a little bit longer just to make sure the boys have come," responded Avrum.

For the past three nights Meyer had gone to Salki's house for the food, just as they'd agreed. But tonight it was to be delivered, for Salki felt that changing the routine would avoid suspicion. It was decided that Janek and Henrik Gorski, the police chief's son, would bring the food and set it ouside the haystack. There would be no signal, no communication. The quicker it was done, the better. Only in an emergency would Janek break the code of silence and speak to the hidden family.

Everyone was pleased that Meyer wouldn't be making the journey anymore. Each night they suffered through the same ordeal. Would he make it? Had he been caught? It seemed that each time he left, it took longer for him to return. They would rather have spread what they had over a longer period or even gone a day without anything to eat than have Meyer go out every night.

But there was one person who wasn't pleased: Meyer. He had now been in this haystack for nearly three weeks. He was tired of being trapped in the small enclosure. He knew it worried everyone when he left, especially Malka and Manya, but it relieved his anxieties to be out and doing something useful. Why couldn't they understand? Manya of all people should realize how important it was. No, he thought, she understands, it's me who doesn't always try to understand. She cares so much and doesn't want anything bad to happen. Manya's only thinking of me.

"Meyer, let's go see if they've come," said Avrum.

Meyer squeezed Manya's shoulder lovingly and made his way through the tunnel with his father. They could see the food wasn't at the entrance when they emerged, so they walked around the haystack. Nothing!

"Maybe they buried it under the hay, Meyer," Avrum suggested, prodding the base of the pile and circling again. Then Avrum felt something. He dug the hay away, and sure enough, there were the baskets.

"Very clever," murmured Meyer.

Avrum picked up the baskets. Meyer replaced the hay, then followed his father into the hideout.

"Listen to me, everyone," said Avrum when they finished eating. "Tonight we aren't going out in twos. We'll all go together. It won't take as long. After what we heard today, we don't want to spend any more time than necessary outside."

"What do you think that noise was, Papa?" asked Cyvia.

"I don't have any more of an idea now than when you asked me before," Avrum snapped.

Cyvia struggled to keep the tears from coming.

"She was just asking," Malka shot back, hugging her youngest daughter.

"I know—it's just that I'm worried about the commotion we heard, too. It was very close." Avrum opened his arms and motioned for Cyvia to come to him. She threw her arms around his neck. Avrum squeezed back, and kissed her on the cheek. "I didn't mean it, Cyvia. I'm just worried about our safety. I wouldn't do anything to hurt you, my baby," he said tenderly.

"It's all right, Papa. I love you."

"And I love you, Cyvia." Avrum hugged his daughter again, then started for the tunnel. Before removing the bale of hay from the opening, he whispered over his shoulder, "Remember, be as quick as possible, and don't make any noise."

Once outside, they broke into two groups, with Malka, Rela, and the girls going to one area and Avrum, Moniek, and the boys to another. After a few moments, when Avrum turned to walk back to the haystack, Meyer had disappeared.

"Moniek," Avrum whispered, "where did Meyer go?"

"I don't know," Moniek answered, surprised. "He was here just a second ago."

"Chaim, did you see him?" asked Avrum.

"No, I didn't notice anything. Maybe he went back to the haystack with Manya," Chaim answered very quietly.

When the three got to the entrance, there was no Meyer. Soon they were joined by Malka and the girls, but not Meyer. Avrum hoped they wouldn't notice he was missing. He should have known better.

"Where's Meyer?" asked Manya.

"He'll be back in a few minutes," Avrum answered, trying not to sound concerned and averting his eyes from Moniek and Chaim. "I wanted him to check the area to see if he could pick up any clues about the voices." He hated to mislead her, but how could he say he didn't know? They would just start worrying again. They were worn out by the tension and fear. Meyer wasn't helping by running off like this.

"Everyone go inside," Avrum instructed. "I'll wait out here for Meyer."

"Can't we stay, too, Papa, until Meyer gets back?" asked Minka.

"No, Minka, it's too dangerous for everyone to be standing outside."

"But it feels so good out here," she pleaded. "It's like being buried in there."

"I'll tell you what, Minka," he offered. "We won't close the entrance—then the fresh air will go inside. Remember not to turn on any flashlights."

Slowly they made their way into the sanctuary, reluctant to have their few minutes of freedom end. Five, ten, fifteen minutes passed. Still no Meyer. Where could he be? He was probably doing something to help, but what? No sure answer came to mind as Avrum searched the darkness for some sign.

Five more minutes passed. Finally he heard some rustling in the field.

"Meyer," he whispered, "Is that you?"

"Yes, Papa," said Meyer, approaching his father.

"Where have you been?"

Meyer's coat was slung over his shoulder like a satchel, and it was bulging. "I have a surprise, Papa. I'm sorry if I worried you."

"Meyer, you can't run off like that without telling me. Your mother and Manya get very upset. I run out of excuses for you."

"I know, Papa, I'll try to remember," Meyer promised, laying the bundle on the ground.

"What is that?" asked Avrum.

"The surprise," said Meyer. "I'll show you inside."

When Cyvia saw the big bundle her brother was dragging, her questions started. "What's in your coat? Is it something to play with? Is it for me?"

"On my way back from Salki's the last time, I took a different route across Josef's farm and found these. When we went out tonight, I decided to get some." He pulled out a round object.

"What is it?" asked Toba.

"They're sweet turnips," said Meyer. "Since we haven't had anything sweet in so long, I thought it would be nice."

Avrum just shook his head, and Manya threw him a knowing glance as she wrapped her arms around Meyer.

17

The pattern for the next seven days was the same. Every day the voices returned. How much longer could they go on this way? The pressure was unbearable. How many people are there? Why do they keep coming back? Are they Nazis or Poles? Do they know we're in here and are they just waiting for us? No, that couldn't be, or they'd have grabbed us when we went outside at night. They would have stopped Janek and Henrik from bringing the food. Those two boys would be dead by now, along with Salki and Gorski. Maybe the Germans have set up this sadistic routine for their pleasure. No, thought Avrum, they might play with one Jew to frighten a group, but here there was no audience for the Nazis to terrify.

In the beginning, it had been so much easier. They had talked, told stories, prayed, and at times even laughed. But there was very little talking now because of the cloying voices that pierced the haystack. And when they did talk, many times tempers flared.

Once in a while Meyer would even get mad at Manya, and this above all made Avrum uncomfortable. He wished that Meyer would try to consider what Manya and Chaim must be going through. They had no idea about their mother, father, brother, and sisters. Were they still alive? Had they been found? Deported? How much could a seventeen- and fourteen-year-old be expected to endure? At least we're all here together as a family, thought Avrum. How long can they go on without cracking? Their parents would be very proud of the way they were holding up. But as each day passed, Manya clung to Meyer for support, and Chaim clutched steadfastly to Manya.

"We have to get out of here," said Meyer. "I don't know what those voices are, but we can't stay here much longer without finding out what's going on."

"If there was a problem, Salki would let us know, wouldn't he?" asked Malka. "He'd leave a note with the food, maybe."

"Yes, he'd get word to us, Malka, but I don't think he'd dare write anything down. If the wrong person came across the note—"

"So," Meyer interrupted, "you think as long as the food is delivered, we should stay where we are?"

"That's exactly right, Meyer. We have no reason to believe we're in any more danger now than when we first arrived," said Avrum.

"But the voices, Papa," Meyer retorted, "the voices are causing us a problem!"

"Perhaps, but so far they've brought us no real danger, Meyer. If somebody knew we were here, they would've taken us already.

We must be patient—as hard as that may be. We can't give up the hope that we'll survive this, and that it will be over soon Someone will stop them."

"Don't you want to know what's going on out there? It's been seven days since we've had any news."

"Of course I want to know, but there's nothing we can do," answered Avrum.

"Yes there is—I can go talk to Salki," said Meyer.

Avrum stared at his son. Maybe that would be the best solution for all of them. It would help to reassure everyone. "Okay, Meyer," he said softly, "go to Salki's."

Manya held him tightly, not wanting him to leave. Slowly she released her grip, knowing it was best for all of them that he go, especially himself.

Meyer kissed her tenderly on the lips and whispered, "I love you."

She grabbed Chaim and held on to her little brother.

Meyer was gone a long time, and as usual, everybody was tense waiting for his return.

Meyer, please come back, please, Manya thought. I want to be with you now. I only came because you wanted me with you and because I love you. I don't want to be here without you. I shouldn't have come. I should have stayed with my family. Why can't this be over?

Chaim tried to comfort his older sister—just as she'd always comforted him. "It'll be all right, Manya. Meyer will be back soon and it'll be fine." He felt helpless; what else could he say? He cried with her.

"I was going to send for you in a day or so," Salki said, looking at the haggard boy in front of him. "The Nazis have changed their orders. They're no longer going to deport or kill Jews—young and healthy Jews," he added. "They've put out a bulletin calling for any Jews who are hiding in the area to come out. They need them for work," explained Salki.

"But is it safe? Can I bring my whole family in?" asked Meyer with cautious enthusiasm.

"I don't think everyone should come. They've set up a small ghetto. There are only young people in it—between the ages of fifteen and about thirty. I didn't trust what the Nazis were doing at first. I was sure it was a damn trick so the murderers could finish their filthy work. But from what I have seen, it may be true—for now. What happens when the work is done, I don't know," Salki said straightforwardly. "It's up to you to decide what you want to do. I'll help all of you any way I can."

"Have you ever been trapped in a dug-out haystack for almost a month like a caged animal? Not knowing when someone was going to come busting in and kill you—not knowing anything that's going on?" Meyer challenged. "It's not that we aren't grateful for everything you've done for us. We've just got to get out of there."

"Meyer, sometimes even when you know what's going on, it doesn't help. You're still helpless," Salki responded dejectedly.

"You hate them, don't you?" asked Meyer. He could see the anger on Salki's face, the tightening of his jaw, and knew the answer before Salki spoke.

"They're murderous bastards who care nothing about life. But it's not just the Germans. There are many Poles who are helping them. They're just as bad as the Nazis, maybe worse. Someday they'll all get what's coming to them," Salki answered angrily.

"Why don't you leave?" asked Meyer.

"I do what I can here to make it a little easier for some people. I'm not a heroic person, Meyer. I've done some things I'm not proud of, believe me. I only try to do what I think is right, what anybody should do. It may not be a lot, but it might help a few people a little."

"Is that why Gorski does it, too?" asked Meyer.

"Yes, he's helping because it's the right thing to do. No one will ever know how much he is doing to help people. He's a very decent man," responded Salki. "But we have more important things to discuss. What have you decided to do?"

"I think the best thing would be for me to sneak into the ghetto and see if it's safe. Then I can tell the others," answered Meyer.

"If that's what you want, fine. I'll send Janek around to find you once you're in the ghetto to see if you need anything. Remember, Meyer, you can't just walk in. You should find a man named Silberstein. Report to him and he'll inform the proper authorities about you. He's a good man."

"I know his family. I'm glad they're alive."

"It's time for you to go, Meyer—you've been here a long time and your family will be worried. I'll be in touch with you."

Meyer started for the door, then abruptly turned around. "I almost forgot one of the things I came here to find out," he said. "Every day for the past week we've heard voices outside. Sometimes they're very close, other times they're farther away. There's yelling and screaming and even laughter. Do you have any idea who's out there?"

Salki tried to keep from smiling as he responded very apologetically, "Yes, Meyer, I know who's out there. I should've let you know, but I didn't want to startle everyone by sending for you or having my son talk to you. Every day I've sent Janek and Henrik to the field to keep an eye on the haystack. They were to warn you if they saw anyone coming."

Meyer stood there dumbfounded. This whole time, they had been terrified that the Nazis were closing in, when it had only been the two boys watching out for their safety.

18

It was difficult for Meyer to explain to his parents that he wanted to see the ghetto for himself. They were frightened for themselves and for him. Meyer was sure his father understood, but his mother most assuredly did not. She wanted them all to stay together. The mood lightened a bit when Meyer told them about their young guardians. Now they would know that the voices were protecting them. Besides, he had assured Malka, if things weren't right in town, he'd come back. With that she seemed more content and even promised to watch over Manya.

He made it to town without incident, but shivered a bit when he entered the ghetto area and saw doors standing open and windows smashed. He wondered if any of the houses were occupied—they all looked disemboweled and deserted.

Salki had said to go to a house behind the old Jewish Center. Mr. Silberstein admitted Meyer without comment—a far cry from the furtive watchfulness of five weeks ago. He assured Meyer that

Jews were welcome to return and were very much needed by the Nazis. The work wouldn't be pleasant. They'd have to clean out the belongings of their former neighbors. It would certainly be backbreaking—they would build roads, haul tons of household goods, work in the brick factory—but they'd be quartered in acceptable housing and, it seemed, protected from indiscriminate slaughter. There were no guarantees, he said, but for now it could be a livable situation, definitely more so than hiding in the woods or trying to leave the country. Didn't Meyer agree? Meyer wasn't sure, and indicated that he'd have to go back to his hiding place and discuss it with his family before making a decision. Silberstein reacted sharply against this idea, explaining that Meyer would jeopardize the ghetto and his family's safety by trying to go back. The Germans could be watching, and they would get the idea that the ghetto leadership was mixed up in the resistance.

Meyer finally agreed to stay in town for two or three days to witness the conditions under which they would live if he decided to stay. He presented himself for work the next morning, and spent twelve hours muscling furniture down flights of stairs and into trucks, yanking down draperies, piling up pots and pans, dishes, utensils, linens, and lamps, dumping out drawers of shirts, socks, underwear, and baby clothes. He felt ashamed as he and the others handled, even evaluated, the personal belongings of their faceless owners, and he realized that sooner or later someone, perhaps he, would perform the same sickening task at his own house or Manya's.

He wasn't able to reach the Nagelsztajns' house—it was too far in toward the center of town. The small ghetto area was an isolated section near the Zamosc bridge and adjacent to the Jewish cemetery. The streets—alleys, really—were unpaved and the houses run-down, but that was of no consequence to Meyer. It was far more important that the Nazis were inviting the Jews to come out of hiding and work. For the last seventy-two hours Meyer had watched and thought while he worked, attempting to examine the Nazis' motives from every angle. Each day more Jews arrived in the ghetto, so Meyer could see he wasn't alone in accepting the Nazi invitation. But he made one decision. He couldn't recommend that his parents join him. John Salki had confirmed Meyer's suspicion that "Jews to work" meant Jews deemed capable of work, and the Nazis translated that to mean young but not too young. It wasn't the kind of message he wanted to send to the haystack, but it was the only one he could send. Perhaps his parents and little sisters could make it to Mislavitch now. Maybe the apparent easing of the situation meant the worst was over for the Jews. No, he thought, if that were true, the whole family would be safe in the ghetto, and he knew this was not the case.

He'd send for Manya and Chaim and perhaps Toba. They could get along quite well; in fact, he was really hopeful about setting up a little home with Manya, and he had already informed the head of the ghetto to expect three more members of his family. He even had the house picked out. They wouldn't have it all to themselves, of course, and it looked about ready to slide down the embankment into the creek behind it, but anything was better than being trapped in that haystack. He couldn't face going back.

Meyer was standing in the trees by the creek waiting for Janek. Salki's son had been sent by his father to the Jewish section ostensibly to carry an official communiqué to the ghetto, but really to talk to Meyer. Somehow the boy always appeared when Meyer needed him—sometimes to deliver information, but more often ready to carry it back. He never looked suspicious, sauntering along as he did with a broken tree limb or pitching rocks into the creek.

Janek didn't break stride when he saw Meyer, but plucked his slingshot from his back pocket and stopped to gather a pebble or two. Pausing to fit the stone into the sling, he moved a few more feet in Meyer's direction, then turned his back and aimed the slingshot at the ice-crusted water.

"Janek," whispered Meyer. The boy held his stance as if waiting to spot just the right target.

"Janek," Meyer repeated, "you have to go to the haystack. Tell my family that I'm going to stay here and that I want Manya to join me. Tell them it's all right for Chaim and Toba, too."

Janek let the sling loose and watched the stone ricochet across the creek's surface. He nodded very faintly as he placed another pebble into the sling and took aim again, panning the opposite bank.

"Janek," Meyer continued, "you must tell my father that the

rest of them wouldn't be safe here. They should go to Mislavitch. Let him know we'll be fine and that I'll get word to him somehow. Tell him"—he paused, swallowing hard—"tell them all, I love them."

The boy lowered his hands and waited to hear more. When Meyer said nothing, Janek raised the slingshot again and fired the stone skyward, following its trajectory and finally hearing the crunch of its landing on dried leaves. He tapped the V-shaped wood against the palm of his hand, then held out a foot to test the water's icy edge. He trotted away, alternating his feet between the bank and the ice. Two minutes later he was cavorting through the bare trees, kicking leaves and swinging around tree trunks, but always moving efficiently toward his destination. Soon he was in the fields running full blast, using outstretched arms like the wings of a plane. Once in a while he pirouetted, angling his arms to aim imaginary guns at make-believe cities; then, mission completed, he'd be off again. He playfully circled the haystack twice before collapsing against it and sliding down to sit on the ground. The entrance was precisely to his left. He looked all around him, decided it was safe, and yanked the bale of hay outward. In seconds he had fit his small frame into the tunnel and replaced the door.

Holding their breaths, the inhabitants of the haystack strained to see the figure entering their refuge.

"Mr. Korenblit, Mr. Korenblit, I have news from Meyer," he began, and transmitted Meyer's message. Avrum passed the boy some water and thanked him. Janek's eyes shone with excitement and pride. "So you understand, then? Manya and Chaim and Toba should sneak into town. Meyer will be waiting for them."

"I understand, Janek. They'll go in a few hours. But quick, my boy, you must be on your way. We don't want your father to be concerned."

"Do you have any message to send back?" asked Janek, crawling toward the tunnel.

"No, I think Meyer will expect them to come. There's no sense in your taking any more risks today. Thank you again, Janek. You are a very brave young man."

The boy smiled and scooted out.

"Maybe we could go right now," said Manya. "It sounds like it's safe."

"Well, yes," said Avrum, "but the rest of us can't go yet. We'll have to wait for darkness. Maybe you should, too."

"I really want to go now. It could be more dangerous to go into town after dark. Maybe there are more guards around at night. Toba, Chaim, what do you think?"

"I think Avrum is right, Manya," said Chaim. "We should wait until it's dark. I don't think you and Toba should go yet. Let me go first. I'll make sure it's absolutely safe for you to come."

"But Meyer has already said it's safe," she responded.

"Just one more day, Manya. Please stay here."

Manya reached out her hands to his face and gently held him. She began to cry. "All right, Chaim, you go first."

The hours passed very slowly for Manya. There was no sleep for her that night. She could only think about Chaim. She was responsible for her little brother. Her parents had expected her to take care of him, watch out for him. Why had she let him go alone? If they'd gone together, they'd all be safe in the ghetto now.

Manya looked across the haystack. Malka was cradling Toba. She wanted to hold her eldest daughter as long as possible. The older woman knew she wouldn't be seeing her for a long time.

Manya had promised Chaim she'd wait until he sent word for her and Toba to come, but she couldn't wait any longer. Four days had passed since Meyer had left. She had to see him, to know he was safe, to touch him.

Manya drew a deep breath. "I think Toba and I should leave now."

Startled by Manya's announcement, everyone sat up and began fidgeting.

"But Manya, we haven't heard from Chaim yet," responded Avrum.

"I know. But we don't have any idea what's happening. The Germans may not let anyone else into the ghetto. Then I couldn't be with Meyer or Chaim."

Avrum knew it would be useless to argue with Manya. She was determined to leave. Avrum nodded his head.

Toba reached for Malka, who could only groan a farewell; then the others moved to envelop the eldest Korenblit daughter. Manya winced as she watched the replay of her own heartache.

The two girls scrambled through the tunnel to the outside. With squinting eyes they tried to seal the entrance and cover their tracks. They were out! They stood up on quaking legs and for the first time in thirty days looked at the tree-rimmed city. It was beautiful. They moved indecisively into the fields a few hundred yards. Then Manya saw the army jeep. It was about half a mile from them.

"My God!" she breathed, raising a spastic finger to point. "It's the SS! Run! Run!" she croaked, grabbing Toba's hand. "This way!"

They streaked across the field, not quite sure where they were going. Manya scanned the horizon for anything that could hide them—anything! Then she saw Wisniewski's barn dead ahead. She was almost dragging Toba along, but fixed her eyes on the slightly canted brownish-red doors that might save them.

Heaving one of the barn doors open, Manya pulled Toba inside. Her brain screamed with panic as she searched their wake. She yanked the door shut, shoved Toba up the ladder, scaled it herself, threw it to the ground, and dived to the bottom of the hay. She tried to listen, but all she could hear was her heart and the rasp of her breathing. Oh, Meyer, she thought, I may not make it now, but I love you. She could hear the engine, closer and closer. It stopped just outside the barn. The girls stopped breathing lest they set a single blade of hay in motion.

"Raus!" came the bellowing from below. "Kommt raus, Ihr verflucte Hunde!"

Manya heard slamming and banging as the stalls were searched; then the ladder struck the edge of the loft. She couldn't feel her heart beating. She heard the grunts and pants of a heavyset man climbing a ladder. Hay flew everywhere as the Nazi continued to scream his demand that they give themselves up. Then there was a thud just beside her head and she saw the prongs of a pitchfork cut through the straw again and again. She lay there waiting for the tool to pierce her chest and hoped she would die immediately. I love you, Meyer, she chanted, I love you forever.

Then it stopped. There were a couple of hideous laughs as the soldiers made departing sounds. The engine coughed to life and carried the terror away. Am I alive? thought Manya. I'm alive! she answered herself. Don't be too quick to come out, she thought; they might be hiding down there. It could be a trick. She lay very still and drew a long, glorious breath, holding it to listen some more, then slowly exhaled. After a while—she didn't know how long—she felt all around her under the hay. Fear struck again. Oh, God! The pitchfork! What if Toba . . . ? How could she tell Meyer . . . ?

In a moment, though, she felt something brush against her shoulder and saw Toba's own hand reaching out to find her.

"Toba!" Manya whispered. "Are you all right? Are you hurt?"

Meyer's sister choked back a sob and dug her fingers into Manya's shoulder. "I think I'm all right," she said. "I think so."

The girls gradually extracted themselves and peeked over the edge, surveying the barn. Everything looked normal. Very carefully they descended the ladder.

"Nice of them to set it up for us," whispered Manya to Toba.

"What now?" asked Toba. "Do we go back to the haystack? Can we please go back to the haystack? I want to be with my mother and father. I want to stay with them."

"We can't go now, Toba. We have to wait until it's dark." She was silent for a moment, then added, "We'll have to ask Josef to hide us. I hate to do it, but there's no choice."

The girls cracked the barn door and peered outside. It was only a few hundred feet to Josef's door. Somehow they both knew to cross the yard casually. If they were seen, they hoped to be taken for the two Wisniewski women. They didn't knock, but tripped the latch and slipped inside. Josef Wisniewski jumped when he saw them. Manya conveyed her regret with apologetic eyes. Josef must have seen the Germans search the barn, for he said nothing, but scurried them to a back room.

"Just till it gets dark," promised Manya as he shut the door.

They heard a steady hum of voices coming from the kitchen, then a high-pitched, emphatic, "We can't!"

A few minutes later Josef tapped on the door and entered. "I'm sorry, really sorry," he said in a low tone, "but you can't stay in the house. My mother—it's too dangerous. Those Germans could come back. I just . . . I'm sorry."

He started to leave, then seeing the stunned expressions on the girls' faces, added in a whisper, "If you want to hide in the barn, it's all right."

The girls looked at his serious face, nodded, and filed silently down the hall and out the front. They slipped across the yard and into the barn. An hour or so later, Josef opened the barn door and slid a tray of food and water to them. They devoured the simple meal and savored every drop of the soothing liquid. They began to shiver with the cold and snuggled together for warmth.

It seemed to take forever for the sun to set and the night to descend, and they waited at least another hour before leaving the barn and entering the fields.

"I'll go with you, Toba, to make sure you're all right," offered Manya.

"You don't have to, Manya, I can do it. You'd better go to town. Meyer and Chaim will be waiting."

"I'm responsible for you, Toba."

"I'll be fine. I can make my way back to the haystack. Really, it's all right. Go on," she insisted, turning Manya in the other direction. "Meyer's waiting."

They hugged each other like sisters, then drew away. Toba waved and Manya blew a kiss. I wish she would come with me, Manya thought, but I know what it's like to want your mother and father. I know what it's like.

She took a deep breath and gazed at the silhouette of the city. Yes, Meyer was waiting, and maybe, just maybe, he'd know something about her parents. She had to go.

19

Manya squeezed her eyes shut against the shards of early sunlight that penetrated the room from the blanket-covered window. Where was she? Maybe it had been a dream and the last month had never happened. She rolled over on her side and bumped into someone lying next to her. No, it hadn't been a dream. The slumbering form next to her was Meyer. He looked so peaceful stretched out on the bed. Of course. She was no longer in the haystack, she was in the ghetto.

They were relatively safe, or so Meyer had said. The Germans needed them to work. She'd been out of the haystack for less than twenty-four hours, yet already she felt free. She had slept in a bed. It was so comfortable she didn't want to get up. She could roll over, stretch out, without worrying about waking anyone. She hadn't slept so well in a long time.

She couldn't quite remember how she'd gotten to the ghetto the night before. She'd been so intent on being with Meyer that it was all a blur. She hadn't seen any soldiers or jeeps, nothing military, and she had no memory of the cold of the late-fall night. When she entered the city, she felt calmer than she had in three years or more. Indeed, the town appeared very much as it had in the old days. Maybe things would be better now, no more beatings or killings. Perhaps she could find out about her family.

Meyer stirred next to her. She opened her eyes to watch him, and pictured their reunion the night before. When she had reached the ghetto, Meyer stepped out of the shadows and seized her in his arms, hugging the breath out of her and barraging her with kisses and questions. He drew away, holding her by the shoulders and asking, "Is everyone all right? Have you been getting the food? Where's Toba? Have my parents gone to Mislavitch? Is Chaim with you?" This last shattered her, since she had fully expected Chaim to have found Meyer already.

Seeing her tears, Meyer held her close again, then turned her around and guided her down the dark street and into a small house.

"Tell me," he pleaded, and she had done her best to fill in the days he had missed with his family. Yes, they had gotten food all right. Toba had gone back to her parents. They were fine and about to leave for Mislavitch. She didn't know where Chaim was, she explained, telling Meyer that Chaim had insisted on leaving the haystack first to make sure the ghetto was safe for girls. It was the last time she had seen him. Then she told Meyer what had happened in Josef's barn, her voice rising with hysteria toward the end.

"And that's when Toba went back to the haystack?" he asked, shaking his head with disapproval and insisting that she should have come to the ghetto, that it was more dangerous for Toba to stay with her parents.

If only Meyer could understand poor Toba, thought Manya. She wanted to be with her parents. Sometimes Meyer just didn't understand emotions. But Manya stopped when she realized why he was insensitive to feelings: safety was his first priority.

Manya couldn't help but feel she had let Meyer down, and began to cry again. He had crushed her to him, stroking her hair and saying, "Don't worry. Chaim will be fine . . . Toba will be fine." But she knew he was only saying that to soften her hurt and his own. She had to recognize that Chaim might be gone forever. They had to face reality, no matter how painful, for the next time it might be worse. They had to concentrate on the positive, be thankful that they had each other, that they were together.

Manya's thoughts were interrupted by the smell of something wonderful filtering through the air. She hadn't smelled the delicate aroma for a long time, and then only rarely. It was coffee. Meyer explained that they were given rations. While they weren't going to get fat on what they were given, they certainly wouldn't starve to death. And there were ways of getting extra food.

Then Manya heard sounds coming from elsewhere in the house and lifted her head to listen.

"Shhh," said a sleepy Meyer, pulling her closer. "It's all right. It's only Sam."

"Sam?"

"He shares this house with us. Lie down, Manya, just two more minutes."

She lay back contentedly, wishing they could stay like this forever. Maybe today we'll find out something about my family or Chaim, she thought. Maybe I can get to my house somehow. If only Meyer had been able to find out something. He felt so bad about telling her he hadn't been able to check on them. She tried to console him, to tell him it was all right. But Meyer was so stubborn. He always felt that if he didn't have an answer he hadn't done enough.

She felt a warm kiss on her shoulder and a sound pat on her backside as Meyer rolled out of bed.

"Up, Manya, get up," he called, "You have to report to the office, and I have to go to work. They'll give you a work assignment in a day or two, but after you check with them, you'll just stay in the ghetto today. Don't leave. I'm sure you can find plenty to do to fix up this house."

"Do you just go to work? That's it?" she asked.

"Well, no, first we all go down to be counted. Then we go to work," he explained.

"Why do they count you? Should I be counted, too?"

"Not until after you've been registered with the head of the ghetto. The Germans want to keep track of us, so they count in the morning and again when we come back at night."

"How many Jews are here? Anyone we know?" she asked.

"About forty-five or fifty in all, but there are a few more every day. Some we know and some we don't. Sam is from a little town . . . Ach, I can't remember the name right now—it's not far away. Manya, I really think we'll be all right here, at least for a while. The Nazis need us."

"But what will we do?"

"Oh, different things. I dug vegetables one day, but most of the time, we've helped clear out houses, move furniture—you know, empty everything out."

"But what are they doing with all the furniture and everything?" she asked.

"They're shipping it all to Germany, every bit of it. I've seen some beautiful things, believe me," he said.

"Doesn't it make you feel terrible to take all those things away? Meyer, we knew those people!"

"The first day, it made me sick, Manya, really sick. But another fellow working with me told me I'd better get over it. 'That's why you're here,' he said, 'so you better do it.' I realized he was right. You can't think about it, that's all—you just do it," Meyer said soberly. He sat silently on the edge of the bed for a moment, then pulled on his boots.

"They'll be lining up soon," he announced, giving her a kiss. "I'm so glad you're here, Manya. Come, let's eat breakfast, then I must go."

All too quickly they finished eating and were standing at the door.

"Remember, wait about a half-hour and then go to the office. They'll take care of you."

"Would they know something about my family?" Manya asked timidly.

"Ask them. Things change every day; they could have information today that they didn't have yesterday. Just promise me that you won't do anything foolish like trying to get to your house. If Silberstein has any news about them, we'll talk about it when I return tonight." Meyer could sense Manya's uneasiness and added, "Just be patient and take no risks. I want you here when I get back. Promise?"

She nodded with tear-filled eyes and watched as he slipped out the door and into the street. She'd try to keep her promise, but if Silberstein knew where her family was, it would be very difficult to sit idle and alone all day. She'd have to conquer the impulse to rush to her house, where she fantasized them waiting for her. She'd be able to help them. Oh, how wonderful it would be to see her mother again. And her father and . . . . But then she thought of Chaim, knew that he wouldn't be at the old house. They would expect her to explain where he was. How could she tell her family she didn't know? How could she possibly face them? Where could he be? He'd gone to find Meyer. What had gone wrong? Maybe someone had seen him and he'd gone back to the haystack.

Right after Meyer left, Manya went to register at the office. As Meyer predicted, she received no work order for that day. She returned to their little house and walked through the rooms straightening the beds and pulling back the window covering to admit the sunshine. The sunlight perked up the shabby rooms, but cold air blew through the window frames and she knew she'd have to replace the blanket curtains before the sun set. She washed up their cups from breakfast and checked over the food supplies and decided to make some noodles for the evening meal.

She watched out the window for a while, seeing a figure here and there, but no one she knew. It was very quiet in the ghetto, which surprised her, but maybe most of the people were elsewhere working. For hours she delighted in staring into the sun-filled street and feeling the sun's warmth on her face. She could see a grove of trees from the back window and knew that to the right, beyond it, lay the fields and the route to the towering haystack. Was Meyer's family still there? And maybe Chaim?

It wasn't long before Meyer and Sam came clumping through the door that evening. Meyer had stopped off at the central provisions building and had some beets and carrots with him. Sam had somehow come into possession of a chicken and was proudly thrusting the scrawny thing at her, saying, "Here's something special. Tonight we celebrate your arrival!"

Manya was so touched by Sam's thoughtfulness and their spirited homecoming was so infectious that she was carried along. For a few hours she forgot her day full of worrying and remembering. She plopped the bony bird into a pot and stewed it, adding the delicate noodles toward the end to the chorused oohs and aahs of the two ravenous men. They devoured the tasty meal and lingered over the empty plates, talking. When Manya rose to clear the table, Meyer reached for the dominoes and they laughed as they clacked the spotted tiles on the table and Manya drew one after another, unsuccessful at matching. Time stopped for them that evening; memories and expectations were muted. Like children they made a game of everything, and giggled at each other's laughter. They were breathless and exhausted when they blew out the candles—all together, one, two, three—and started for the bedroom.

There was a tapping at the front door. Everyone froze. Who could it be at this hour? No one from the ghetto was allowed out after curfew.

Meyer walked toward the door very quietly. "Who's there?" he whispered.

"It's Chaim," came the response.

Sam looked at Manya and Meyer, puzzled. Meyer grabbed at the door latch, unable to open it quickly enough. One second he was alone at the door and the next instant Manya was crowding him away, reaching out to get anxious hands on her little brother.

"Oh, Chaim, Chaim, you're safe. I was so worried. Where were you?"

"Take it easy, Manya, let the poor boy breathe," said Meyer, bestowing his own hugs on the young boy. Even Sam joined the happy trio, depositing a sloppy kiss on one cheek of the startled boy's tear-washed face.

"Manya," Meyer finally interrupted, "Chaim must be hungry. Can you fix him something?"

"Just some water," Chaim broke in. "I'm very thirsty."

"I'll get it," Sam volunteered, relighting the candles.

"Please, tell me what happened to you," Manya insisted.

Chaim explained that he had hidden throughout the night and most of the next day. He didn't mention that he had been at his parents' house.

"I wanted to see what was going on in the ghetto, what people were doing, what the Gestapo was up to. After I was sure it was safe, I came out. I was going to report to the office like Janek told us to do, but while I was walking into the ghetto, I ran into Damone."

"Damone!" said Manya. "He was one of the Gestapo who beat up Daddy all the time."

"I know," said Chaim. "I was hoping he wouldn't recognize me from the times I went to work with Daddy, but he did, so I walked up to him. He looked at me and said, 'So, you are still here!' I just nodded and said I heard there was work to be done. He told me there were jobs if I was willing to work hard, and then he added, 'You look a little skinny for hard work.' He told me to report to the office in the ghetto. By the time I did that, everyone else had gone to work. I was assigned to live in a house and told to report to work the next morning. I was trying to figure out how I could get back to the haystack to let you and Toba know to join me here. It seemed best to find Meyer, so I asked if Meyer had registered. They told me he had and where he lived. I was sure you were at work, Meyer, so I waited till now to come."

"Chaim, you'll live here with us," Meyer said.

"Oh, yes, Chaim. We'll be a family again," Manya added, wiping the tears from her eyes. "I'm so glad you're safe—and to think you were nearby all day and we didn't know it. Oy"—she feigned disapproval—"why didn't you come sooner?"

"I was afraid, I guess . . . I don't know," he said, avoiding her eyes. He looked around the room. "Where's Toba?"

"She went back to the haystack, Chaim, to be with her parents." There was an awkward silence, so Manya changed the subject. "Do you think you could eat a little something now?"

"Not too much, maybe a slice of bread."

"I've got something better than that," she said, running to the kitchen. For at least an hour they talked while Chaim devoured the leftovers from their dinner, rekindling the gaiety that had infected them all evening. It was only when they saw Chaim struggling to stay awake that they ushered him to bed and collapsed themselves.

The next day Manya was sent to the fields to dig vegetables. She was weary and sore when she returned to the ghetto that night. It had been weeks since she'd had so much exertion. But as she walked home, the thought of Chaim waiting there erased some of the fatigue from her bones.

20

Manya had been in the ghetto for four days. She stood in line next to Meyer, holding his hand.

"Sixty-two, sixty-three, sixty-four . . ."

It had been difficult the first day she went out to work. She had hoped that she and Meyer would be assigned to the same work detail, but it didn't happen. She was sent to one area of town and Meyer to another.

Meyer was right about the people in the ghetto. While some of the faces in line were familiar, most weren't. She was happy to see two people she had gone to school with, Tovah and Molly. It was comforting to know that at least a few people from Hrubieszow had survived the deportations.

Manya still knew nothing about her family. Maybe today would be different. She would ask some of the Poles who worked around her if they knew her family or what had happened to them.

The last number was counted. Everyone was there, and why not? Where else did they have to go? Manya squeezed Meyer's hand and released it as the group broke up and headed for various destinations. She said good-bye to Meyer and Chaim and joined her group going into the city.

She walked into the first house and saw clothes, furniture, and dishes thrown all over the floor. She just stood and stared. It looked the same as her house the first time the SS had barged in looking for her family. She wanted to turn and run, but Meyer's words came back to her. "You have to get used to it. That's why we're here. If we weren't working, they'd send us off or kill us." Meyer was right. It was far more important to do as you were told and survive.

It was nearly lunchtime when Manya came out of the house, her arms laden with clothes. She tossed her bundle onto the pile and looked up. Her heart stopped for a moment, then started beating twice as fast. There, strutting down the sidewalk toward her, was Wagner. Would he remember her? If he did, what would he do? Kill her or be nice, as he had in the past? This was the same man who had given her father extra food when Shlomo had worked at Gestapo headquarters, and told him how much he liked him and would take good care of him. Other times he had beaten her father so badly he could hardly walk home. She had also seen him beat other Jews in the street for no reason. Yet she couldn't help but think about what he'd done to save the Nagelsztajn family one time.

She could still feel the closeness of the jail cell, the panic of being alone, the terror of being ordered out onto the street with her mother and brothers and sisters. Hundreds of people had been pushed and dragged this way and that, and finally herded to the jail and crammed into a small basement room. Manya and her mother clung to the little ones, and pushed others out of the way in a frenzied effort to stay together.

It was a tiny enclosure which normally held twenty-five people, but the Nazis had crammed more than one hundred people inside. There was nowhere to move, no room to turn. The heat became unbearable. She could smell the sweat in the room and felt the moisture running down her own body. Everyone around her was crying and wailing. There was a little window at the back of the cell. Metal bars and glass covered it, keeping the sounds confined within. People shoved each other trying to get to that window, to look out one last time.

For hours they huddled together until, miraculously, the door to the underground cell opened and the guard called out, "Nagelsztajn! Nagelsztajn!" Numb with dread, Mincha Nagelsztajn hesitated, weighing the situation, turned to the door, drew the rest of her family closer to her, and motioned Manya to bring up the rear. They stumbled through the maze of people, at times forcing their way clear and trying to ignore the murmured protests of the crowd. Reaching the door, Mincha exited past the impatient guard, followed by the younger children, but just as Manya was about to step through, the door slammed shut.

"No!" she screamed, pounding her fists against it. "Wait! I belong with them! Mama! Mama! Help me!"

She sobbed and pleaded through the planks, but no rescue came. Worn out and terrified, she slouched limply against the wall.

It was twenty-four hours before she heard the bolt slide on the door and her name called out. The throng surged forward again to the exit, blocking her path and complaining noisily. Manya fought her way through them, trying to identify herself over their angry cries, but her voice failed her. Instead she waved her arm aloft as she battled to reach the door with the others. When she stood before the guard at last, he shoved her through and re-bolted the door. Manya followed him down the hall and up the stairs, then stood trembling before him. He pointed to the exit. "Go on," he spat, "you're free to go."

Very slowly Manya moved toward the door, expecting them to drag her back any second. Touching the door latch, she hunched over, prepared to receive the bullet she felt certain would cut short her escape. But there was no sound, no threat from behind, and her fingers had tightened on the latch and disengaged the lock. In an instant she was outside.

Her knees buckled as she descended the step from the wooden sidewalk to the street. But then her mother was at her side, hugging her and crying, and her father and Meyer. Some hours later they explained that her father had gone to Wagner, had begged the German to free the Nagelsztajns. Wagner had done it, but something had gone wrong, and Manya had been left behind. Her father went to Wagner again to plead. No one could understand why this man who so easily performed countless acts of brutality could also show mercy. But he did.

Now as Manya stared across the ghetto at Wagner, she wondered if he knew where her family was. Would he remember her? Should she risk talking to him? His cold eyes and aloof manner frightened her, yet she felt oddly sentimental toward him. It might be better to pass him by and go back to work. But what if Wagner knew something? She had to speak to him, she decided, moving closer to the Gestapo sergeant. His steely eyes met hers, and she stopped in front of him. She wanted to run.

"Good day, Herr Wagner," she began in a weak voice. Wagner ignored her greeting, his face passive.

"I don't know if you remember me, sir," Manya continued. "My father used to work for you. Shlomo Nagelsztajn is his name. I . . ." She stopped when she saw the beginning of a smile—or was it a leer, a preamble to death?

Then he spoke, and his face was friendly, his eyes almost kind.

"Of course I remember," he said. "You were the one who was forgotten in the jail that time, yes?"

She nodded. "You were responsible for getting me out."

"Yes, I know," he responded with no emotion.

Manya hesitated. Maybe she should save her questions for another time. She didn't want to make him angry.

"Herr Wagner," she went on, in spite of herself, "I haven't seen my family for a long time. Do you know where they are? If they are all right?"

His expression cooled slightly, then softened again. "They're in a good place, young lady," he said. "We have sent them to a good place to work. Don't worry about them."

"It's just that I . . . no one has seen them or knows anything," she stammered. "I . . . Will I see them again?"

"I told you they're in a good place," he said, the ice returning to his eyes. "You'd better take care of yourself and not worry about them."

She wanted to ask where this place was, how long they'd been there, when they'd be back. But his demeanor told her he would say no more. She forced herself to smile and nodded gratefully as he turned his back and strode away.

Manya couldn't wait for the work day to be finished so she could rush home and tell Chaim and Meyer the news. It wasn't really good news, but at least she had some idea about her family. They were alive, according to Wagner. That would help Chaim. He continued to feel guilty about leaving them. Now he would know they were all right, that he'd made the right decision. She kept reminding Chaim of those last words Mincha said that agonizing night when they parted: "If we are separated, maybe one of us will survive."

After Manya's group returned and was counted, she went running back to the house. She burst through the door yelling, "Meyer! Chaim!"

"Manya what is it?" asked Meyer, coming from the kitchen to meet her.

"Where's Chaim?" puffed Manya, trying to recover her breath.

"He's in the other room. What is it, Manya?" Meyer demanded.

"Chaim, come here! I have news!"

Chaim was soon standing in the middle of the room with Meyer and Manya. The two young men's faces were pleading for her to spit out the news.

"Mama and Daddy are alive! Everybody is still alive! I found out today. They were taken to a place to work. They're safe! They aren't dead."

Chaim's body, which for so long had sagged and looked numb, came to life. There was a glimmer in his eyes as they began to swell with tears, and he managed a small smile.

Manya grabbed him and hugged with all her might. "You see, Chaim, everything is all right. We're alive and the rest of the family is alive. We may even be able to see them."

"How do you know all this?" asked Meyer.

"I found out from Wagner."

"Wagner!" Meyer snapped. "Did he just come walking up to you?"

"Of course not," answered Manya."I went up to him."

Meyer stared at her in disbelief. "Are you crazy?"

"Why shouldn't I? My father used to work for him."

"Yes, and Wagner beat him up all the time, too!"

"Don't forget that Wagner saved our lives one time—yours too—when my father went to him for help!"

"No, I'm not forgetting anything. It's you who should remember that none of us would be here if your father hadn't had the courage to go to Wagner in the first place. That man is a beast and you shouldn't trust him!"

"Hey, wait a minute," Sam interrupted, "why are you two arguing? What are you talking about?"

"It's not an argument, Sam. I got excited because I don't think it's good to draw attention to yourself that way. Wagner is unpredictable. Instead of talking to you, he might have . . . well, you know what I mean."

Manya nodded soberly and continued to hug Chaim. A small thrill of relief rushed through Meyer's body. Yesterday Janek Salki had told Meyer that the food left outside the haystack the previous night had not been picked up. That meant his family had gone to Mislavitch to hide. Now Manya knew about her family. Both the Korenblits and the Nagelsztajns were still alive.

21

Manya had just finished cleaning the dinner dishes when Meyer called everyone together.

"We've all been here for two weeks. I think it's time to make plans."

"What do you mean—make plans?" asked Manya.

"There's still a lot of work to be done here in Hrubieszow. But what happens when all the work is finished? Do you think the Nazis are just going to leave us here in peace? They'll probably send us away to work or something worse," responded Meyer.

Meyer looked around the small circle of housemates, half-expecting one of them to say something. The only movement came from the newest member of their household, Leon, who fidgeted in his chair. He'd been brought to the ghetto by the SS a few days earlier.

"Do you have something in mind?" asked Sam.

"Yes, I do. We've all been taking small amounts of goods from the houses we've been working in to trade for extra food and other things we need. What if we took a little bit more and stored it here in the house?"

"But what good would that do?" asked Leon.

"When the time comes, we can trade it for money, papers, passports, whatever we can get. Then we can use the money and papers to get away," Meyer answered.

"Where would we go and who would we trade the goods with?" asked Manya.

"We'll find someone to sell everything to. Then we would try to get to one of the neutral countries, like Switzerland."

"Do you really think we could make it?" asked Leon.

"It's worth a try," Sam quickly responded. "Anything is better than just waiting. Besides, Meyer is right, the Germans aren't going to just leave us here when we're finished. Other people are probably thinking of the same thing. I think it's a good idea, Meyer."

"What if the Gestapo comes and searches the house? Where do we hide it?" asked Manya.

"Manya, the Nazis would kill us for taking as little as we have already. We'll just have to be very careful. If someone is suspicious, just don't take anything. We have time. They aren't going to move us out tomorrow or the next day. We'll figure out a place to hide the goods," Meyer answered.

Meyer was relieved. They weren't going to sit around and wait for the day when the Germans would send them away. It gave them all something to look to for the future.

Lying in bed that night, Meyer could sense Manya's uneasiness about their plan. He pulled her close. "It's the right thing to do, Manya. We can't just sit around and do nothing."

"I know, Meyer, it's just that I am scared, scared something bad will happen," she whispered.

"Nothing will happen, everything will be fine. We've made it this far together and we'll make it the rest of the way. We have each other, and I wouldn't jeopardize that. I want to be with you forever."

Manya closed her eyes. She let the words settle in her mind; words that were always so confident and comforting. She prayed to God that He would make Meyer's words come true, that they'd be together always.

For the next two weeks everyone brought various items to the house. While they hadn't amassed much yet, Meyer could see a problem in the future if they didn't find someone to take the goods.

As he walked to the morning count, he thought about Salki. His son Janek was still coming into the ghetto, at great risk, to check on them. Maybe Meyer could start giving some things to the young boy to take back to his father. Salki would surely know what to do with it. Even if he couldn't get rid of the materials, perhaps he could store some of them temporarily.

Meyer was still thinking about the problem when he heard his name called. It was Isaac Hipps, who had been assigned to dispense work orders today. He announced some more names, told them to stay behind, then dismissed the rest of the group to their designated work.

Meyer watched the group break up and go in various directions. There were nearly 150 people now in the ghetto. Hardly a day had gone by without a new face popping up in line for the count. He saw Manya waving good-bye to him as she made her way up the street to her assignment. He waved back, then turned to get his instructions.

"You twelve will be going to work at the fort," Isaac informed them.

"Do you know how long we'll be there or what kind of work we'll be doing?" asked one of the young men.

"I'm not sure. All they said was to send twelve men to the fort today. It could be just for the day or for a while. I'm sorry, I just don't know. You'll probably be cleaning up there. No one will be going with you—you'll be your own watch guards. I think you all know what would happen if one of you didn't show up or come back. They know how many are expected."

Yes, Meyer thought, they did know what would happen. Although one person might get away, others would pay with their lives.

The twelve young men turned and started walking out of the ghetto. Meyer didn't know the others very well. He'd seen them before, but most of them weren't from Hrubieszow.

It was a long walk to the fort, and none of them were in a hurry to get there. The longer it took, the less time they'd have to work, since they would still have to be back for the curfew. There was very little talking as they left the ghetto. The SS guard hardly gave them a glance as the group walked into the Polish section of town.

Meyer walked on with the group, up a little hill and down another few blocks, and saw the marketplace just ahead. The Nagelsztajn house overlooked the market area. He hoped that Wagner wasn't lying to Manya about her parents—the thought of being reunited with them kept Manya and Chaim going.

Walking through the city brought back memories to Meyer. So many times he had played in the streets, being yelled at for making too much noise or messing up someone's flowerbed. So often he got into mischief, with Chaim tagging along, afraid Chaim would get caught because he couldn't run as fast as the older boys.

Before Meyer realized it, they were at the main street of the city. There, in the fork in the road, sat the cannon still pointing straight down the brick avenue that led into town. This was the weapon that was to keep unwanted invaders out and stop those who would come to harm the people of Hrubieszow.

Meyer remembered that first day of the war as if it were yesterday, when hundreds, maybe thousands of Poles of all ages, both Jews and non-Jews, marched to the fork in the road where the cannon stood, vowing to fight the Nazis to the very end. People put away their differences and stood there proudly, together. They had marched to the fort singing the national anthem.

Now the fork of the road was empty except for twelve Jewish workers. The once menacing cannon looked small and tame, having never fired a shot. And some of those same Poles who pledged to kill the Nazis had helped this sworn enemy to murder the very people they had marched with so short a time ago.

They were nearing the fort when Meyer noticed a woman standing in a robe outside her house, broom in hand, sweeping the porch. It was Anna, an old friend of the Korenblits'. Her husband was away, of course, since he was a colonel in the Polish Army. Hearing their approach, she glanced up from her chore. She stared at Meyer with a puzzled look on her face. Would she recognize him? If she did, would she acknowledge him? It would certainly feel good to be greeted—instead of ignored—by an old friend. But he'd better not count on it. He didn't want to be disappointed.

Then he saw her wave and heard her call out his name. She hesitated, scanning both sides of the street. Then she moved off her porch and came toward him, capturing him in a warm embrace. "Meyer how are you? It's been so long! Where is the rest of your family? I think about them often."

"I'm fine," he responded. "I don't know where my family is. We were separated during the last deportation."

"That's terrible," she said sympathetically. "When the Nazis started rounding up all the Jews and sending them away, I feared the worst. It's so good to see that you're alive."

"It's good to see you, too. How is your husband?" asked Meyer.

Her expression darkened as she answered, "I haven't seen or heard from him since the Germans came in and the Polish Army left. It's been nearly three years."

"I'm sorry," Meyer said.

"Yes, it's all so terrible," she replied. "But what can I do for you? Do you need anything? Food or clothing?"

"No, they're giving us enough. But thank you anyway," he answered. "I must go now. I've been assigned to work at the fort. I'll see you again," he added as he turned and ran to catch up with the rest of the group.

As he entered the gate to the fort, his mind was racing. He had the seed of an idea, and Anna was the key. Maybe I can help her and she can help us, he thought.

Once inside, the twelve were met by a sergeant from the regular army. He explained why they were in the fort and what was expected of them. He said if they did what they were told, they'd be treated well. Then he proceeded to make work assignments.

Meyer would be working in the horse stalls, cleaning them out and helping to take care of the animals. If he weren't being forced to do it, he'd probably enjoy working with the horses. Well, he'd make the best of it, do a very good job. If his idea was going to succeed, he'd have to keep his work assignment at the fort as long as possible.

There was a great deal of work to do, since no one had been assigned to the fort before, but the day went very quickly for Meyer. He swept and shoveled, laid fresh hay, and repaired bridles. He curried the animals and polished the saddles. It was mid-afternoon before he unwrapped the slab of bread and cheese he had brought to eat. He took only a few minutes for his lunch break, choosing instead to take up his chores in the next stall, and the next. Then it was time to go home.

As he walked out of the fort and past Anna's house, he thought about the plan he had been formulating all day. He knew it was risky, but if Anna would cooperate, it could be productive for all of them. He'd ask her in a few days. Meyer couldn't wait to get home to tell the others.

22

That same day, Manya walked along to work with her group. For weeks she had stripped her neighbors' houses bare. Everything was removed, right down to the mezuzah beside each front door. Since the talk with Meyer and their plan to salvage everything they could, she had faced the grim task more calmly, even hopefully. She had a goal now, and had to put aside her feelings of dread and guilt as she handled and evaluated the goods in each house.

There was no truly precious jewelry; that was confiscated years before. But there was a market for silverware, fine table linens, velvet bedspreads and draperies, and the occasional piece of silk she found here and there. The bulky, heavy items were difficult to smuggle away, but winter coats helped to camouflage the valuables they wound around themselves and held secure with make-do belts.

It didn't matter that they would garner far less than the true value of the items. Before, they had been content to trade for meat or sugar or vodka, but now they would somehow try to sell the items, perhaps through Salki. Now a scarf or a piece of porcelain or a clock would bring them a few coins closer to financing their escape.

As Manya moved along through the streets with the others, she wondered what she would come across this time. She hardly noticed the bakery in her old neighborhood as they passed it. But then they turned right toward the marketplace and she saw the shoemaker's and the tailor's, and now the group had stopped precisely in front of Manya's house. She spun around, searching for a reason—any reason—that would explain away the devastating realization of why they were here.

Wait! she wanted to scream. Don't you know this is my house? But they didn't know. I can't do this! But they didn't care. It was just another house. The faces of her co-workers swam before her eyes and she felt herself spinning down and down, down further still. Then there were arms tight around her, holding her. She saw her mother's face, but the voice that called her name wasn't right, and she had to abandon oblivion and allow daylight to flood the blackness of her thoughts.

"Manya, you fainted. Manya, are you all right?" the voice continued. "What is it? Are you ill?"

Manya tried to focus on the concerned face that peered into hers. It was Esther, a young girl from the same work group. "You have to snap out of it, Manya. Quick," Esther went on, rubbing Manya's hands and slapping her face. "The Germans might see you like this. Here, lean on me. Yes, that's better. We'll be inside this house in a minute; you can sit down in there until you feel better."

"Nooo," Manya howled, covering her eyes. "I can't. It's . . . I can't!"

"What is it? What's wrong?"

"Oh, don't you see? It's *my* house," she cried, burying her face to muffle the sound.

"Oh, my God, Manya. I'm sorry! I didn't know. Those depraved bastards; they're savages," her friend snapped. "Manya, you have to go inside, you know that. You have no choice."

"How can I?" she moaned. "Could you?"

"I'd have to, just as you do. If you refuse, it's over for you. Isn't that right? Manya! Answer me!" Esther insisted, shaking her. "They'll kill you or ship you off. Think of Meyer, Manya. Do you want never to see him again? You're going in, Manya! There's no other choice. You must force yourself to pretend it's another house, another family. Move up now, before the guards get suspicious. Go . . . move!"

Meyer. She wondered what he would do in her place. Do what they say, he'd told her. He would go in, and so should she. In a few hours he would share this hurt and wipe her tears. His consolation was more important than anyone else's. Manya allowed herself to be propelled forward through the door and up the steps. She kept her eyes lowered as they climbed, for she didn't have to see to know what it would look like. It would be no different from the twenty-five other homes she'd been forced to pick clean, except that here they would find no silver or velvet. In this house there was glass instead of crystal, cotton instead of silk, the rough sheets laboriously and lovingly patched, the Sabbath tablecloth long ago bartered for a sack of flour.

They reached the first landing and Manya stopped. Her friend tried to push her on, but Manya shook her head.

"We must start at the top, Manya," Esther urged in a soft voice . But Manya shook her head again.

"I . . . I have to see . . . I'll come upstairs in a minute."

"I don't know, Manya—you're not going to run off, are you?"

"No really. I just have to see something. It won't take long, I promise."

Checking for guards behind her, Manya ducked down the hallway off the landing. She could hear noises from the workers above. How could she allow those people, mostly strangers, to dismantle the fixtures of her childhood? She should be up there, overseeing the task, drinking it all in. She would never see those things again. But she had to go to the basement first.

When she reached the steps, her heart pounded as if it would explode. They *could* be there, she thought. It was possible. But Wagner said they'd been taken away. Still, if he was wrong . . .

She crouched by the top step, trying to see below, and held her breath in an effort to catch the faintest hint of sound. Nothing. She descended on tiptoe, keeping her back to the rough brick wall that bordered the right flank of the familiar stairwell, and remembering to avoid the creaky second step from the bottom. Pausing to listen again, she turned to her right very slowly. What she saw made her gasp.

There in front of her was the haven Shlomo had so carefully crafted, the work he was so sure would save his loved ones. The bricks that had served to seal her family's hiding place were strewn about and broken.

"Daddy?" she whispered at the jagged opening. "Mama?" she called, bending down to peer inside.

It was empty—no sign of any of them. The window was wide open; wooden slats that had boarded it up hung at angles where they had previously been nailed. The scene showed evidence of a hasty departure. Had it also been violent? She couldn't be sure. The solace that she had taken from Wagner's words disappeared.

She crawled inside. With shaking fingers she picked up a dress that lay in a heap on the floor. It was hers. She clutched it to her, trying to squeeze out the memories of its wear. She felt dizzy again as she saw a broken cup, a comb, a small nightgown, a man's shirt. She gathered the odd bits of clothing, stroking her cheek with the shirt, nuzzling the nightgown, tracing the teeth of the comb with her fingers.

"Oh, Mama," she began, "I pray you are all alive as Wagner says you are. I want to believe him, but sitting here in this house, this room that kept us safe and together, makes me wonder if that German is telling the truth. I love you," she said to the absent occupants of the handcrafted enclosure. "I miss you—I miss you so much," she moaned. "God, please watch over them, wherever they may be." Then she raised her fists to her head; she almost screamed: "I wish we weren't Jews!"

She let herself cry this time, and it didn't take long before the tears were gone. Stuffing the old dress down her front, she dragged herself back through the hideout entrance and up the steps to join the others. At least she had seen it for herself, knew for sure that her family was gone. Maybe now the nightmares would stop.

23

Meyer jogged down the dead-end street to his house in the ghetto. The day had crawled by, and he had cursed the distance he had to cover between the fort and the ghetto. Manya would be there already, waiting for him.

Seeing Anna that morning had been a stroke of luck. He couldn't wait to tell Manya and the rest. Their dream of escape could quite possibly be within reach now. He was sure of it.

He bounded up the steps and charged through the front door. "Manya!" he called when he didn't see her. "Manya, come here. I have exciting news! Where are you?" he yelled. He looked in the kitchen, then peeked out the little window toward the outhouse. Its door was standing open, so she wasn't in there. He strode back to the main room, and then he saw it, flung over the back of one of the chairs. He reached out and fingered the softness of the washed-out fabric.

This was Manya's dress. He had seen it so many times, but not recently, not since . . . Where had it come from? He knew Chaim was working on a clean-up detail; perhaps he, or Leon . . . maybe Sam? . . . But as fast as the excuses came to mind, they couldn't silence what he feared to be true. His previous delight and excitement turned into an aching weariness as he acknowledged it. Manya. He crashed his fist into the already seam-split overstuffed chair. Damn the sons-of-bitches, the stinking pigs! He touched the dress again as if it were made of the most treasured brocade, as if his precious Manya herself were inside it. Then he moved toward the bedroom.

Manya lay curled up on the bed. Her cheeks were wet and her eyes swollen. When she opened them, he saw a dull, glazed look. He'd seen it before, but never on this face. It frightened him. He bent down and cradled her face with his hand, then wrapped himself around her tenderly, protectively. He felt the tremor of her sobs. He rocked her when she tried to choke out words but could only wail. He soothed her when she failed, murmuring, "I know, I know," over and over. "It'll be all right," he whispered, "I'll make it all right. We'll get out of here and somehow we'll find your Mama and Daddy. We'll do it, Manya. I know we will. And do you know why?" he asked. It surprised him when he felt her shake her head. She was coming back to him, climbing out of the gloom.

"I'll tell you why, my darling," he said. "Because we are strong and we love each other. Isn't that right? Yes?"

He felt her nod.

"Yes, I thought so," he went on, then squeezed her very tight. "And I'll tell you something else, Manya Nagelsztajn. We're going to have a big wedding one day like no one ever saw before in Hrubieszow. And both of our families will be there. We're going to have a big house with electricity and faucets, even a bathroom inside. And babies, we're going to have lots of babies. You'd like that, yes?" he asked, drawing away to look at her. He laughed when he saw her shy smile, and hugged her some more.

Then they heard an excited voice from the other room. "Meyer, Manya, look what I have!" yelled Sam. Getting no response, he came bursting into the inner room. "Oh, I'm sorry," he said when he saw Meyer holding Manya in his arms. "I didn't mean to interrupt."

"No, no. It's all right, Sam. We were just coming out."

"Is something the matter, Meyer? Can I help?"

"Manya was upset about something she saw today. She's better now," Meyer answered.

The outside door opened and Chaim and Leon walked in just as Meyer and Manya came out of the inner room holding hands.

"What's the matter, Manya?" Chaim asked.

She let go of Meyer, reached out and grabbed her little brother, and squeezed him very tightly, half-whispering in his ear, "I love you so much, Chaim."

He hugged her back, taking in every second of his sister's warmth and closeness.

"I was in our house today, Chaim."

She could feel him stiffen, but he didn't say a word. He just held on to her, not wanting to let go. Finally in a choked voice he acknowledged what she had said. "I already know, Manya. I've been there."

She drew away, staring into his eyes. "When?"

"The first night I came here," he said softly.

"Oh, Chaim, no! Why didn't you tell me . . . ?" she began, but stopped when she read the message in his eyes. He had meant to shield her from this hurt. She hugged him again. "I love you," she whispered, and felt his nod echo the endearment.

Meyer saw Sam and Leon shift awkwardly at the emotional exchange. He placed an arm around the brother and sister and drew them apart tenderly. "Let's see what Sam brought," he said. "Then I have some news to tell everyone."

Sam picked up a small bundle. He had hidden something under a dirty brown rag. When he unwrapped the cloth, he was holding a fine china bowl.

"Where did you get that?" asked Leon, admiring the piece.

"Someone had hidden it under a loose board in one of the houses I was in today. We should be able to get a good price for this, once we find someone who'll buy it."

"It's beautiful, Sam," Meyer agreed. "That's what my news is about. I may have found someone who'll help us."

"You have? Who is it?" asked Leon.

"An old friend of my family."

"Are you sure you can trust this person?"

"I really think so. She and her husband were very good friends of our family. I saw her today and she spoke to me. She seemed very pleased to see me, and asked about my parents."

"What are the details, when do we start taking things to her. . . and how?"

"Not so fast, Leon. I haven't asked her yet."

"But shouldn't you have asked her when you were talking to her? How can you be sure you'll see her again?"

"I'll see her, don't worry. Just leave it to me."

"I don't see why she would risk doing this. I understand she's a friend, but this is dangerous," said Sam.

"Because I'm going to make her a proposition that will help her as well. Her husband is in the army. She's alone, and I think she would welcome a chance to make some extra money. I'll offer her half of what she collects from selling what we bring her."

"Do you think she'll do it, Meyer?" Manya asked.

"I believe she will. She was so happy to see me. She offered me food, clothes, whatever I needed. She wants to help. All I have to do is tell her how. I'm sure she'll agree."

They worked on Manya's street for nearly a week. Every house was empty, so she was surprised that Saturday when they were led back to the three-story brick building that had been her home. The roof was gone, and half of the top floor. A rickety scaffolding hugged one side of the structure; some ladders were propped against the front. There were piles of baskets and coils of rope. Hammers and chisels were distributed to the men in the group of workers. As they ascended the ladders and scaffolding, each man pulled up a length of rope and secured one end, letting the other trail to the ground. The women were called forward and handed baskets.

"You are going to tear down this building," the officer began. "The men will crack the mortar and load the loosened bricks into the baskets and lower them to you. Each of you will untie a basket and fasten an empty one to the rope. Then you'll carry the bricks and stack them in that truck. You will not throw them. When that truck is full, another will arrive. Get to work!"

Manya couldn't believe her eyes or her ears! This was her home! Were they crazy? This fine brick building had been here for more than a hundred years! Her mother's family had lived here all that time! Why should it be knocked down? Why was she being punished like this? Oh, Meyer, Meyer, if you could see what they are doing! It's too much. I can't help them erase the last trace of my family's existence in this town. I won't! I can't!

Yes, you can, she knew Meyer would say. Yes, you can. Say it, Manya: Yes, I can. Say it! the thought of his voice insisted.

"Yes, I . . . Yes, I can," she stammered out loud.

She heard a man shout something from above, and looked up. He shook the loose rope impatiently. Manya caught the swinging line, then fumbled with its ragged end. Her numb fingers finally cinched the cord securely to the basket handles.

Up it went like an autumn leaf floating on an updraft. A mo-

ment later it descended, swaying to and fro. She steadied it with
her arms and guided it to the ground. Releasing the knot, she
refastened the line to her other straw container.

There were perhaps fifteen or twenty bricks in the first basket,
which she tugged and pushed toward the truck. She had moved it
only half the necessary distance when she saw the second basket-
ful descending from its taut rope. Beads of sweat trickled down
her chest; needles of panic shot up her back. She'd have to work
faster.

I don't understand why this must be done, she thought. But I'll
do it. I'll do it to stay alive and to be with Meyer.

She stooped over, picked up the basket, and staggered to the
ramp at the rear of the vehicle. Pitching her body forward for
leverage, she dragged the bricks onto the bed of the truck. One
by one she stacked them in a neat pile, alternating the rows as she
had seen her father do so many times. There was a tear on every
brick.

24

As Meyer finished up his chores at the fort and put away his
tools, he thought about his visit to Anna's that morning. When his
work group left the ghetto, he had explained to the other men
that he had to make a stop on the way to the fort. They had seen
Anna and Meyer talking a few days ago, so they asked if that was
where he was going. Meyer had told them that Anna thought he
might hear something about her husband at the fort and asked
him to stop by her house now and then to talk.

Meyer went on to explain that he'd promised Anna he would
find out what he could and that he'd stop at her house every
other day or so to report. He hated to mislead them, but he knew
he couldn't divulge the arrangements he had made with Anna to
transfer the smuggled goods. When he approached her with the
plan, she jumped at it. "I'll do anything I can to help you," she
said. "Your family was always very kind to me and my husband."
She even knew someone who would pay a good price for the
items, but she didn't tell Meyer who it was and he didn't ask. The

only way to be safe was to keep quiet. The more people who knew the details, the more dangerous the exchange would be. Besides, he was quite aware that most of the people in the ghetto were trying to do the same thing and were perhaps far ahead of him in achieving their goals.

The men agreed to take their time as they passed Anna's house so that Meyer could run around to her back door. They were pleased to hear that Anna had promised to give Meyer a little something for his trouble, although they were surprised that Meyer would take such a chance for her. He told them that he was willing to do this because he liked her and because one day she might be able to help him. That was something they could understand.

So as they approached Anna's house, they walked very slowly and Meyer slipped away from the group. It went without a hitch. Now, as Meyer aligned the brooms and shovels and pitchforks in the stable's storage area, he was anxious to get home to tell Manya and the others all about Anna. He left the stable and joined the group of men for the walk back to the ghetto. His feet hardly touched the ground en route, but he stood patiently for the count, then ran lightning fast down the street to his house. He burst through the door yelling: "Manya, Manya!"

She was standing in the kitchen when she heard him. He sounded breathless and excited. Was it good or bad? She never knew what to expect when he came running in like this. She worried all day about the delivery he was planning to make.

"Meyer, is everything all right?" she asked.

"Yes, yes," he answered, "everything went perfectly!" He grabbed her and spun her around, grinning and hooting.

"Wait!" she laughed "Wait! Tell me what happened! Don't act so silly!" She giggled, giving him a hug and pulling him toward a chair. "I want to hear every word! Chaim! Sam! Leon! Come in here, quick—Meyer's home!"

The three young men joined the couple in a rush, all talking at once.

"So, tell us, Meyer, *tell* us!" said Sam. "From the beginning!"

"All right, all right. When we left the ghetto this morning, I explained to the other men that I had to stop at Anna's house, and they agreed to help. We got near her house, and I sneaked

away and went to her back door. She was standing there waiting. I
pulled the silverware out of my pants, handed it to her, and left.
The whole thing didn't even take two minutes. I ran around the
other side of the house and caught up with the others. They were
just sauntering along."

"And no one saw you leave?" asked Leon.

"There was nothing to see! For all anyone knew, I ran back
there to use the outhouse!" Meyer exclaimed, tousling Chaim's
hair.

"It's going to work!" Sam cried, dancing Leon around. "We're
going to get out of this!"

Meyer, Manya, and Chaim latched on to the joyous pair, exchanging hugs and laughter and pounding each other on the
back. It was the first time in a long time that they accepted the
moment for what it was. No one injected words of caution, no one
worried about how long it would take. They had the will to find
freedom; now they had the means. It was wonderful!

"Manya!" Meyer roared finally, "Manya, we're hungry—what
have you got for four starving men?"

Reluctantly Manya returned to the kitchen. She could hear
Meyer's voice continuing to recount the stories of the day to Sam,
Leon, and Chaim. How she wanted to sit with them instead of
being alone in the kitchen making dinner. It would be nice to
celebrate with something special to eat, but of course that was
impossible. She reached for the bowl of cooked beets and potatoes
that sat on the windowsill, and began to chop. She sliced a mound
of paper-thin onion, then dumped everything into a pot with a
splash of oil. She had a little piece of sausage, which she cut into
thin circles and added to the sputtering pan. She shredded a
mountain of cabbage, then dropped it in by double handfuls,
along with a few precious ounces of reserved chicken stock, and
covered the pot.

As the heavy odor of steaming cabbage masked the enticing
aroma of the sautéed onion, she let her thoughts carry her away.
If she closed her eyes, she could let the smells and sounds of the
dinner cooking convince her that she was at home in her mother's
kitchen. But as wonderful as that was to imagine, she was in the
ghetto, in her own house, her own kitchen. She'd cook, clean,
wash, and scrub here just as she had before. But the dishes she

washed, the floors she scrubbed, didn't belong to her, had not been tended by generations of her family, and would not be cared for by her own children in the future.

They spent twelve hours each day laboring for the SS, digging, dragging, and hauling—whatever they were told to do. They resisted passively, elongating each process to guarantee that they'd be needed tomorrow, and the tomorrow after that. When they tramped home each day, they were stooped with fatigue and heartache, but they fixed their eyes on the front doors of the houses that could shut out the Gestapo, the lineups, and the threat of death. There were no bolts to throw or keys to turn; the Germans could burst in on them at will, but they were determined not to think about that.

The second half of the day belonged to them, and they used it as much to create a sense of normalcy in their lives as they did to renew their energies for what they would face the next day. In the evening they talked, reminisced, worried and made plans, exchanged rumors or quoted news overheard from a talkative German soldier. They analyzed and examined it all, searching, picking over the often garbled pieces of information, looking for truth and meaning and the effect it would have on them.

Then they played cards or dominoes and sipped glasses of tea. Despite the curfew, Tovah frequently sneaked from house to house in the evenings. She exuded friendship and cheer with her energetic manner. It was her way of helping others, making it possible for them to forget, for a little while, the reality outside. They were smitten with her sweet, gifted voice as it sang the old songs and carried them along a trail of memories. "She has a presence, that one," they would say; or, "She should be on the stage, that's for sure." Then Tovah would blush and radiate pleasure to hear her now impossible goal recognized.

At some point most evenings they would select the items Meyer would carry to Anna. Many times this proved to be exceptional entertainment, although Meyer didn't always share their amusement. "This is serious," he'd remind them, and they knew it was, knew that none of them would have wanted to make the dangerous exchange in his place, but they couldn't stifle their giggles—not when he had that bowl under his shirt or when the silverware jingled in his boots!

During the past month they had had a few rather pleasant evenings. By now they were starting to retell some of their own stories, letting the old days fade. It felt good to laugh. But there had
been some chilling nights, like when Meyer came home with a
gun. He found out that a few men in the ghetto had weapons.
"We're behind not to have a gun," he told Manya. "If something
happens in the ghetto, we have to be prepared." She begged him
to think of the consequences if the weapon were discovered.
"They'll kill us if they find it!" she cried. "It's too dangerous." But
Meyer hadn't listened to her pleas and produced the pistol and
forty rounds of ammunition one evening after work. Manya was
furious and very frightened, but Meyer drew her aside and
calmed her down, assuring her he had no intention of being foolish with it. "We have it just in case, Manya," he told her, "and no
one outside of this house is to be told we have it. I don't plan to
use it unless I have to, do you understand?" he promised.

"Where did you get it?" Manya finally asked.

"It's best that you don't know," Meyer replied, ending her
questions.

And so, several times a week, Meyer would bring out the pistol
from its hiding place in an old boot and instruct them in its use.
"What is the first thing you do?" he challenged Manya.

"Undo the safety catch," she retorted.

He'd nod approvingly, remove the ammunition, and go on with
the lesson, making each of them practice at aiming and pulling
the trigger.

The presence of the gun made Chaim feel safer, but he
wouldn't touch the thing. He sat patiently and listened, but as the
pistol was passed to him, he always motioned for Manya to take it.
He couldn't seem to shake the thought of what it could do.

Noise from the cooking pot got louder. "Ach," Manya said out
loud as she snatched it off the fire and peeked under the lid.
Whew, it was all right, not burned, thank goodness. "Sit down at
the table," she called to the men in the next room. "Dinner is
ready." She moved quickly and automatically, gathering a handful
of utensils and a chunk of bread. In just a moment they'd be
sitting together and she could ask Meyer to tell her again about
Anna and the goods he had delivered. Like a sumptuous meal,
she wanted to taste the victory, feel it, smell it over and over. Oh,

Mama and Daddy, I'll see you soon, she thought. I just know it! The thought of it gave her a feeling of strength she hadn't had for a long time.

25

It was a great relief to Manya to be reassigned. Today she'd be working in the ghetto, and she was pleased. There was more independence and serenity here. No one watched over her to make certain she was working, No kicks to her body if she drifted off into her own thoughts. Even when a Gestapo came walking through the ghetto, he could be avoided.

She had gradually become accustomed to cleaning out the uninhabited Jewish homes, convincing herself that the previous occupants were alive and had simply been sent away to work, like her own parents. When all this was over, they, like her family, would return to Hrubieszow.

But there were times when she came across something in one of the houses, perhaps a doll, that challenged her selective logic. With trembling hands she'd smooth its tiny hand-stitched garments, feeling the love of the mother who had made them and the delight of the child who had dreamed with them. Cradling the abandoned plaything, she thought of her own little sisters and the doll dress her mother cut from the back of a too-ragged-to-mend shirt. It was painful for Manya to relinquish the doll to the pile of goods destined for Germany. How disappointed the child of the house would be to return and find it gone.

Not being part of a cleanout brigade would eliminate any possibility of picking up something that Meyer could take to Anna's. But that was all right for a day. They still had goods hidden under their bed that were waiting to be delivered. Soon after Meyer had made the arrangements with Anna, some three months ago now, they decided that going there every other day was too risky for Meyer, and perhaps too much for Anna to handle. They wanted to be careful about the pressure they put on her, so they settled on a frequency of twice a week.

Meyer knew that Anna didn't sell everything he brought her — that was part of the agreement. One time he actually went inside her house. Draped over her bed was a beautiful plush bedspread that he had deposited with her some days before. He couldn't help but smile to himself when he thought about the trouble he had had in getting it to her. Manya must have wound it around him four or five times. His coat had barely fit over his body. It was almost too obvious for him to take. And to make matters worse, it had been a warm day. There wouldn't be any money coming from that ordeal. But he didn't mind—he considered it partial payment of the debt he owed her for helping them.

They had no idea who was buying the goods or for how much. Meyer told Anna to get what she could and she agreed to hold the money for him. As the weeks rolled by, Anna repeatedly offered encouragement. She told Meyer not to worry, everything was going well, that he was due quite a sum of money already and soon—very soon—there would be enough. It was good news, and, feeling grateful, Meyer insisted that she keep a generous share for herself. He wasn't quite sure how he would repay the men who went to work with him every day and who delayed their progress long enough for Meyer to slip away. They knew if Meyer was caught they'd all be punished by the Gestapo. But that didn't deter them. Each time the ruse worked, they felt victorious, their morale boosted.

When Meyer announced to Manya, Chaim, Sam and Leon at dinner one night that their goal was almost within reach, they sat and talked all night about how they would escape. They were sure they wouldn't have to wait much longer.

Soon Meyer will ask Anna for the money, Manya thought as she set aside her chores for the lunch break and headed for her house. Aside from waking up each morning and knowing that she had Meyer and Chaim close, escape was her only ray of hope. She was standing in the kitchen warming up some vegetables left over from last night's dinner when someone knocked on the door. It couldn't be the Gestapo; they didn't bother to knock. Then she heard a voice call out her name. "Manya! Manya Nagelsztajn! Are you in there?" The voice sounded urgent.

She rushed to the door. "Mr. Silberstein, what is it? Why are you here?"

The older man checked over his shoulder before he stepped through the door and shut it. Manya stared at his face. His lips were tight and his jaw set. She saw him swallow hard before he spoke. "The Gestapo just left the office, Manya. They want to see Meyer when he comes back from work," he said solemnly.

The words pierced her body. She couldn't believe she'd heard right. There must be some mistake. Not Meyer, he hadn't done anything.

"Oh, my God," she cried, pulling at her face with her hands. Silberstein offered a comforting arm. "Why do they want him? What did he do? What will they do to him?" she implored.

"I'm sorry, Manya, but I don't know the answer to any of your questions. It can't be good—it was that butcher, Alex, who came. And he asked for Meyer by name. I wish I could tell you more, but he didn't say anything else. He just said to have Meyer Korenblit report to Gestapo headquarters when he returns," the man replied apologetically.

"What should I do?" she begged.

"That's for you to decide, Manya. The best I can do is pass on the information I have. What happens now is up to you," he responded.

No! She wanted to scream, but the word was trapped in her throat. It was just as well, for she knew he'd done enough already. She knew what the Nazis would do if they found out Mr. Silberstein had told anyone they were looking for Meyer. She had to think of a way to handle this by herself. She nodded at the man and he loosened his grip on her and turned toward the door.

The next thing Manya knew, she was standing outside alone. Something had to be done quickly. The Gestapo might not wait for Meyer to return from work—they might go directly to the fort and pick him up. She had to get to him before they did, or she might never see him again! She would change clothes and walk to the ghetto entrance. Then she would tie a scarf around her head and cross into the Polish area. Dressed this way, she'd look like a Polish woman and could make it across town to the fort. She'd have to remember to take off her armband. . . . How long had it been since the Gestapo was at the office asking for Meyer? How long had she been standing outside her house? Maybe it was too late already! Please, God, she prayed, don't let them find him!

She turned to go inside, then heard her name. "Manya, what is it? Is something wrong? Why are you crying?"

It was Isaac Hipps.

"Oh, Isaac, I don't know what to do," she cried. "I have to go and warn Meyer. The Gestapo is looking for him. Something terrible is going to happen!"

"How do you know this, Manya?"

"Someone just told me. They want him to report when he gets back from work. I don't know what else to do, so I am going to sneak over to the fort and tell Meyer not to come back."

"That will be very dangerous, Manya. You could get caught. You know they don't let people near the fort without permission."

"I don't care. If he comes back here, they'll take him away. I'll never see him again. I have to go," she insisted.

"Listen to me, Manya. I'll go instead. I have a pass. I can get through without any trouble. I can also get there a lot faster than you can," he asserted with a grim smile. "Doesn't that make sense, Manya?"

"Yes," she responded "but why should you take such a risk? I should go—it's my responsibility!"

"Nonsense, Manya, we have to help each other. It's much smarter for me to go, and that's what I'm going to do. Do you hear?"

"Yes, Isaac," she answered, gratefully obedient. "But, Isaac, please hurry!"

"I'll find him right now," he replied, gently touching her on the shoulder. "Do you know exactly where Meyer is working?" he asked.

"In the stable with the horses."

"All right," he said, "I'm on my way. Stay calm, Manya, whatever you do, stay calm and don't do anything foolish."

As Manya watched Isaac run down the street, she knew he was right. His long strides would carry him out of the ghetto and on his way to the fort much faster than she could have managed. Meyer's life was now in Isaac's hands—and legs.

It was a miracle she'd run into Isaac. He was such a good friend, although considerably older than she. There was no one better to send to warn Meyer. He was a very trustworthy person who wouldn't tell anyone about what was happening. Isaac was also one of the few Jews who had a pass that enabled him to walk around the city without being stopped. He got the pass because of the work he was able to do for the Germans—the same kind of skilled labor that Manya's father had done for them—plus, Isaac knew about electricity, and the Nazis needed his talents at various places during the day.

Manya didn't know what to do or where to go. What if Isaac didn't get there in time? Or couldn't find Meyer? Or was ordered to work by a passing SS officer? Why hadn't she told Isaac to come back as soon as he'd seen Meyer? Oh, God, please help Meyer . . . help Isaac . . . please! Manya stood there long after Isaac was out of sight. She kept whispering, "Hurry, Isaac, hurry!"

26

Isaac showed his pass to the guard on duty at the front gate and walked into the fort, acting as nonchalant as possible. He made his way across the grounds toward the stables as if he had an official job to do. If Manya was correct, he would find Meyer inside.

Meyer was hard at work when he heard someone call out his name. "Meyer," the voice said, "are you here?"

He walked out of one of the stalls and came face to face with Isaac. "What are you doing here?" Meyer greeted his friend with a smile. There was no return smile, and Meyer could see that something was terribly wrong.

"Speak Polish, Meyer, so the Germans can't understand. I have come here to warn you. The Gestapo is looking for you. They asked for you by name. Don't come back to the ghetto!"

Meyer was stunned. He couldn't believe what Isaac was telling him. "Why do they want me? How did you find out?"

"Somehow Manya found out and told me. She was going to come herself, but I talked her out of it," he answered. "If you have somewhere to go, you better leave as quickly as possible. Don't wait until the work day is over. If the Gestapo checks to see where you're working, they may come here to get you."

Isaac made a helpless gesture. There was nothing more he could say or do for the young man with the stricken look on his face. He turned away and walked out of the stable.

Meyer just stood there. He usually knew just what to do, but this had happened too quickly. He had to make up his mind—

why couldn't he think? He had to get out of the fort, but which side of the fence was the safest, the least patrolled? Finally an idea got through the jumble in his mind. He'd try to make his way to Salki's or Gorski's. Yes, that was it.

Walking out of the stables, he headed to one side of the fort grounds. Behind one of the outer buildings, he could get close to the fence. His instincts were firing instructions to his brain like pistons out of rhythm, but Meyer knew he had to look calm. With each step he took, his heart pounded five times. His feet felt like they were attached to the grinding stones of his father's flour mill. Would he ever get to the fence? Meyer was terrified. This wasn't some general roundup of Jews. This was personal. The Nazis wanted *him,* Meyer Korenblit.

He was at the fence. The building shielded him from view. Outside the fence, open fields. Danger. Then a grove of trees. Refuge. He dived to the ground, and lying on his stomach, reached under the lowest wire. His outstretched fingers, like talons, gouged the hard ground, the toes of his boots dug the turf for traction, and everything in between elongated and flattened to avoid the chiseled prongs of the barbed wire that could ensnare him. It seemed to take forever to slide under. Like a frenzied nightmare, he imagined them just behind him, inching closer and closer, gaining on him as he fell, and yet he eluded their every lunge, scrambling and weaving and dodging out of reach. There was a ringing in his ears that might muffle the first shouts of discovery, but he wouldn't look back—didn't want to know if they had noticed his escape, couldn't think what to do if they really were in pursuit.

Then he was out! He jumped up and headed straight for the trees. He leaned gratefully against one, knees like jelly, looking back. Nobody had seen him; no one was coming. He took his first breath in minutes.

He'd go to Salki's. Fewer neighbors. Less chance of being seen.

A very tired Manya took her place in line after work that afternoon. Seeing Chaim approach, she motioned him to stand beside her and linked her arm tightly around his. The count proceeded. It took all her determination to scan the line of faces—desperate to see Meyer, knowing that either way, escaped or arrested, he wouldn't be there. When she saw Isaac, she avoided his eyes, afraid to look, more afraid not to, thirsting for information but dreading to hear it. She had to know, and looked up again. Did she read something in his stare?

Damn! Why couldn't they hurry up with this stupid counting—if it went on much longer, she was going to scream! Then she heard the SS shouting angrily. She hadn't noticed the group of workers return from the fort.

"There are only eleven," she heard a German say. "There were twelve this morning."

Manya watched another SS stride menacingly toward the group of men. "Who is missing?" he bellowed.

No one spoke.

"I asked a question—you will answer. Who is missing?" he repeated, then accosted the silent group one by one. "Do you know? You? You?" Eleven shakes of the head.

Manya thought she would faint. She stole another look at Isaac. Not a muscle moved on his face, but she saw it in his eyes. Isaac had delivered the message to Meyer in time. She was sure of it. She turned to look straight ahead and found herself staring directly into Silberstein's face. He had the customary passive expression, but then Manya caught an almost imperceptible nod. She looked away.

The SS spun around and faced the rest of the Jewish workers. "You know it's useless to keep quiet—more useless to try to escape. No one will help a Jew escape. We'll find out who is missing—someone will tell us . . . perhaps one of you, eh?" he said with a leer. "We'll bring him back and make an example of him so you can be reminded again of what happens to someone who doesn't cooperate. And I promise you one more thing: if any of you have helped him, you, too, will be punished, do you hear?" he screamed. His piercing eyes seemed to examine the very souls of the weary figures before him; then he whirled around and spat a command for dismissal over his shoulder.

Still linked together, Manya steered Chaim toward their little house. She imagined that everyone was looking at her, knowing that she was responsible for this Nazi tirade. She expected to hear the SS threaten to shoot fifty people if no one came forward to confess. Perhaps they would think of that tomorrow, she thought with a shudder.

"I didn't see M—" Chaim began in a guarded whisper, but was

cut short by an elbow in his ribs and an abrupt shake of Manya's head. Seeing Isaac ahead, she hurried on to catch up with him. Maybe he had a message for her from Meyer, or had heard why Meyer was wanted. But more important, she had to thank Isaac. If only she could think how.

27

Meyer was sitting in the attic hideout Salki had built. He had taken a long route around the brick factory, outside the town, and through the back fields to get to Salki's. He didn't think anyone had seen him. Mrs. Salki was at home alone when he came bursting through the back door. He quickly explained the situation, and she immediately sent him up to the hiding place, telling him to be absolutely quiet and that John would be home in a few hours.

He was alone. There was no one to talk to. No one to tell him everything would be all right. He was as scared now as he had been when Isaac first told him he was wanted. Even the seemingly safe sanctuary of the attic hideout did nothing to curb his terror. He was trapped again, knowing any second the Gestapo could come bursting into the attic and drag him off.

He kept trying to think why they wanted him. Maybe the Gestapo had gone into the house and found the gun. That must be it, they found the gun. If that was true, then Manya, Chaim, Sam, and Leon were also in danger. He'd have to get word to them. He could ask Janek to go. But wait. Manya had been the one to warn him. She would have taken steps to protect herself and the others already. They may have gone to Josef's haystack.

Meyer heard a door open downstairs. The voices of two people talking came through the wooden boards in the ceiling. Then silence. He held his breath; there were footsteps on the ladder leading to the attic. He peeked through the slats of the hidden room and saw the trapdoor to the attic open. He waited, scarcely breathing, to see who it was. Then he heard a familiar friendly voice say, "Meyer, it's me, John."

The young man had never been so glad to see anyone in his life. For a brief moment relief rushed through his entire body. He removed the planks from the hiding place and stepped out to greet his friend. "Salki, they're looking for me. I didn't know what else to do."

"I know, Meyer, my wife told me. You made the right decision by coming here. Do you have any idea why they want you?" he asked.

"No!" responded the frightened teenager. "The only thing I can think of is they found the gun I had hidden . . ." He stopped short when he saw the look on John's face. Meyer had never told him about getting the gun.

The older man was obviously struggling for control. He'd warned Meyer about this. Why hadn't the boy listened to him? Well, it couldn't be helped now; there was nothing to be gained by looking back.

"I told you what the Nazis would do if they caught a Jew with a gun—they don't even allow Poles to have weapons without special permission," he said softly. "This is serious, Meyer, very serious."

Meyer nodded sheepishly. He wished he had listened to Salki.

"I . . . uh, did you hear anything about this today?" Meyer asked. "I mean, I'm worried about Manya and Chaim. Are they still there? Should we warn them?"

"Meyer, Manya was the one who warned *you*. She would surely have known if the Gestapo was looking for her as well. She and Chaim would have come here—I'm sure of it."

Meyer knew his friend was probably right. She would figure out a way for them to escape if it was necessary.

"Maybe she went back to the haystack!"

"I can send Janek there to find out, but it's far too dangerous for him to go to the ghetto today. The Nazis will no doubt be watching the house for you to return. Tomorrow or the next day will be safer. I'll check with Gorski—he can find out what's going on."

"What am I going to do, Salki?"

"I don't know. We'll put together as much information as possible; then we'll decide. Patience must be our ally, Meyer, and that's a quality you would do well to develop. I'll send something up for you to eat; then you must try to get some rest."

As the man turned to leave, Meyer asked him for one more favor. "Please let me know as soon as you find out if Manya and the others are in the haystack."

Meyer's benefactor nodded his head in agreement, then made his way down the ladder.

Meyer was alone again. Alone to think of the past. He was no longer confident of the future.

It was hours before Commissioner Salki returned to tell him that Janek had found no one at the haystack. Salki had gone to Gorski, but the chief of police had no knowledge of why the Gestapo was looking for Meyer. Gorski hadn't even known that Meyer was wanted, and the Nazis usually kept him informed of such things. Gorski assured Salki he'd get what news he could tomorrow. The only other bit of information that Salki was able to pass on was that there had been no killings in the ghetto that day.

Meyer gave a heavy sigh. Manya must still be all right. He would just have to wait until Gorski and Salki could manipulate the Nazis for the information. If the Germans didn't destroy him, he thought, the waiting would.

28

It was morning at last. Manya sat straight up in bed. She looked around and realized she must have fallen asleep after all. How long she had lain in bed the night before—how many times she had gotten up, how she had won the struggle against racing out in the darkness to find Meyer—she didn't know. But she had finally convinced herself that waiting was her only alternative. The Germans might be watching her, and she had no intention of leading them to Meyer. Not that she was certain where he could be found.

She had to see him, to talk to him, to hold him. She had been careful and sensible for the last two nights, but tonight, after work, she would go to Salki's. That seemed to be the most likely place for Meyer to be. John Salki wouldn't let them down.

She would have to put on her Polish garb, sneak through the ghetto after curfew, and remove her armband. Once in the Polish section, she'd be all right. Now all she had to do was to get through the day. She'd work very hard; then the time would pass quickly. She could feel Meyer's arms around her already.

She leaped out of bed, straightened the sheets and blankets, and drew a comb through her hair. She decided not to change her slept-in clothes and dipped some water to clean up.

Then she thought of Chaim. Already quiet-natured, he had withdrawn even further when she told him that Meyer was wanted by the Gestapo. Chaim would be very upset to hear what she planned to do. Somehow Manya would try to make him understand that she wasn't abandoning him by going to Meyer. She had to convince Chaim that she loved him, too, and would be back. Perhaps if she asked Chaim to help her, he would feel more a part of her plan. She didn't want to frighten him, but—

What was that? Walking into the next room, she heard it again. It was at the front door. Very cautiously she cracked open the door and peeked out. There was no one there. Puzzled, she looked around again, then started to close the door.

"Here!" came a voice. "Over here!"

Manya snatched the door open wide.

"Where?" she called. "Who's there?"

"It's me, Janek Salki. My father sent me with a message."

Finally Manya could see the boy crouched between some bushes. "Wait," she warned, looking all around. Satisfied that no one was about, she nodded for Janek to continue.

"It's Meyer. He's at our house," whispered the boy.

"Is he all right?" Manya interrupted.

Ignoring her question, the boy continued. "He wants you to come tonight. Can you do it?"

"Yes, yes. I was just planning . . . tell him . . . I still don't know why he's wanted," she stammered.

"Will you come?" Janek asked again.

"Yes, of course. It may be quite late, but I will come."

"I'll tell him. He asked me to come back right away."

"Janek, I . . . God bless you, Janek. I was so worried. Thank you—thank you for coming."

The boy made no reply as he edged his way from the house and disappeared. It was all arranged. Tonight she'd see Meyer. He'd hold her and reassure her, and together they'd figure out what to do. She'd definitely explain to Meyer that it was because of Silberstein that he was safe in Salki's attic instead of rotting or worse in the Gestapo jail.

A few hours later at work, Manya's workmates cleared shelves and drawers while she ran a dustrag around the empty surfaces. Reaching to a high ledge, she flicked the cloth along its length. Something skittered at the back of the shelf, and she reached up to investigate. She found a small carved box inlaid with mother-of-pearl. A nice treasure to deposit with Anna, she thought wryly, starting to toss it on a nearby pile. But wait, the thought continued, perhaps there was a use for it even without Anna.

Meyer was at Salki's. If she could work out a way to continue smuggling goods, it might help raise money for Meyer's escape. Manya would pick up the plan where Meyer had left off. She would take everything she could to John Salki. She slipped the little box deep into her coat pocket and took up the dusting again.

With her cleaning task completed, Manya stooped over, picked up a pile of clothing, and headed outside. As she stepped from the doorway, she saw Wagner coming down the street. She watched him gesture with his riding crop to another group of workers and heard him bark an order or two. Oh, God, she thought, not him—not today. Please let him go right by. She dumped her bundle onto a larger pile in the street and turned to rush back inside. She had almost made it through the door when she heard her name.

"You there, Nagelsztajn!" he shouted. "Just a minute. I want to talk to you!"

Manya stopped short, and with great effort turned around.

"It is you—yes, I thought so," he said, coming closer.

"Good day, Herr Wagner," Manya stammered, watching him stop in front of her. He stared at her for long moments without speaking, casually slapping the palm of his gloved left hand with the riding crop. The strokes of leather on leather and his piercing eyes achieved their intended effect. Manya's knees began to tremble. She made herself speak. "You wanted to talk to me, Herr Wagner?"

He gave her another long, purposeful look, then broke the spell. "Yes, I want to talk to you, Miss Nagelsztajn," he said, accentuating the "Miss" in a contrivance of respect. "Your boyfriend—Meyer, isn't it?" he began, hesitating to examine her reaction. "I thought you might be able to tell me where he is."

"Meyer?" she repeated, borrowing time to think.

"Well?" he added impatiently.

"No, Herr Wagner," she answered. "I can't tell you. He isn't here. I . . . I don't know where he is. He went to work a few days ago and never came back. He didn't say anything to me—not even good-bye—and I thought we were very close."

His eyes searched Manya's face for a ripple of deception. Manya returned his stare directly and innocently.

"It figures he just ran off without telling you. You Jews are all alike, thinking only about yourselves. My superiors want to talk to him," he continued in a lame effort to gain her confidence. "So, you aren't able to help me—you have no information?"

Manya shook her head.

"You'd tell me if you knew something, wouldn't you?"

Manya nodded, but didn't speak.

Wagner studied her intently. "You're perspiring a lot for such a cold day," he said slowly.

"I . . . It's the work, Herr Wagner," Manya answered. "I was working very hard."

"Ach! Working hard! You people don't even know what hard work is," he said in a disgusted tone. "Well, I can see you'll be no help to me—you'd better get busy." He turned to go, then spoke again. "If you hear from your young man, you should tell him to give himself up. He'll be better off—and so will you."

Manya stared her reply as Wagner proceeded down the street.

29

Returning to the house after work that evening, Manya dashed into the bedroom and pulled off her clothes. She bathed as quickly as she could and redressed, pulling on her Jewish arm-band and stuffing a scarf into the pocket of her dark dress. As she started for the next room, Chaim appeared in the doorway. "What are you doing?" he asked quietly.

"I just got cleaned up a little bit, that's all," she replied as casually as she could. "Are you hungry?"

"Manya, what are you going to do?"

"We're going to eat something as soon as I—"

"I didn't say 'we,' Manya, I said 'you.' You're getting ready for something. Tell me what it is!"

Manya wrapped her arms around Chaim. He was close to tears, and his slight frame welcomed the comfort.

"I'm so afraid, Manya," he choked. "Every time I see a German, I think he's after me . . . every time I hear a sound at night, I think they're coming to get us. Now I see you preparing for something, and you're keeping it a secret. Are you going to leave me behind? I just don't know what to expect anymore!"

"No, Chaim, no," she said, squeezing him tighter. "I'd never run off and leave you—you have to believe that. Come," she said, leading him toward the bed. "Sit down with me. We must talk."

They sat together for some time. Manya explained that Meyer was at Salki's house hiding, that she had to see him. She told Chaim that tonight she'd sneak over there, and she asked him if he would go with her to the gate of the ghetto. At first he shook his head, and she didn't know if he was disagreeing with her decision to go or refusing to accompany her. Then she knew that he was trying to shake off the urge to cry. She realized how very young he was—how brave, how lonely he'd been. She had Meyer, but Chaim had only a part of her. She imagined him lying alone in bed each night, and winced to think how he must have envied the closeness she shared with Meyer. It was only natural that Chaim might think she'd leave him behind.

She hugged him and kissed him and told him she loved him, swearing that he was as important to her as Meyer. She promised that she'd always take care of him, and pleaded with him to understand that she had to go to Salki's. She told him he didn't have to come with her, he could stay in the house. She assured him over and over that she'd be all right and would be back.

Then Sam called to her from the other room, wanting to know where everyone was and if they were going to have dinner.

"Chaim and I are talking, Sam. We'll be out in a little while." Just fix yourself something to eat. I don't feel like cooking tonight." She heard Sam grumbling to Leon, but brushed it aside and turned back to her brother. They sat in the darkness for a while, holding each other.

"You know, Chaim," she began, "Sam knows that Meyer got away, but he doesn't know where. You can't tell anyone what I've told you. Not even Sam. No one must know where Meyer is. It isn't that we don't trust Sam or Leon, we just can't put Meyer or Salki in danger. We have to be strong enough to keep this secret. Do you think you can do it?"

Chaim looked very tired as he gave her a slight nod.

Manya tried to rub some energy into his hunched form, then stood and drew him upright. "You must be hungry by now— maybe just a little bit?" she chided, pinching his cheek and smiling. "Come on, let's see if Sam and Leon left anything for us!"

Chaim pulled back and looked at her through sober eyes. "I'll go with you to the gate tonight, Manya," he said shyly.

"But you don't have to. It's all right—"

"No, I'll go. I want to help you. I love Meyer, too, and if I help you, I'll be helping him."

"Just knowing you're with me is a help, Chaim," she said, stroking his curly hair. "I'm not as brave as I sound. But Meyer needs me, and I have to see him."

They stumbled into the dark kitchen and lit a candle . Manya found some leftover noodles and potato and dropped them into a soup plate for Chaim. She poured milk over it all and tore off a piece of rye bread.

"Milk soup," he said with a grin. It was his favorite.

She sat down with him and nibbled a hunk of bread while he wolfed down the pasty concoction. He livened up and talked easily, obviously enjoying the special attention. Sam and Leon soon yawned their good nights and headed for bed.

Perhaps an hour or more later the conversation trailed off and Chaim noticed a certain preoccupation come over his sister. He was silent for a time, then spoke. "Do you want to go?"

Manya looked at Chaim's thin face. Should she wait a bit longer? Sit with Chaim a little more? She couldn't! It was getting too late. Staring at him intently, she searched his eyes for a flicker of doubt. There was none. She nodded.

He managed a nervous smile and stood up. "Let's go, then," he said, snuffing the candle flame with his fingers.

They tripped the door latch and crouched very low. As their eyes adjusted to the darkness, they listened to the night. There was no sound or sign of activity in the ghetto streets. Hand in hand they slipped through the doorway and outside, finding cover in the same bushes that had hidden the Salki boy earlier in the day.

Cautiously they inched their way three blocks to the ghetto entrance. The customary guards were on duty, but it didn't matter, for they wouldn't leave the ghetto at that point. Not far away, there was a slim passageway between two buildings. There was just enough room for them to slither through if they turned their bodies sideways. The opening emptied into an alley on the Polish side.

Manya could feel Chaim's terrified trembling—or was it her own? She saw the ghetto office just ahead. They had made it! She pulled Chaim's arm and they both knelt down. Yanking off her armband, she stuffed it down the front of her dress, then tied the scarf around her head. Taking his face in her hands, Manya felt his wet cheeks, then gave him a kiss. "I'll be back, brother," she promised. "I'll be back."

He settled in to wait.

The streets were deserted. Manya walked briskly but not too fast. She was almost dizzy from looking ahead, then to the rear, then forward again, but she had to make sure no one was watching or following, Her breath came hard with the pressure of her pace, painting the freezing black night with a trail of vapor like steam from a locomotive.

It was very cold, and Manya's teeth were chattering when she got to Salki's house. She tiptoed up the front steps and placed an ear to the door. The house was silent. She knocked. In a moment the door cracked open and John Salki peered out. Behind him she could see the dim flickering of a single candle. His practiced eyes scanned her wake before he motioned her inside and closed the door.

Silently she followed him up the stairs to the second floor and into one of the bedrooms. Placing a hand on her shoulder, he held her still for a moment so that she would know to wait. He disappeared into the upper hallway and returned lugging something heavy. It was a ladder. It took him a few moments to maneuver it soundlessly through the doorway and into position against one of the bedroom walls.

He climbed up and, arms outstretched, pushed hard against the ceiling. A two-by-three-foot section slid heavily away with a scrape and a thud. She heard him breathe a curse. He descended the ladder and reached for her hand, pointing up. She mimicked his gesture with her own extended arm, looking overhead and whispering, "Up there?" When she glanced down again, he was gone.

She stepped on the first rung and felt the old ladder bow with her weight. It seemed to tremble more with each step she took. Then her groping hands felt the floor of the attic. Her feet advanced another rung. Her upper body cleared the opening and she flopped forward. The cold attic floor felt good against her burning cheeks.

Something touched her arm. Before she could raise her head, she was lifted bodily and pulled away from the trapdoor opening. Familiar arms locked around her; a beloved voice whispered unintelligibly in her ear. When the shaking stopped, Meyer led her into his hiding place and repositioned the planks to seal the entrance.

They were unable to speak at first. She just kept saying, "Oh, Meyer . . . oh, Meyer, why?" They held each other the entire time, not able to let go, trying to make up for the days apart. He squeezed her hand and stroked her soft hair. Then they cried and cried until no more tears would come. They lingered over each embrace, knowing that it would be a while before they could share each other's touch again.

It was two hours before Manya crawled back to the waiting ladder. She nearly jumped out of her skin when she saw John Salki reach to steady her descent. They exchanged no words and she went on downstairs alone as he removed the ladder and watched Meyer replace the trapdoor above.

Manya drew the curtain aside from a front window of the house. It was as still outside as it had been when she arrived. In seconds she was on her way back to the ghetto. Poor Chaim, she thought. He must be freezing by now. She decided to quicken her pace. She wouldn't appear suspicious—after all, anyone out on a night like this would hurry. She pulled the scarf a little lower on her face and was grateful she had it to help shield the cold.

She passed the cannon in its mantle of ice. Not too much farther and she would reach the passageway to the ghetto and Chaim. Then only a few blocks to the house, and bed. She would sleep tonight, she was sure of it. Perhaps Chaim would climb in with her and they could snuggle together like the old days. He would like that, and so would she.

30

Meyer had decided to find his parents. He was going to Mislavitch. It was a cold, clear evening when he stepped from the back door of Salki's house. The moonlight cast silhouettes of the two men against the building. It was nine o'clock, plenty of time for Meyer to reach his destination.

"Be careful, Meyer. Remember, it's still not wise to trust everyone who is an old friend. Times have changed," Salki warned Meyer.

"I know, John, I'll be careful. You don't have to worry about that," Meyer assured his mentor.

"Good, I'll see you in a few days."

They shook hands and said their farewells. Meyer turned and began walking toward the fields. It had been most difficult to explain to Manya that he was leaving for a few days. She finally gave her consent only after he said he wanted to find his family. He knew it was a somewhat dishonest way to get her approval, but he just couldn't stay confined in that attic.

Five days had passed since his escape from the fort. Five grueling days of sitting, wondering what was going on, worrying about what might happen, fearing it would happen any minute.

Meyer wasn't the only one worried. Salki knew that when the Gestapo was looking for someone, they put the pressure on everyone. That was why he reluctantly agreed to Meyer's idea. Neither he nor Gorski had found out why the Gestapo wanted him. They didn't want to push the Germans for information for fear it would arouse suspicion. With Meyer gone, they could more aggressively pursue the answer. If the Nazis became suspicious and watched, or even searched their houses, Meyer wouldn't be there.

Salki extracted Meyer's promise to return within two or three days, believing that by then they would know why the Gestapo was hunting him and could decide what to do.

But Meyer knew that was only part of the reason his friend had made him promise to come back. He didn't want Meyer to make any decisions without first conferring with him and Gorski.

Now Meyer was out, walking into the unknown, with no assurance that when he got to his destination there would be anyone who would help him.

The moon had reached its peak and was making its descent when Meyer reached the outlying farms of Mislavitch. He couldn't go to the Achlers' house while it was dark. If he woke them, it would surely send them into a panic. He'd wait until daybreak. He knew they were early risers.

There were few sounds in the predawn air, but each one was intensified by the quiet that surrounded him. He was scared.

Crouched in the underbrush, he could see the farm. Just down the road was the flour mill. He hadn't been there for a long time. Did Achler still live there? Would he help? Could he be trusted? Salki's words of caution ran through Meyer's head. No, he would trust these old friends; there was no one else he could turn to.

He was standing at the back door. It was too late to turn back. His fist hit the door.

"Isaac, it's Meyer Korenblit."

Seconds later the door flew open. There, standing in the doorway, was the man who had taken over the Korenblit flour mill. His arms opened to greet the young man he hadn't seen for almost a year, grabbing Meyer in a powerful hug. "Come inside quickly. You must be hungry." He yelled to his wife to bring food. "How are you, Meyer? Why are you here?"

"I'm fine Isaac, just fine. Tell me, did my parents come here? Are they safe? Can I see them?

"Yes, yes, Meyer. Avrum came with the family and they're safe. They are being watched over," the man answered.

"Where are they? Are they close by? When can I see them?"

"They aren't far away, but I don't think you should go to them. Not everyone here is still your family's friend. Many people work with the Germans, both for material gain and their dislike of Jews. If the wrong person saw you, it would be very dangerous."

His mind was flooded. He'd been so sure he'd be with his family very soon. He needed them. He missed them so much. Together, he and Avrum could have made the decision about what they should do, just as they'd done in the past.

"I can go at night," Meyer insisted.

"Don't think the darkness always protects you, Meyer. The Nazis and their collaborators are perpetually watching. I'll get word to Avrum and let him know you're here and safe."

The man's logic was on target, but in accepting it, Meyer was filled with sadness. He was fearful and lonely, and fought to conceal his disappointment.

Of course Isaac was right. Especially since the Gestapo was looking for him. Any move he made would be dangerous. The last thing in the world he wanted was to lead the Nazis to his family. Taking a deep breath, he finally agreed with his friend. "I understand, Isaac. It's better that I don't go to see them now."

Seeing the boy's struggle, the Pole asked, "Meyer, is everything all right in the ghetto? What's the matter?"

Trying to hold back the tears, the scared young man answered, "They're looking for me!"

"I know, Meyer, the Nazis are looking for all the Jews."

"No, Isaac, the Gestapo is hunting *me*, Meyer Korenblit!"

Meyer explained to his friend what had happened five days ago. Achler didn't know how to respond. He just sat there shaking his head.

"I'm sorry, Isaac, I don't mean to cause you any trouble."

"Don't be ridiculous, Meyer. I want to help you. Now, let's get you some food. Then you can hide in the barn while I go to Tomitzki to see what we can do."

"Thank you, Isaac, you're still the same old friend. Please do me one favor. When you talk to my parents, don't tell them why I'm here. I don't want them to worry."

As Meyer sat in the barn, he had the feeling that waiting was the only thing he had done for five days. He couldn't stand it anymore. He had to think of a way out. Maybe now would be the time to join the underground. But what about Manya? He couldn't leave her, and she wouldn't leave Chaim.

Opening the barn doors ever so slightly, he peeked through the crack at the flour mill down the road. Was it still the same, or had it been changed? Avrum had devoted so much time and work to make it successful. Meyer loved being there beside his father, watching the stones grind the grain, then shoveling the fine flour into the sacks. He had to make sure there was just the right amount in each bag. Avrum would scold him as much for not having enough in the sack as he would for having too much. Then the struggle would ensue. Meyer against the flour. The first few years, he wasn't strong enough to pick up the bundle, throw it over his shoulder, and carry it to the chute like his older brothers could. He would yank and pull, dragging it across the floor. Wanting to keep up with his brothers, he would try to move too quickly, often tripping over some object left in the middle of the room or getting his feet tangled up under the sack. Finally he managed to get the sack on his shoulder. With knees ready to buckle, he staggered like a drunk to the chute and heaved the burden off his shoulder. His weight carried him forward. It was a race to see if he or the flour would hit the bottom first. Lying on his back looking up, he could see the others holding their sides and pointing. Even Avrum was chuckling as he looked down at his youngest son sprawled out on the floor with the sack lying across his body and his face covered with flour.

Soon after the war had started, Avrum turned over the flour mill to Achler and Tomitzki, but continued to work there. Avrum hoped that if the Nazis thought it belonged to these two Poles it wouldn't be confiscated or torn down. The Poles had taken care of it with the understanding that after the war Avrum would take it back. Many times during the past three years Meyer had been able to sneak back and get flour to sell on the black market. He'd even been able to give some to the Nagelsztajns after food rationing went into effect.

Then there had been the time he'd gotten boots for Manya. She had never had a pair of boots. The winter was approaching and Meyer knew there was no way Shlomo would ever be able to get them for her now; he couldn't even afford them before the war. It was in the fall of 1941 and Meyer asked Achler for an extra amount of flour for his black-market activities. He took it to the shoemaker, and that winter Manya had her first pair of boots. They became her most prized possession. Now the boots were gone, along with all the other possessions from the Nagelsztajn house.

Meyer shook his head to bring himself back to the present. Tomitzki and Achler were once again helping his family, and now they were going to help Meyer.

He continued to wait. The morning passed into the early afternoon. Still no Isaac or Tomitzki. Mrs. Achler brought him lunch but stayed only a few minutes to talk.

Four walls surrounded him; nowhere to go. He didn't know how much more of this he'd be able to take. After what seemed like an eternity, he saw Achler and Tomitzki walking down the road toward the barn.

Meyer greeted the two older men happily. If nothing else, he would at least have someone to talk with.

"Meyer, I saw your family, and they're fine. Avrum wanted to come and see you, but I talked him out of it," Achler said.

"You didn't tell them why I was here, did you?"

"Oh no!" the Pole responded. "But they were concerned about why you had come. I told them you just wanted to check on them, since you hadn't had any word in so long. I think they accepted that," he said, rather proud of himself. "They send you their love. Your mother continues to pray for the day you'll all be back together."

"Now, we must get down to business, Meyer," interjected Tomitzki. "I think we have a plan that might work. It'll be very dangerous, but if you are willing to try it, we'll help you."

"I'll try anything," Meyer answered eagerly. "Tell me what it is."

"You know," Tomitzki continued, "my boy Antonio and you are about the same age and build. We're going to go to the magistrate's office and explain that Antonio has lost his identification papers. Hopefully, they'll give us another set of papers—for a price, of course. Then we'll substitute your picture for his."

"But how will you get my picture? And what about the stamp?" Meyer asked.

"You let us worry about that, Meyer," Achler responded. "Just remember, you won't be able to use the papers around here. Too many people know both Antonio and you."

"You are taking a big risk by doing this," Meyer said.

"Are *you* willing to take the chance, Meyer?" Achler asked.

Meyer nodded his head. "I hardly know what to say. How can I ever thank you?"

"Avrum and your family have been our friends for many years, Meyer. Your father has always been good to us. He's done a lot over the years to help us, and we want to repay him," Tomitzki responded.

Meyer stayed in Achler's house that night. His wife prepared a meal that seemed like a feast. She even made the brown noodles he loved so much. He savored them, making them last as long as possible. They talked late into the night, exchanging stories of the past and the present situation. Meyer explained what had been going on in the ghetto.

It was painful to recall the stories, and Meyer could see the anger on Isaac's face.

Then the Pole filled in with stories about the Korenblits in the past months. They'd been set up in a good place and were well taken care of.

"The girls are fine, a little restless, especially Minka. She always talks about you, Meyer. How soon the two of you will play together," Achler said with a smile.

"Malka is grateful that she, Avrum, and the girls are safe. But the hurt grows every day inside her, Meyer. Not having her sons there and not knowing if they're safe," he continued.

Meyer cringed when he heard those words. He wanted to jump up and demand that Isaac take him to his family. But he knew it was wrong. He must wait and do nothing foolish. They were alive, together, and safe. That was the most important thing. And Malka knew that he was alive and well. That knowledge would give her the strength she needed to continue the fight.

As he lay in bed, he couldn't help but feel better, not quite as scared as before. Once more his fate was back in his own hands.

The next day Tomitzki managed to get a camera. The last time Meyer could remember being photographed was for a family portrait taken in 1938. He wished he had that photo to look at every day.

It was decided that Meyer would return to his hiding place in Hrubieszow and wait for two weeks until the papers were processed and then changed. Achler and Tomitzki didn't know exactly how long it would take, and they didn't want Meyer running back and forth if the documents weren't ready. He'd return in two weeks and pick up the papers. Then he'd be on his own.

Achler had gone to the Korenblits earlier in the day to explain that Meyer was going back to the ghetto now that he was sure

Three of the Nagelsztajn children in 1938 in Hrubieszow:
Chaim, Gittel and Joshua.

The Korenblit family in 1938: *(standing)* Toba, Aunt Rivka, Motl,
Aunt Tovah, Minka and Meyer; *(seated)* Malka, Cyvia and Avrum.

Meyer in 1981 at the Korenblit flour mill with Isaac Achler *(far right)*, who took over its operation in 1939. (MIKE KORENBLIT)

Entrance to the ghetto where the last Jews of Hrubieszow lived. The building on the left served as the Jewish Center. Photo taken in 1981. (MIKE KORENBLIT)

In the center is the house where Manya, Meyer and Chaim lived after they left the haystack. Photo taken in 1981. (MIKE KORENBLIT)

Police Chief Gorski, Mrs. Gorski, and their daughter.

Manya and Meyer Korenblit in 1946, just after their marriage.

January 30, 1982, Manya and Chaim in Newcastle upon Tyne, England.
(Newcastle Chronicle & Journal, Ltd.)

Together again after 39 years. (Cecilia Nagelsztajn, far right).
(Newcastle Chronicle & Journal, Ltd.)

Manya, Chaim and Meyer.
(Newcastle Chronicle & Journal, Ltd.)

Brother and sister in Newcastle, January 31, 1982.
(Newcastle Chronicle & Journal, Ltd.)

Roast beef and yorkshire pudding on Sunday with some of the family. *(standing)* Kathie Janger, Joan Korenblit, Mike Korenblit, Cecilia Nagelsztajn, Meyer Korenblit, Judith and Michael Nagelsztajn; *(seated)* Manya Korenblit and Chaim Nagelsztajn.

(ALLEN GLENWRIGHT)

they were safe. Meyer told Isaac to tell his family that he'd be in touch with them every two weeks or so, depending on when he could get out, that he'd be fine, and not to worry about him. He also sent word that Manya and Chaim were well and sent their love. The last part of his message was that they had learned the Nagelsztajns were alive and safe.

When Isaac returned and told Meyer that Malka's face had lit up after hearing all the news, he felt relieved. He also knew he must continue the charade until this was over. He could never let them know he was being hunted.

Meyer looked out the window to make sure it was dark.

"Isaac, I think I should go now," Meyer told the older man.

Meyer's journey back to Salki's was by the same route he had taken to get to Mislavitch. He was glad it seemed shorter going than coming.

Again, people were putting their lives in danger for Meyer. For three months Achler and Tomitzki had taken care of his family. Now, with their help once more, he wouldn't just be sitting in the attic at Salki's. Meyer was ecstatic about the plan they'd come up with. He hadn't even thought about what he was going to do with the papers once he got them. He knew he wouldn't leave the country without Manya and Chaim. Maybe he could go to a town not far away and get a job. Then he could return every few weeks to see Manya. He'd also be able to get word to his parents that he was still alive and well. They'd never know he wasn't in the ghetto and wouldn't be more worried than necessary.

Meyer smiled to himself when he thought about an incident that had taken place early during the occupation. Because of it, Meyer was confident this scheme would work. He was returning home with Avrum and the other Jews who worked at the brick factory. They were ordered to line up upon their arrival at the plaza. The SS wanted to look them over. The Germans walked up and down the lines, yelling and screaming at some, beating others. One of them finally made his way to Meyer's line, stopping directly in front of him. Meyer was shaking inside, sure the Nazi was going to hit him. Instead, looking right into Meyer's eyes he said, "What are you doing in this line? Don't you know this work is only for the filthy Jews?"

Shocked, Meyer had not known what to say.

"Well?" he repeated.

"I am Jewish," Meyer responded.

"You are? Are you sure?" he demanded.

"Yes, sir," Meyer told him. "This is my father."

He stood there looking at Meyer for a few seconds; then he stormed away. It seemed that Meyer didn't look Jewish. The German was obviously upset that he'd been wrong. If I could pass as a Pole then, I could surely pass as one now, he thought.

Meyer expected to have trouble convincing Manya that this scheme would work. She'd want him to remain at Salki's indefinitely, but he just couldn't stand being cooped up. Even though Salki would have let Meyer stay as long as he needed, it would become more dangerous as each day went by, and he didn't want to continuously jeopardize the family.

He'd make Manya understand. He was definitely going through with the plan. He knew John would be somewhat relieved even if he didn't show it. Meyer could hardly wait to get there and tell him.

31

"I tell you, I don't believe it." Meyer hollered.

"It's true—Gorski found out yesterday," said John Salki.

"But she's my friend, she offered to help—why would she report me to the Gestapo?"

Salki sighed wearily. Meyer had just returned from Mislavitch. The teenager's face was a mask of rage.

"Meyer," Salki began, "you know that Anna's husband has been gone a long time—"

"Of course—she used to talk to me about it. But what's that got to do with this?"

"Please, let me finish. It has a lot to do with this. So she talked with you about her husband. Did she ever mention Damone?"

"Never."

"No, I suppose not," Salki said, shaking his head. "But she knew him, Meyer, she knew him very well."

"What are you saying?"

"Use your head, Meyer. Tell me—where is her house?"

"Across the street from the fort, but—"

"Yes, across the street from the fort. In other words, across the street from one of Damone's offices. Meyer, Anna is Damone's girlfriend!"

Damone's girlfriend! The words echoed in Meyer's head. How could he have been so stupid? Why didn't he guess? But there had never been a clue. Meyer had never seen the Gestapo officer at Anna's house. Had Anna been planning this all along?

"No!" he said out loud in a dual rejection of his poor judgment and her betrayal.

"I swear it's true, Meyer. Gorski found out that those two have been carrying on for months!"

Salki saw the anger fading into hurt. The eyes took on a doleful look. The older man softened his tone. "I know how you feel—" he began.

"*You* know how *I* feel? How could you know how I feel?"

Salki nodded his acceptance of Meyer's point, but shrugged off the boy's affront.

"Feeling sorry for yourself won't help, Meyer," he continued in a calm voice. "It's over. We have to plan for today and tomorrow."

Meyer finally lifted his gaze and looked directly into Salki's eyes.

"There's something else to consider, my friend," Salki went on. "We know that Manya and Chaim are still in the ghetto. If Anna is responsible for reporting you, then they're probably not in great danger—they can stay where they are. We should be thankful for that."

"Thankful?" Meyer said sarcastically. "How thankful will they be when I tell them how stupid I was, that we'll never get out of this? How will they feel when they find out I let that woman cheat us out of our freedom? I've failed them!"

"That's enough!" John Salki yelled over Meyer's tirade. "I'll hear no more of this self-pity! Do you think that being free is all Manya thinks about? Or is it to be free with you?"

"With me," the boy responded.

"Does she sneak over here to be free? Or to help keep you safe?"

Meyer shifted uncomfortably and looked away, then nodded.

"Does she seem to care why you are wanted by the Germans?"

"No—"

"All right, then, that's what you must think about. Never mind that you used bad judgment—it's not the first time. Manya still believes in you. You have to show her that even when you make a mistake, you can bounce back."

It was two days since Meyer had made the return visit to Mislavitch to pick up the invaluable identity papers. Tomitzki and Achler had done their job well. They'd also gotten Meyer another gun. At first he was hesitant about taking the weapon, but he finally gave in.

Mrs. Salki came into the room. "It's all clear outside, Meyer," she said softly.

Meyer rose from the table and headed for the back door, checking to make sure he had the precious papers in his pocket. The older woman turned out the light in the kitchen and quietly opened the door. As he moved past her and out the opening, he heard her whisper, "Be careful. I'll see you later."

John Salki had left the house a half-hour ago. Meyer was to wait until the commissioner had enough time to get to Gorski's and then he was to meet them there and go over the plan one final time. Gorski wanted to check everything in detail.

Meyer went to Gorski's back door, where he'd gone so many times as a young boy, illegally bringing his friend meat from his father. He didn't bother to knock. He turned the doorknob and pushed. It wasn't locked.

"Gorski! Salki!"

"Come in, Meyer, we're in here," came the response.

Meyer followed the voice to the living room. The two men were seated and looked up at him with grim smiles as he walked into the room.

"Any problems, Meyer?" asked Salki.

"No, it was very quiet," he answered.

"Good," responded Gorski. "Do you have the papers with you?"

Meyer pulled the papers from his pocket and handed them to the chief of police, who took the document and with trained eyes scrutinized the paper, word by word, line by line. He got up and walked to the lamp on the table. Holding the papers to the light, he nodded his head every once in a while. Then he went back to his chair and examined them again.

Finally he announced his verdict: "Perfect! They're excellent. They'll do fine."

All three men smiled happily.

"If you lose your papers, you have to go in person to get new ones. How did they get your picture stamped?"

"They stole the stamp," he stated.

Gorski gave a small snicker. "Well, we can't let all that trouble go for nothing. We must prepare you for your trip. From now on you are Antonio Tomitzki, not Meyer Korenblit. You must think 'Antonio' at all times. You must think and act like a Pole. You are no longer a Jew."

The words stung. He was being told to forget who he was and what he was. No matter how much it might hurt, he had to do it.

"My name is Antonio Tomitzki. I'm from Mislavitch," he repeated.

For the next hour, while Meyer studied the papers, Gorski and Salki fed him information, grilled him with questions, and drilled the proper responses into him.

"You must always stay calm, no matter what is happening. Be sure of yourself at all times and be respectful of anyone who stops you. Give nobody a reason to get mad or suspicious," Gorski instructed.

Then the interrogation began.

"What is your name? Where are you from? How old are you? When were you born? What is your father's name? Your mother's? How many people live in Mislavitch?"

The answers from Meyer were automatic.

"Where are you going?"

"To Lublin."

"Why?"

"To visit a sick uncle."

"Why aren't your parents with you?"

"They couldn't leave work."

Then they'd start over.

"What is your name? How tall are you? How many brothers and sisters do you have? Where is Mislavitch?"

"Why are you so far from home?"

"I'm on my way to Warsaw. I have a job there."

"What kind of job?"

"I work in a factory making steel ball bearings."

"That's a good job. If Jews still owned the factories, you wouldn't have work. You're happy with what we're doing to the filthy swine?"

Meyer hesitated, then stammered.

"No! You can't do that," yelled Gorski.

Lowering his voice, he put his arm around Meyer. "I know it's hard. But you must answer quickly and correctly. Answer like a Pole would, whether he means what he's saying or not. You are Antonio Tomitzki. You have to respond as he would. You can't let them shake you up."

Gorski stepped in front of Meyer, placing his hands lightly on his shoulders. "Do you understand? Can you do it?"

"Yes," came the reluctant response.

"Good, let's start over."

For two more hours Salki and Gorski questioned, and the new Antonio Tomitzki answered, until they were satisfied they could do no more to help. The training session was over.

John Salki left first, through the front door, Meyer waiting to give him enough time to get home.

"How are Avrum and the family?" Gorski asked.

"They're fine. I wasn't able to see them, but we've sent messages to each other," answered Meyer sadly.

"Good. I'm glad to hear that, Meyer. Maybe next year we'll again be able to celebrate Passover together. You know I love your mother's cooking."

"I hope we can too, Gorski."

They got up and moved to the back door. Before opening it, the chief of police turned and faced Meyer. "Tonight was just practice, a game. The day after tomorrow it'll be for real. Remember what we told you, Meyer. Remember it well." He put his arm around Meyer's shoulders. "Good luck, my friend. I'll see you in a few weeks."

32

"Manya, you know it's the only thing I can do. If there were any other way, I'd try. Do you think I want to leave you, not to be close by, to know you and Chaim are safe? The longer I stay here, the more danger I put everyone in. You see, we can trust very few people."

She must be strong. Now wasn't the time to show fear. Meyer was leaving. She would show him she had the fortitude to go on. There was a lot she could do to help Meyer while he was away. She wouldn't tell him about the plan she had formulated with Chaim and Salki. He'd need money and clothes when he returned, and she'd get them. She let the tears flow, not even attempting to stop them, instead letting Meyer's powerful hand tenderly brush them aside.

"I know, Meyer," she finally responded. "I'll be strong and take care of Chaim. We'll be here when you return. We'll do what we must to survive, just as you will. We have so much more of life to share. Do you remember, Meyer, the first time you told me you loved me?"

Meyer nodded his head rather bashfully, his face turning light red.

Manya was using the same kind of ploy on Meyer that he used on her when things were very bad: thinking back to the past to help you get through the present. It didn't always work, but when it did, that feeling of hope got them by one more day.

"You cried like a little baby at my bedside. You were so afraid of how sick I was. You said you loved me so much and if I got well you'd never again look at another girl. That made me so happy. I knew you thought I was on my deathbed or something—remember?" said Manya, poking his shoulder playfully until his embarrassed nod admitted it.

They shared a smile, then sat quietly. Meyer gently stroked her arm in a continuous motion while Manya held him tight knowing in a few moments he would say those words she so dreaded to hear.

"Manya, it's time for me to leave."

She squeezed hard, as if that might change his mind, but she knew he had to go. They stood and walked to the back door, where Salki was waiting.

"It's clear, Meyer," the commissioner informed him. "Good luck, and be careful. I'll see you in a few weeks," he continued, reaching out his hand to Meyer. Then he turned and left the room to give the two young people a minute alone.

Meyer pulled Manya close. "I'll be fine. You must take care of yourself and Chaim. He needs you," Meyer whispered in her ear. "I'll be back, Manya. I love you more than anything."

Their lips met, and each could feel the wetness from the other's cheek. Meyer pulled away and opened the door. He turned to look at her one more time.

No sound came forth; Manya could only mouth the words "I love you."

Meyer was gone. She peeked through the curtains to catch one fading glimpse of the man she loved before the darkness swallowed him. "I love you, Meyer. I'll be strong."

Meyer made his way to Mislavitch, where Isaac Achler was waiting for him. He watched as Achler hitched the horse to the cart; then Meyer climbed in and lay down. Taking a tarpaulin, Isaac threw it over the young man and proceeded to pile vegetables and other goods on top of him.

Meyer felt the cart jerk forward.

"Are you all right, Meyer?" came the voice in front of him.

"Yes," was the muffled reply.

"You won't have to stay there long, just until we get a few miles outside town."

Meyer had traveled this road many times with his father, but he never realized how many bumps there were. The cart shimmied across the cobblestones, bouncing him up and down and sideways. He moved around in the V-shaped area, trying to get comfortable without disturbing the goods that concealed him. There was no room to lie flat, so he assumed a fetal position, bracing his feet against one side of the cart, pressing his shoulders to the other. The steady clip-clop of the horse's hooves added a syncopated rhythm to the swaying wagon. It seemed like hours before the cart stopped.

"Okay, Meyer, I think it's safe now."

A thankful Meyer scrambled out from under the smelly blanket. He joined Achler in the front of the cart and they lurched forward once again, at a snail's pace. There was no need to hurry. Neither man spoke, each sitting with his own thoughts.

Meyer saw the sign: "DUBIENKA ANOTHER 4."

"I think this is far enough, Isaac," Meyer said.

The Pole stopped the cart for a second time and Meyer jumped down. He'd walk the rest of the way so the two men wouldn't be seen together. Meyer would catch the train in Dubienka for Chelm.

"Thank you, my friend. I'll see you in a few weeks. Please tell my parents everything is fine."

"I will, Meyer, and good luck. May God go with you."

Meyer threw his bundle over his shoulder and began walking leisurely along the road. Mrs. Salki had wrapped some food which would last for a couple of days; he had two extra shirts and a change of underwear in the cloth bag. In his pocket was the money Salki had given him for food and lodging, along with the invaluable papers.

Before very long Meyer was standing at the train stop on the other side of town. It was too early for the train to arrive. There was nobody else around yet. He sat down to wait, and wondered what he would do once he got to Chelm. He was still scared. It would take only one person to recognize him, only one mistake on his part, and it would all be over.

"Antonio Tomitzki. I'm going to visit a sick uncle in Lublin," he whispered under his breath.

Meyer felt very much alone.

33

"Where are you going?"

"To Chelm," Meyer quickly answered.

"That will be two zlotys," the man told him.

Meyer thrust his hand into his pocket and counted out the correct change while the conductor tore off a ticket and punched it. Taking the money from Meyer, he turned and walked down the aisle to the next passenger. Meyer couldn't help but glance over his shoulder to see if the conductor was looking at him. He wasn't. The car wasn't full, and Meyer was glad. The fewer people there were, the less likely it would be that anyone would recognize him. Only four people had gotten on the train in Dubienka. So far, everything had gone well, but he knew next time it would be different. There was no ticket counter in Dubienka; he just got on the train and paid. In Chelm and the larger cities, this wouldn't be the case. He'd have to buy his ticket ahead of time, and there would no doubt be many more people at the train station.

The whistle blew. They were coming into another town. A few more people got on. Meyer began making mental notes. How many stops were there between Dubienka and Chelm? How long between each one? How big was each town? At what times and where did the most people get on? He played with all the options. Was it better to get on with a lot of people or not many? Should he sit down beside someone or always try to find an empty bench?

He reached into his bundle and pulled out a hunk of bread and cheese. He was careful how much he ate, since he didn't know how easy it would be to get more. Where he was going, food couldn't be obtained the way it had been in Hrubieszow. There was rationing, and he didn't have coupons. Meyer knew that was the least of his problems and he could deal with it when the time came.

He looked out the window. It was so peaceful. The countryside had begun its spring ritual. The grass beside the tracks was turning a beautiful shade of green. The open fields were coming to life. Cattle grazed lazily, turning their heads as the train sped past. Birds soared in a pattern in the clear blue sky; occasionally one swooped down to fly alongside the moving train. Poland was beautiful at this time of year, but Meyer knew this wasn't a spring he would enjoy.

"Next stop is Chelm," the conductor announced.

Meyer held tightly to his bundle, checking his pocket one more time to make sure his papers were there. The train slowed, then came to a jerky stop. Taking a deep breath and slowly letting it out, Meyer rose and headed toward the exit, careful to avoid looking anyone directly in the face, per Gorski's instructions. Pulling his hat down lower on his forehead, he stepped out onto the platform, hoping no one could hear his heart pounding against his chest. Now what? The first thing to do was find a place to stay. He walked through the station and out into the city.

Chelm! So many times he'd come here with his father on business. There was so much to see and do—the excitement of being in the big city, walking down the streets, looking in store windows, and watching all the people. But Avrum wasn't with him this time, and Meyer hadn't come on business.

Knowing he couldn't avoid talking to people forever, he strode up to two men standing on the corner.

"Excuse me, could you tell me where there might be an inexpensive place to stay not far from here?"

The two men looked at Meyer, then at each other. One of them recommended a hotel, but the other man didn't agree. Then the second man mentioned a place. Meyer saw the first man give a half-smile.

"Is it a good place?" Meyer asked.

"Oh, yes indeed, it's a very nice place," the man responded.

"If I were from out of town, I would stay there," the first man added.

"And it isn't expensive? I don't have much money."

"For what you get, it is very cheap."

Meyer got the address and directions, thanked the two men, and left. He looked around as he walked, to remember how to get back to the train station. There were German soldiers standing here and there, some talking to each other, others conversing with Poles.

Looking up the street, he saw two SS men walking toward him. Meyer's instincts didn't fail him. He immediately started to move off the sidewalk into the street, to let them pass, as he reached to tip his hat. Meyer stopped dead in his tracks! He wasn't wearing a yellow Star of David. He wasn't Jewish. He wasn't even Meyer Korenblit. He was Antonio Tomitzki, a Pole, on his way to Lublin to visit a sick uncle. Continuing on the same course, the three men passed, with neither the SS nor Meyer taking notice of the other.

"Thank you, Gorski," Meyer whispered to himself.

Meyer found the address the men had given him without much difficulty. The neighborhood had seen better days, which was probably why it was a cheap place to stay. There were also no Germans in the area. He walked inside the three-story brick building to a small lobby. There were a few chairs, a couch, and a table to the right. In the far corner were two women whispering to each other, wearing some rather strange clothes. To the left was a counter. Meyer walked over to it. Behind it was an older man reading a paper. In back of him on the wall hung two rows of keys, each key on its own nail.

"I'd like a room, please," Meyer said, as if he had done this many times before.

The older man got up slowly, looking Meyer over very well. "Aren't you rather young?" the man asked.

Meyer was taken aback by the man's question.

"I just want a room to stay in for the night," Meyer insisted.

"That's all anyone comes in here for," the man responded with a leer.

Meyer was still puzzled. He looked around the room again and spotted the two women. He stared at them for a moment, noticing how they were dressed. Then it hit him.

"Oh, no, sir! I . . . I just wanted a room," he stammered. "To sleep in, nothing more. I'm from out of town. I didn't know where to go, so I asked these two men, and they recommended you highly. They said your place was very cheap for what you get. That's why I came."

"Uh-huh," the man said, staring at Meyer.

"No, I didn't mean it like that. Maybe I better leave."

"No, no, it's all right. But next time you better make sure what kind of place you're going to."

Meyer paid the necessary amount for one night as the man handed him a key. As he lay in bed, he couldn't help but think of what Manya would say if she knew he was sleeping in this kind of place. Manya—what about his mother?

That first day in Chelm seemed like a month ago, but only two weeks had passed. It was a tormented and lonely time. For fourteen days, everywhere he went, every step he took, he was sure he was being watched. Yet, each day as the deception worked, his confidence grew. Meyer stayed in Chelm for three days, inquiring for work at a few of the places Avrum had done business. None of these people knew the Korenblits were Jewish, so it was relatively safe for Meyer to go to them. They knew the flour mill was in Mislavitch and assumed that to be the Korenblits' hometown, which could only help to verify Meyer's story. Chelm was very close to Hrubieszow, and it was a familiar town. Meyer would have liked to find a job there, some way of passing the time constructively while he was a fugitive. From Chelm he could visit Hrubieszow and Manya frequently, perhaps even find a way for his parents to join him. No. It would never work. The only plan he could make was to ride the train. If he settled in a particular area, he would have to go through dangerous channels to get work and a ration card for food. He couldn't draw attention to himself that way, didn't really want to be tied down without Manya. He had to keep moving. He left for Lublin, and after four days went on to Radom. Then Ostrowiec and finally Zamosc. He decided to get off the train at a small village a few miles outside his hometown, and make his way to Mislavitch to check on his family and assure Achler that all had gone well. Isaac informed him the Korenblits were safe but getting somewhat anxious. Meyer was concerned when he heard this and urged the older man to tell his father not to move, that it was too dangerous. Achler said he'd do his best to convince Avrum to stay where he was. Mrs. Achler served Meyer a delicious hot meal, the first decent food he'd had in two weeks.

Then he headed for Hrubieszow. Soon he would be at Salki's, among friends. He would hold Manya in his arms. Oh, how he longed for her warmth, to feel her touch, to receive her love. He needed to be with her, to know somebody still cared that he was alive.

John Salki welcomed Meyer as if he were his own lost son. He fired rapid questions at Meyer, who matched them with his own about Manya and Chaim. Janek left the house, returning shortly with Gorski, and the three stayed up most of the night talking.

Meyer was shocked to learn what time it was when he awoke the next day. He knew he was tired, but he hadn't intended to sleep the clock around. Mrs. Salki awakened him by offering a hearty stew and telling him that Janek had been to the ghetto to inform Manya that he was back. She would be coming tonight—little more than two hours from now.

Meyer didn't wait in the attic for Manya's arrival. He was downstairs as Manya walked through the door. He grabbed her and squeezed until he could squeeze no longer. They kissed and kissed.

"Oh, Meyer! Meyer! Is it really you?"

"Yes, Manya, I'm here. I missed you so much."

"I was so worried. All I could think about was you—if you were alive, when you'd be back."

"It's all right now, Manya. There's nothing to be worried about. We're together again and that's all that is important."

He hugged her again to be sure she was real. They cried and laughed, never once letting the other go. Manya filled Meyer in on the lost days, and he shared his experiences. He told her of being scared and frightened, how much he missed and loved her. They laughed together when he told her about the night in the whorehouse, and they spoke of Chaim.

They touched and loved for the three nights Meyer was there, but all too quickly it was over. Tonight he would leave again.

Salki walked into the room carrying a bundle. "Here is some food, Meyer. I'm afraid it isn't the same as you've been eating here for the last three days, but it'll keep you going," he said, smiling.

"It'll be fine, John," Meyer responded, tucking the package into his knapsack.

"Here, take this. It should be enough for the next few weeks."

"I can't keep taking your money. You need it," Meyer responded, rejecting the crumpled bills.

"It isn't my money, Meyer. It's yours."

"What do you mean, my money?" he asked.

Salki looked at Manya, then back to Meyer.

"Manya has continued your operation, Meyer, and she's doing quite well," he answered with a huge smile on his face. "You should be very proud of her and Chaim."

"It's you and Janek we should thank," she shot back. "Janek is the one who comes into the ghetto to retrieve the goods, and you're the one who sells them."

"Manya, you must stop. It is far too dangerous. And, John, you're doing enough by letting me stay here," Meyer protested.

"Meyer, you have only one thing to worry about—staying alive," he said in a commanding voice. "We'll be fine. I'll take care of Manya and Chaim. If I think it's becoming excessively dangerous, I'll make them stop."

The risks are already too high, Meyer thought, but it was useless to argue with his friend. "Manya—"

She didn't let him finish the sentence. "I'll be all right, Meyer. And Chaim wants to do all he can to help. He loves you like a brother."

Meyer knew they were determined. There was nothing he could say to change their minds. "Someday, John, someday . . ."

"I know, Meyer," he said, smiling as he took Meyer's outstretched hand.

Manya and Meyer moved to the back door. They stepped outside into the cool night air, embracing and kissing. Slowly Meyer pulled away. Manya held on to his hand, then his fingertips, and then he was gone.

34

"I had a crush on him a long time ago," Tovah admitted to Manya late one night after Meyer's departure. "But he loves you, Manya. I see him watching you."

"He used to watch *you*," Manya retorted, "and it made me so mad I wouldn't speak to him. Then he would ignore me and flirt with you even more. I felt so sorry for myself and moped around the house until my mother was ready to shake me! It was so silly." She giggled.

"Oh, I don't know, Manya. I was ready to snatch him away from you, but I really think he paid attention to me only to make you jealous. You better watch out," she joked, creeping up Manya's arm with playful fingers. "If you don't treat him right, I might capture him yet!"

"Well," said Manya pridefully, "I could have another young man if I wanted. . . ."

"What?" Tovah cried. "Who? What are you talking about?"

"Oh, nothing," Manya answered coyly.

"Manya Nagelsztajn, you tell me right now!" Tovah demanded.

"Oh, maybe Sam—he's pretty good-looking."

"Sam! Do you like Sam?"

"It's not me—it's Sam. I think he hopes I'll forget about Meyer now that he's gone. He does little things—touches my hand, brushes against me, you know what I mean. He talks about taking me away."

"Would you go?" Tovah's question cut short the girlish exchange.

Manya's laughing face grew serious and the corners of her mouth quivered as she spoke. "Oh, Tovah, I miss Meyer so much! I can never stop thinking about him. You're the only one I can talk to. What would I do without you?"

"And what would Meyer do without you?" said Tovah, acknowledging Manya's compliment with a hug. "Every day, you take risks for him. You take things from the houses you work in—no, don't deny it, I've seen you. Then you and Chaim sneak out at night—God knows where you go. Someday I'll tell Meyer how much he should appreciate what you've done for him."

"I love him, Tovah, I have to do what I can to help him—he'd do the same for me. He *has* done the same for me and my family."

"I just want you to be careful, Manya. You have Chaim to think about, too. You know, it's almost a miracle that Meyer has been riding the trains for nearly a month now, and so far he hasn't had any trouble. That's something to be grateful for."

"I know, I know, but he's so homesick—so lonely. The first time he came back . . ." Manya finished the sentence with a helpless gesture.

The room fell silent. Tovah and Manya were becoming very close. With her old feelings of jealousy dispelled, Manya was able to revive the friendship she had enjoyed with Tovah as a child. They confided in each other, laughed and cried together. During the day, Tovah worked in the office at the Jewish Center, performing various clerical duties.

Sam and Leon always perked up when she appeared. Chaim, too, seemed to come out of himself when Tovah was in the house, although his deepening depression continued to worry Manya. She shared her concern with Tovah, who made extra efforts to draw Chaim out of his shell. Sam and Leon tried also, but their attempts, though well-intentioned, were clumsy, and Manya could see that Sam especially was having a difficult time coping with his own fears.

In four weeks Meyer had come back to Hrubieszow once since his departure—about two weeks ago now. Manya knew that if all went well, he was due to return in a few days.

She hadn't thought very much about the rest of her family recently, devoting all of her energy instead to the needs of Chaim and Meyer. Helping them somehow acted as a source of self-renewal. When she had doubts, she whispered them in Tovah's sympathetic ear late at night, long after the others had fallen into bed, and other times Tovah reached to Manya for reassurance. The two reinforced the positive in each other. Together they quashed the darkest of thoughts by admitting them, then casting them away.

As the weeks passed, Sam's attitude became more and more distressing to Manya. Not only did he pressure her about being his girlfriend, but hour after hour he would sit in the room with them, ears deaf to their attempts at conversation, vacant eyes signaling a mind elsewhere engaged. When he did speak, it was always about escape. He was obsessed with the necessity for it. They tried to give consideration to his latest plan, but he seemed to realize that their intentions were not serious. They tried to distract him by offering a splash of wine, or hurrying to reheat his untouched dinner, and succeeded only in making him more frustrated with them for not seeing that he was right. Often he would relent after a time, assuring them that he didn't mean to upset them. But with increasing frequency he shattered the hopeful image that Manya and Tovah tried so hard to project upon the little house. Manya wished she knew how to help Sam, wished more that he could find a way to help himself.

The morning dawned clear and the sun was beaming its promise of warmer temperatures.

"The air feels good," Manya commented to Chaim as they walked along to the count.

"Mmm," he answered, inhaling a lungful through his nose.

"Do you have your lunch?" she asked maternally, then smiled as he patted a bulge in the pocket of his jacket.

They turned a familiar corner. The routine morning lineup didn't look at all like it had the day before. The faces of the Jewish workers showed panic and confusion. Too many commands were being shouted by twice as many gun-wielding soldiers. And there was something else that clawed at the pit of Manya's stomach: trucks. She looked around again. Guns . . . soldiers . . . fear . . . trucks: deportation. She put her arm around Chaim and the two of them joined a partially formed line, as more of the Jewish workers lined up in front of her, still more in front of them.

There were probably 270 people standing within the cordon of military personnel. Manya heard soft crying, saw previously proud shoulders heave with soundless sobs, was startled by a tormented wail from a female voice. She watched 270 heads turn—ever so slightly—to monitor Officer Damone's taunting appraisal of his slave laborers. Manya saw the sun reflect off the brass of Damone's rank insignia as he paced the columns, then caught her breath when he stopped at the head of her row. She saw him raise an arm and flick his wrist as if to create a line of separation, while his aide Wagner leaned forward to listen. Then Wagner clicked his heels, about-faced, and sharply repeated the command to his inferiors, who surged forward to carry it out.

Which group would go? Which would stay? About fifty people were herded away and prodded up the tonguelike ramps that protruded from the gaping rear entrances of the trucks. She and Chaim stood absolutely still, holding hands in what was now the front line of the group. The 220 Jews left standing in the street had succeeded in stifling their emotions. The only movement came from the special-detail soldiers as they assumed their guard positions on the truck. The last sound of the deportation came as the trucks groaned into gear.

The rest of the day was normal.

35

Clickety-clack, clickety-clack, clickety-clack. Like a metronome, the swaying motion and monotonous sound of the train lulled Meyer to sleep, though only briefly, for it was not far between stops. The squealing of the train's slowed approach to the next depot brought his bobbing head to attention, and he had to struggle to remember where he was, where he had been, and the destination he had chosen this time. Then it would start all over again. Clickety-clack, clickety-clack. North and south, east and west, were scrambled in his mind, but he had to keep it straight. What if he were questioned, gave his practiced sick-uncle-in-Lublin response, and then discovered he was not going north, but west, to Krakow? The thought made him shiver. He settled into a memory game that would keep him alert and oriented. He stared out the window to note landmarks—a burned-out barn here, a high water tower there—then repeated the itinerary of towns and villages connected by the ribbon of track he rode.

Time passed at its own rate, with no help or hindrance from Meyer. Oh, on any given day he might watch the sun set with more than a feeling of admiration for its beauty, but generally he was able to travel as casually as the others who shared his coach. Rarely did he initiate a conversation, knowing he was better off to keep his mouth shut. But at times it was almost impossible to remain silent, like when he overheard conversations on the train.

"It is because of them that there's a war," an old man was telling his grandson. The small boy looked respectfully at his grandfather and waited anxiously to hear more.

"You weren't born yet when Marshal Pilsudski was alive. He was too easy with them. They got away with murder while he was in power. What the Germans are doing should have been done years before. This will teach them a lesson once and for all. The Jews, they're like ticks, sucking up everything around them, caring only for themselves. But you won't have to worry, the Germans are finally taking care of them. They're doing us a favor. Once they've completed their work, our problems will be over," the man finished, smiling.

The young boy nodded his head in approval of what his grandfather had told him. Meyer wanted to jump up and beat the man, to scream at the top of his lungs so everyone could hear, "Are you sick or mad? Do you know what they're doing to us? What have I ever done to you? Do you know my father? Or my little sister, who is younger than your grandson? What did she do to you or anyone?" But he held his tongue, or, rather, he bit it.

Occasionally he would hear someone speak up for the Jews. "It's wrong what they're doing to those poor people," a voice might say. While other times it was more like a whisper: "I don't like them, but they are human beings."

Meyer wanted desperately to believe that there were many more Salkis, Gorskis, Achlers, Tomitzkis, and Wisniewskis sitting on the train with him, behind the ticket counters, in all those stores he saw in Lublin and Lodz, and on the countless farms he passed between Zamosc and Krakow, Krakow to Radom, and Radom back to Zamosc. There had to be more, but where were they?

Meyer had been on the run for more than a month. He was tired. His head throbbed with tension and his body ached with loneliness. He had gotten so sick once that he had to stay in Radom one day longer than planned because he kept throwing up. He wasn't sure if it was because of something he'd eaten or because he was scared.

No more, though; he was finished with this kind of running. He was going to ask Salki to help him go to the underground. And if Salki wouldn't help, he would ask Gorski. Manya would just have to understand, they all must. He just couldn't keep going on like this.

Manya could tell something was the matter the minute she saw Meyer. While there was the happiness of being together and hugs and kisses, Meyer was far too quiet. "What's bothering you?" she finally asked.

"I made a decision, Manya, and you aren't going to be pleased," he answered in a half-commanding, half-apologetic voice.

No, she didn't want to hear what it was. He was back; they were together, holding and touching each other. Don't tell me anything bad, she wanted to beg, just be with me and love me. She looked up at him.

"I can't go on like this, Manya. I just can't. I'm going to ask John to help me get to the underground."

Pain . . . terror . . . shock—they bombarded her from every direction, ricocheting off the walls. "Can't go on . . ." they echoed. "Going to underground! . . ."

"No, Meyer, no!" she wailed. "It'll be all right. I'll stay here with you. Salki will let us stay."

"I have to, Manya, don't you see?"

"No, I don't see," she screamed. "You'll be killed. That's what I see. What about your family?"

He didn't know what to say or do. Pulling her close, he held her. She had to understand, but he couldn't seem to find the words to describe what he'd been going through. "Shh, Manya. Let's talk about it. Maybe I can explain why I must do this," he said, knowing how much he was hurting her.

The commotion brought Salki to the living room to see what was going on. "Meyer! Manya! What's the matter with you two?" he demanded.

"He wants to go to the underground," Manya said angrily, pointing an accusing finger in Meyer's face. "He's tired of running," she added a little more sympathetically.

"It's not just being tired of running. It's more than that. I'm disgusted with everything I have to do. Moving to a different place each night so people won't be suspicious."

"And you think it's so different in the underground, that you have the luxury of staying in one place, moving only when it's convenient for you?"

"I'm sick of listening to people talk about Jews, about me, as though we were some sort of subhumans."

"Oh, I see," the commissioner said, turning to Manya. "I guess our friendly Gestapo and SS are now treating you with respect in the ghetto, addressing you as 'Miss' Nagelsztajn. Right, Manya?"

Salki's voice dripped with sarcasm and Meyer could hardly have missed his point. He knew what Manya, Chaim, and the rest of the Jews in the ghetto went through. They heard the same words day in and day out as he did. Only they couldn't turn their backs and walk away as he was usually able to do.

"I'm scared, Salki—scared of being caught. And worrying if I'm caught what it could mean for you and your family. I'm scared for the people in Mislavitch who are helping my family, and scared for Manya and Chaim."

"I'm scared, too, Meyer. Every time I pick up something in a house and hide it down my dress, I'm terrified. But I know it will help you, so I do it," Manya said gently, taking Meyer's hand lightly in hers.

"Meyer, you're barely seventeen years old. Of course you're scared, and you damn well better be. I know what you're doing is difficult, but you've got to keep trying. Push a little harder. I realize it's easy for me to say—the bastards aren't looking for me—not yet anyway," Salki added with a rueful grin.

"John, you know how much I . . . we appreciate—" Meyer began.

"I'm not asking for your thanks," Salki interrupted with a sweep of his hand. "And I don't mean to make too much of what we're doing. I know very well we can never do enough. I only want you to understand that everything is more complicated—involves more people—than it might appear. Going to the underground is out of the question—it's just not a good time. Please trust me. You're still safe with the plan we're using. Think about it, Meyer. We can talk more about this in the morning, when you've had some rest."

"John, can I stay with Meyer tonight?" asked Manya, trying to change the subject.

"No, Manya," Meyer responded quickly, "you must go back. I won't leave. Chaim will be waiting for you."

"He'll be all right," Manya was quick to assure Meyer. "If I don't come back, he'll figure that I'm with you."

"You know it's fine with me, Manya," Salki answered. "I even think it will be safe for you to stay downstairs tonight. Just be sure to leave before anyone might see you," he cautioned as he left the room.

Manya curled up beside Meyer on the too small bed in the tiny spare room. "Hold me, Meyer, and don't let go."

"I won't ever let you go, Manya, I love you."

36

Each time she went, Chaim accompanied her as far as the passageway, helping to carry the goods Manya would take to Salki, and waiting patiently for her return. And each time, she had come back. But tonight she was already long overdue, and Chaim was starting to feel panicky—old worries joining new ones in an assumption of things gone wrong.

He decided to go back to the house. She had told him over and over it would be all right, but he had resisted. Keeping the vigil was a matter of pride. If she could take risks, so could he, and he had waited faithfully in the freezing, junk-filled alley, half-dozing, time after time until he heard her scuffling feet approach. Tonight, though, he was tired—tired of everything—and he knew she would understand if he wasn't there when she sidled through the passageway.

He didn't belong here anymore. Manya spent most of her free time helping Meyer, and although Sam and Leon tried to include him in their conversations, the effort was obvious. Nor could he predict any improvement. He was too young to be considered their equal.

His uneasiness grew as he made his way to the house, and he realized he had not sneaked through these streets alone since the first night after he had left the haystack, six months ago. Manya had always been with him. He wished he didn't have to rely on her to such an extent—resented that so much of his strength came from her. He was old enough—nearly fifteen now—to be more self-sufficient, he'd have to start acting that way. He should accept more responsibility for himself and take on more for others. But he did so enjoy his sister's motherly attention, and rather thought she liked giving it.

With a certain lack of caution he approached the steps of the house, and made more noise than necessary entering the door. He moved toward the bedroom, then stopped. He wasn't really sleepy—tired, yes, but not sleepy. He turned around. What should he do? His eye caught a bottle of vodka sitting on the table. He meandered over to the table under the pretext of lighting a candle. The match flared and he noticed the bottle was nearly full. He had never liked it much, but still . . . Manya should be home by now—what was keeping her? Maybe he should go back to the alley. He didn't want to worry her. Well, she was certainly worrying him.

In one motion he shook out the match and scooped up the bottle. There was a used glass near the candlestick. That Sam, he thought—he always leaves everything for Manya to do. If he were Manya, he would tell Sam to clean up after himself.

He popped the cork on the bottle and smelled the contents. Hmmmm. Not terrific, but not so bad. Why not? he thought, reaching for the glass. He poured an ounce or two. That seemed about right—at least that's how much Sam and Meyer allotted. He held up the glass and peered at it, shrugged, and filled it up. What did he care how much Sam and Meyer drank?

He took a sip, then downed the rest. He felt fine. Of course he felt fine—what had he expected, to faint? He was grown up now, he could drink. He could do a lot of things like a grown-up. He could deliver goods to Salki once in a while. Manya didn't have to take all the chances. He would ask her about it. He refilled the glass and walked over to the overstuffed chair. No, he would *tell* her. When you were an adult, you didn't ask.

He gulped the liquid and plopped into the chair. He hadn't meant to sit down so abruptly. Yes, he would make some of the trips to Salki's. Manya was a girl; he was a b—no, not a boy, a man. Yes, that was a good idea. If they took turns, people wouldn't notice them—less sushp . . . shusp . . . suspicious.

He felt very warm, a little clammy even. Only a few minutes ago he had been freezing. Must be the liquor; he had heard it was a good thing to have when you were cold. He tipped the bottle toward the glass again and heard it glug as it poured. Meyer would let him help if it were up to him. He would say that to Manya. Yes, that would make her think twice before she said no. He toasted the thought and drained the glass.

He seemed to be pouring too fast—the vodka was splashing all over him. He looked closer. The neck of the bottle had slipped over the edge. His arms felt very heavy; they didn't seem to be receiving the message from his brain. He had to concentrate to reaim the flow. He bent his head to meet the glass and save himself the exertion of raising it to his lips. As he gulped it down, one eye caught the level of the liquor in the bottle. It was nearly empty. He wondered if there was more in the kitchen. He would get up to see in a minute. Right now, he thought his eyes were shut.

Sam found him in the morning, and no amount of shaking and yelling penetrated Chaim's stupor or broke his hold on the empty bottle he clutched protectively in the crook of his left arm. Had Chaim been roused, he would have heard a very angry Sam threaten to tell Manya of the transgression. He would have heard a very disgusted Sam exclaim at the smell of Chaim's liquor-soaked clothes. He would have seen a very amused Sam shake his head in genuine enjoyment of the typical manifestation of growing manhood. And he would have felt a very sympathetic Sam hold him while he retched, then swab him with wet cloths.

It was only after work that day that Manya came home. She had stayed the night with Meyer, knowing that was all the time they could count on, and had joined her workmates on the job. So the evening count would be one higher—what could it matter? Meyer was gone. She didn't know when she would see him again. She had almost laughed out loud when the Germans realized they had one more Jew that night than they had had that morning. The soldier had flipped through his chart clumsily and delayed the usually matter-of-fact dismissal while he struggled with the realization that he had caught a mistake. But wait, maybe it was his own error—better let it go—and with a still-uncertain look on his face, he waved their release.

Manya was so lost in her thoughts that she didn't notice Chaim's absence from the lineup. She could hardly put one foot in front of the other, she was so weary. Then she heard Sam calling to her, and looked ahead to see him beckoning.

"Wait till I tell you what your brother did," Sam began.

"Chaim?" she repeated, glancing around. "Where is he? I don't see him."

"No, it's all right, Manya," Sam assured her quickly. "He's at home. But he was a bad boy last night, and I wouldn't want to trade places with him today! Ach!" he said, slapping his own cheek and laughing.

"What are you talking about?" Manya said, stopping dead in the street.

"He got drunk! Oh, boy, he got drunk—guzzled my whole bottle of vodka! I came out this morning and found him passed out in a chair. I shook him and shook him, and the more I did, the more he threw up! He didn't even know where he was, I tell you!"

Manya was not amused. She strode past Sam toward the house.

"Wait, Manya," he called to her back. "What's the matter? Wait for me!"

She ignored him. These men! she thought, shaking her head. You'd think they would learn to grow up another way!

37

Wagner was half a step away before Manya and her friend Esther noticed him. They scrambled to get off the wooden sidewalk and out of his way, praying he would go right by. The two stood in the gutter with their heads bowed, not only to convey a sense of servility but also in an effort to achieve anonymity. His boots thundered on a step or two, then stopped.

"Jew!" he bellowed, advancing toward them in slow, threatening strides. Manya looked up. His black-gloved hands rested haughtily on his hips. She looked back at the ground without answering.

"You . . . Jew!" he screamed again, bending closer. The two

raised their eyes. His face was contorted with rage and loathing.

"Is this your private sidewalk?" he goaded.

"No, Herr Wagner," said Manya.

"Do you belong on the same sidewalk as a German officer?"

"No, Herr Wagner," Manya answered again. "I'm very sorry, we meant no disrespect, Herr Wagner. Please excuse us, we didn't see you—"

"'Please excuse us, we didn't see you,'" he mocked, staring crazily at them. "There *is* no excuse for you!" he screamed. "You never learn! You grovel and crawl to my face, but when my back is turned . . . You think I don't know? You make me sick with your sniveling, do you hear? I'm sick to death of every last one of you!"

Frantic to calm him, Manya tried to catch his eyes with her own, but he stared right through her. She saw a gloved hand move to stroke his chin as he pondered their fate. This was going too far. Didn't he recognize her? Surely he wouldn't harm her if he did. All the other times . . . Had he forgotten?

No, *she* had forgotten: Wagner had never spoken a civil word to Manya when there were other people around. If she could just delay for time, he would come to his senses, think of a way to let them go without losing face. How could she steer him to that course?

"Please, sir—" she began.

"Silence!" he hissed. The voice was cold and evil. He would make them suffer while he decided their punishment. There was nothing Manya could do but stand there. She grabbed Esther's hand.

The motion caught Wagner's attention. Something happened behind his face. "Oh, such good friends, I see," he scoffed. "Such good friends that you ignore your responsibility to a German! I must teach you better manners. Up!" he commanded. "Up on the sidewalk, both of you!"

Manya pleaded with her eyes.

"Move!" he yelled. The two girls jumped to comply, standing tight together in front of him.

"You want to walk on the sidewalk? So! You shall walk on the sidewalk. Perhaps we'll walk together. It seems you feel worthy of such an honor. Very well, we shall walk. But that way," he said, pointing behind them. "Turn around."

Esther hesitated too long for Wagner's patience. He shoved her with one hand, and released the flap of his holster with the other. Stumbling to get her feet under her, Manya's friend turned around very slowly.

"You stay!" he ordered Manya, then turned back to Esther. "Walk!" he shouted. "Now!"

Manya saw Esther put one quaking leg in front of the other. There was a terrific explosion, and Esther sprawled abruptly on the wooden boards a few feet from Manya. Manya froze, sprayed with blood and bone fragments. She couldn't shut her eyes against the sight of Esther's oozing skull. She would look until Wagner's next bullet took away her sight. Get it over with! she felt ready to scream. But no second shot was fired. Instead she heard his boots, then saw them next to Esther's body. As if he were touching a maggot-ridden beast, Wagner slipped a foot under Esther and rolled her off the sidewalk and into the gutter. Esther moaned.

At the sound, Manya glanced up, then stared down again.

"Bury her!" Wagner snapped, his face drained of color.

"But she's not—"

"I said bury her!"

"I . . . A shovel—I'll get—"

"No shovel—use your hands. Then clean up this mess. I want no trace of it the next time I walk here." He brandished his pistol.

Manya bent over and gingerly touched Esther's misshapen head. "Herr Wagner," she said in a hoarse whisper, "couldn't I take her to the cemetery—"

"No! This is a lesson for you swine! You'll bury the bitch here . . . unless"—he leaned over to thrust the gun in Manya's face—"unless you want to die here too!"

Wagner watched the resignation pass over her face as she began digging; then he strutted into the office of the Jewish Center to summon extra hands to the scene.

A few minutes later, Esther stopped breathing.

38

The trucks were coming again. This time Manya wasn't going to line up with the others. She'd take Chaim and they'd hide until the deportation was over. She knew exactly what to do and how.

Why had Chaim left the house early this morning? She knew something had been bothering him the last week. He had become depressed again, thinking more and more about the family and their own situation. How was she ever going to find him among all these people in the street? She had only a few minutes before the Germans would be organized, and she needed every second to make her plan work. But each step she took toward the lineup area was a step in the wrong direction! Why, oh why, hadn't she told Chaim to wait for her?

Then she saw him just ahead. Thank God! She approached him from the rear and placed a hand on each of his bony shoulders. He stiffened as she steered him to the side of a building.

"We're going to run—to hide!" she whispered in his ear. "I know a perfect place. Then we'll go to Salki's. We can't take a chance. They're going to deport some more today, Chaim. Come on!" she urged, grabbing his hand. "Follow me!"

But he pulled back. She turned around and looked into his downturned face.

"No," he said, shaking his head in a double negative.

"No?" she echoed. "What do you mean, 'no'? Chaim, we have to hide—we have to run!" She almost had to scream to be heard over the growing noise in the street.

"No," he repeated. "I'm tired of running. I don't want to run anymore."

Manya glanced behind him and saw the Germans making final preparations.

"Chaim, we have to go. Don't do this, *please!*" she begged.

"No, Manya," he answered, "I'm not running." He couldn't meet her eyes. His determination and resignation were clear.

Manya took a few steps away from him and looked toward the Zamosc bridge. There were more Nazis coming across it. There was so little time. Gunshots rang out. The soldiers were firing warning shots in the air.

"Chaim!" she called again, but he didn't turn around. If I go, she thought, maybe he'll follow me. It was all she could think of. She began to run, glancing over her shoulder to see if Chaim was behind her. He wasn't. But she was committed; she had to keep going. She ducked down a side street, then another, and came back out onto the same street a block away, right by the Zamosc bridge. No guards. She dropped into the high grass that flanked the river, working her way backward, feetfirst, under the low bridge. She couldn't turn her eyes away from the action a block away. The undulating crowd, people choosing this line . . . no, maybe this one, drawing passive veils over their faces as the lines filled. Chaim was in the fourth row.

Manya fixed burning eyes on his face, seeking to transmit courage and support—yes, even luck. If only he would look up. It's all right, she kept telling herself, it's all right. They won't choose him. They'll take someone else. There was a rumbling overhead that made her jump; then the trucks lurched into view and stopped with whining brakes. She sought Chaim's face again, glanced up at his curly hair. He gazed straight ahead. With the trucks in the way, she couldn't see Damone or Wagner, wouldn't be able to catch the first sign of who would be chosen. What was happening?

Save him, she prayed. Oh, God, save him. He's all I have left. Look at his face, God, see how pale he is. He's only fourteen! She heard Wagner's voice but couldn't make out the words. Then a chunk of the straight lines broke off, melding together so fast she couldn't be sure how many rows it represented.

Her frantic eyes skipped over the taller figures. She was looking for a shorter person, hazel eyes, brown hair, thin . . . There! No, it was someone else. She looked for a brown jacket, sleeves too long, and knickers belted in folds around a slender waist—maybe *him!* Then, as the boy turned, wrong again. She was looking for a sweet face grown solemn, with cheeks as yet untouched by a razor's blade, and front teeth that dipped up in the middle. She was looking for her brother, Chaim Nagelsztajn.

The fifty evacuees mounted the truck ramps one by one. Manya's eyes darted from one ramp to the other. Then she saw him. They were taking him. There was a howl from another era—a demonlike baying. Had she heard it or only felt it? Chaim paused only a second before he disappeared into the belly of the truck. But he didn't look around; perhaps he was only waiting for the path to clear in front of him.

As he stepped from her view, Manya collapsed into the grass. She lay there and heard truck doors slamming and ramps scraping their complaint against metal truck beds as they were shoved from the ground to the inside and came to a noisy rest at the feet of the riders. She heard the engines accelerate, but the trucks didn't cross over her head. They rattled their way in the opposite direction.

An order for dismissal echoed through the street; then it grew quiet. She wasn't sure how long she stayed under the bridge. Eventually, however, she made her way to Salki's. He wasn't home when she arrived, but his wife ushered Manya inside and to safety in the attic.

Later that evening, John Salki tapped on the planks of the hidden enclosure in his attic and called to her. Without meaning to, she sobbed her despair to him, sparing him no detail. He tried to console her, first offering words, then strong arms, and finally promises of Meyer's imminent return. He told her she could stay here, that he would send Janek to find out when it was safe for her to return to the ghetto.

But she seemed not to hear him, and through it all could only wail of her brother, "His face . . . oh, his face . . ."

39

Avrum Korenblit lay in a ward of paint-chipped hospital beds in the town of Sokul. His head was swathed in bandages spotted crimson from the wound they covered. Hat in hand, Meyer approached the bed and looked at his father's face.

Despite his unconscious state, the older man's cheeks and chin were peppered with several days' beard, and the intensity of the bruises on one side of his forehead gave evidence that they were at their angriest. Soon, Meyer hoped, they would begin to lighten and fade.

Meyer had to look away when he saw his father's half-closed eyelids flicker open to reveal eyes rolled inward. Then Avrum moaned and muttered words garbled by the injury to his brain.

He had been hit with a metal bar—that's what the men in Sokul had told Meyer—and left to bleed in the street. The men waited for the Nazis to march away and then scrambled to carry Avrum to the ghetto hospital. From what they told Meyer, Avrum had been alone. No, they agreed, there was no woman with him, no children. He was definitely alone. They told Meyer the injury had occurred three days ago. Three days ago Meyer had been in Zamosc, only thirty miles away.

Avrum groaned again, and Meyer leaned close to his father's ear. "Papa?" he whispered. Struggling between his desire to rouse his father and the little-boy instinct not to disturb a sleeping parent, Meyer called to Avrum again. "Papa? It's me, Meyer, Papa. Can you hear me?"

The forty-three-year-old man gave no response.

Meyer continued. "Papa, can you tell me where Mama is? Is she coming here?"

Nothing.

Meyer sat with him for three more days and watched the doctor listen to Avrum's heart and peer under his eyelids. When Meyer asked if his father would get better, the physician turned kind eyes on the son, explaining that the injury was grave and there was nothing further he could do to reverse Avrum's condition. He told Meyer to keep trying to reach his father, to talk to him, prod him, mention other members of the family. He said that the patient might respond if Meyer called him by name, but that he must shout it: "Avrum!" Yes, the doctor admitted, it's hard for a son to yell at his sick father—harder still to make noise in a hospital ward. But one couldn't rely on whispering to break through the dreamy barrier.

Meyer followed the doctor's recommendations faithfully, adding a few remedies of his own. He moistened his father's dry lips with water, swabbed his face and chest, held his hand, smoothed the stubble away with a razor. And Meyer kept a constant dialogue going, hoping something might get through. "You can't leave now, Papa. Mama and the girls need you. I need you. Don't die, Papa, please don't die. Why did you ever leave Mislavitch? You were safe there, protected." Meyer's tone changed from pleading to anger. But he was directing it at the wrong person, he realized. Maybe he was to blame for not going to Avrum the first time Achler told him the Korenblits were nervous about staying in Mislavitch. Or perhaps Isaac had become frightened and hadn't really talked Avrum out of leaving.

No! Stop! It was no one's fault. It was the son-of-a-bitching Poles who were letting this happen, and the Nazi bastards who championed the hideous cause. That's whose fault it was; they were to blame. Meyer stopped his tirade when he realized he was talking out loud.

Avrum remained locked in the coma, moving only in spasms, speaking nothing but twisted words. Hour after hour Meyer sat there, shying away only when the dressing was changed on the wound because he couldn't look, or finding himself pushed aside by the nurses as they hurried to minister to the convulsions when they intensified. More than once Meyer buried his head in the sheets of his father's bed and cried. Sometimes he fell asleep, cradling his father's hand to his cheek.

At night Meyer stumbled to the home of one of the men who had helped Avrum, where he tossed and turned until it was time to take up his vigil again. The fourth morning, a nurse blocked his way into the ward. "I'm sorry—" she began, cut short by Meyer's hand moving her aside. He stared down the row of beds. His father's was empty. He looked back at the nurse. The answer was in her eyes before he asked the question.

"Very early this morning," she said. "It was very peaceful—no convulsions, nothing like that. We wanted you to know," she said, putting a hand on his shoulder. He bowed his head and nodded, covering her hand with his own in thanks for her concern. His voice was hoarse when he asked where they had taken his father.

"Downstairs," she said softly, turning him away from the ward and pointing down the hall.

"Can I leave him for an hour—would that be all right? Half an hour, if that's too long."

"Whenever you're ready," she said. "I'm sure you want to make some arrangements."

"Arrangements . . ." he repeated. "Yes, I . . . I'll need to get a—"

"Whenever you're ready," she interrupted. "We're all so sorry. You hadn't seen him for a long time, had you?" she asked.

"No," Meyer answered. "Not for quite a while." He tried to smile as he took his leave, and heard his feet fall heavily on the steps to the first floor. He blinked away the glare of sunlight as he went through the hospital door. He still didn't know where his mother was. If only his father had been able to explain.

Meyer talked with a number of people about the burial. He was relieved to find out that he could arrange a service and that it was

still legal for his father to be buried in the Jewish cemetery. If this
had to happen, Meyer reasoned, better here than in Hrubieszow.
Here at least he could give his father a proper funeral.

Meyer bought a coffin from a Jewish cabinetmaker who had
turned his craft to more practical pursuits. Since Meyer paid in
cash instead of trading, the man gave him a good price and offered to accompany Meyer to the hospital.

Setting the box down at the hospital entrance, Meyer inquired
at the front desk, then rejoined his helper, and the two carried
the coffin to the morgue, where they claimed the body of the man
who had believed God would save him.

Later that afternoon, Meyer stood silently at the gravesite he
had prepared with his own hands. Ten men circled the coffin,
including Meyer. Nine men chorused the soft chant. Meyer would
not lend his approval to God by joining in. They were fools, the
rest of them. Couldn't they see that God had turned His back on
them? "You have to trust in Him, have faith," a long-ago memory
of Avrum's voice insisted. Meyer cried through the next two reci-
tations. When the last prayer of the service began, Meyer's lips
mouthed the familiar words until his cracking voice found firmer
chords. He knew it would have made his father happy.

It was as if the train's whistle echoed the mourning of the man
it carried home. Meyer sat tensely in his seat, leaning forward to
speed the locomotive on its way.

"Hrubieszow," came the conductor's call at last.

He was home. He stood with feet spread wide and knees un-
locked to be ready for the lurch of the train's altered momentum,
and took wobbly steps toward the exit. The train was still easing
into the station when Meyer swung off. He picked his way across
an unlit siding and up an embankment, then jogged quickly to a
nearby field. He crashed into chuckholes and fell headlong, in
careless need to reach his destination. Manya. Each step a yard
closer, a second less to wait. The image of her face hung in the air
before him. He ran faster in its direction.

John Salki's family was just finishing dinner when Meyer
knocked and entered in one motion.

"Meyer!" Salki exclaimed, standing up. "You look terrible.
Here—sit down. Was it a hard trip?"

Meyer could feel himself caving in, knew he had to hold on a little longer. He coughed away the lump in his throat. Accepting the chair, he leaned forward, propping his forearms on his knees and staring at the floor. With breaths that came and went more like sighs, he tried to compose himself.

As if on cue, Mrs. Salki jumped to her feet, stacking dishes and chattering a greeting and a prescription of food in the awkward silence of the room. From the kitchen she called reminders of chores to her children. Checking his pocket watch, Salki rescued Janek from his mother's bidding. Meyer saw the boy's nods punctuate his father's instructions before Salki relinquished the messenger to his task and rejoined Meyer at the table.

"I've just sent Janek to get Manya," the commissioner explained.

Meyer nodded gratefully. He still couldn't risk trying his voice.

Salki looked uncomfortable. Nicotine-stained fingers dug into his shirt pocket and drew out a pouch and a flat, banded sheaf of papers. Licking his thumb to coax a single sheet from the pack, Salki pried open the gathered end of the pouch. He shook out a measure onto the paper, then caught the strings of the bag in his mouth and pulled. He took too much time spreading, rolling, and sealing the cigarette. A match brought it to life.

"Can you tell me about it?" the commissioner asked, trying to convey with his tone that he was prepared to hear anything Meyer might say.

Meyer told his friend what had happened: the injury, the coma, the death, the funeral. When he had finished, Meyer saw the impact of his words in John Salki's glistening, dark-circled eyes and in the long ash on his untended cigarette. Then the man covered his face with his hands, finally parting them to massage his temples.

"You found no clue about your mother?" Salki asked without looking at Meyer.

"Nothing," Meyer answered in a low voice. "Nothing," he repeated. "I'll have to go to Mislavitch. She's probably waiting for my father to send for her. I don't know," he said wearily, "I don't know."

He followed Salki's circling fingers around and around, then noticed the man's taut lips and clenched jaw. A battle was being fought behind Salki's eyes. The man's arms fell limply to his lap as he made a decision. He took a deep breath and used it to force out the words. "Meyer," he began apologetically, "I have something I must tell you, my friend. I'm afraid it's not good." He paused to summon his courage.

Meyer pulled upright and braced himself.

"I had a report," Salki continued. "It's not confirmed—Gorski is still checking—but it's something you have to know." The commissioner heaved himself from his chair and paced the room slowly. He turned to face Meyer.

"Meyer, there was a shooting. The report came to Gorski that a woman traveling by train was accused of being Jewish. She was removed from the train, questioned, and shot."

Meyer's guarded expression changed to denial.

"There were children with her, Meyer—three girls."

"Shot?" Meyer whispered.

"All of them," Salki replied.

Meyer let heavy lids fall over his eyes. He bent double and buried his head in his arms, rocking his ache away as his mother had done when he was a boy. Abruptly he sprang to his feet. "It was my mother and sisters, wasn't it?" he shrieked.

"Maybe not!" Salki shot back with as much fervor. "I told you it is unconfirmed, and we have no names—it could have been anyone!"

"I have to get to Mislavitch!" said Meyer, moving to the door.

"No, wait, Meyer! Take time to think."

"I have to know, John," Meyer cried.

"But Manya will be here any minute. How will she feel to find you gone? Meyer, she's desperate to see you, has come here nearly every night praying you'll be here! For God's sake, wait!"

Holding the door wide, Meyer hesitated a moment, then another. If he found his mother, she'd have to be told about Avrum. He had to do it. If his mother was dead, he wanted to know now. He couldn't wait for Manya.

"Explain," he pleaded. "My father . . . Mislavitch . . . sorry . . . few days." He crossed the threshold, then turned back. He had thought of something else. "Love," he added, and was gone.

40

There was no moon to light Meyer's way—just darkness. No stars to guide him—just blackness. No sounds to warn him of impending danger—just stillness. The night was lifeless, empty of any feelings, a mirror image of the chain of events that had rocked Meyer's life during the past twenty-four hours.

Salki's words couldn't be true. He had misunderstood Gorski. Yes, that was it. Or Gorski was mistaken, had heard it secondhand. His mother wouldn't have left, not until Avrum sent for her. It was too dangerous. Achler would not have allowed her to go. She would have listened to him.

He ran and ran. Pushing himself to go faster, faster, and still faster. Move, feet! Quicker, legs! You're not tired. We have to get to Mama before she leaves. Yes, before she leaves. They would be there when he arrived. He would comfort his mother and sisters. He would stay with them, watch out for them, take care of them. You see why we must hurry? Don't hinder me, help me, *please*. Don't stop, keep going. His lungs were about to burst. No, not yet. It isn't far. Pain in his stomach. Not now. It'll be all right. We'll be there soon.

This was all a dream. It wasn't happening. A nightmare. He stumbled, tried to balance himself, but he was falling. Down, down, down. He crashed on the hard ground. Get up! It hurts! No, it doesn't!

There was the house. No lights. He didn't care, he'd wake them up.

Thud! Thud! Thud! Meyer's fist beat his demand on the wooden door.

"Isaac! Isaac! It's me, Meyer. Get up!"

Thud! Thud! Thud!

"Get up, dammit!"

Finally a sleepy, bewildered Achler unlatched the barrier.

"You've got to take me to my mother. Right now," Meyer implored.

"But, Meyer—"

"Please, Isaac, you've got to," he begged. "My father is dead!"

The older man went limp, steadying himself against the wall.

His head and shoulders heaved. He sucked in air through his nose, trying to control himself.

"Please take me to them. They may leave."

"I can't, Meyer," Isaac choked, attempting to speak. "They . . ."

"They what, Isaac, *what?* You must tell me!"

"They . . . they left a few days ago," he finally got out.

Wake up, Meyer. Your heart isn't beating. You aren't breathing. You aren't moving. You aren't hearing anything. Open your eyes. They are open. Why is there no sight? He felt his knees buckle, his hands begin to shake, his head pound.

"No!" he screamed. "They haven't left. I'll go to them."

Isaac grabbed the young boy and shook him. "I'm sorry, Meyer. It's true. They're gone."

"But why? They were safe here," Meyer cried.

"I tried to talk them out of it, believe me, but Avrum wouldn't listen. He felt he was putting us in too much danger. He was worried they'd be discovered, and he wanted to find a safer place where nobody knew him. We heard there was a large ghetto in Sokul, so he went there by himself to see if it would be better. Then he was going to come back for Malka and the girls. When he didn't show up or send a message after three days, your mother was sure something must have happened. So Malka took the girls and left for Sokul. I tried to make them stay. I even said I'd go and try to find Avrum. But . . . I'm sorry, Meyer, there was nothing more I could do or say to change her mind."

"It's . . . I . . ." He wanted to tell the man he understood, that it wasn't his fault, that there was nothing more he could have done. What had gone wrong? Just one week ago everything was fine. Now it was all falling apart. He had to look for his mother and bring her back.

"I've got to find them."

"Meyer, you don't know where they are!"

"You said they went to Sokul. When?"

"Two days ago, but—"

"I'll find them there. Yes, they'll be there. I'm sure of it."

Isaac wouldn't argue with him. What could he possibly say? "Be careful, Meyer," he warned, but he was talking to himself.

There would be no train to speed his journey until the morning hours. He wasn't going to wait, even if it meant running the whole way. He would go as far as possible on foot and hope he'd be near enough to a town to catch a ride or a train when the sun came up.

Bypassing Hrubieszow, he continued, each step becoming more strenuous. He had to rest, to lie down for a few minutes. No, he'd fall asleep and never wake up. What did it matter? Damn you, Meyer, it does matter. Salki was wrong. Malka, Toba, Minka, and little Cyvia were waiting for him in Sokul. It mattered to them, and it mattered to Manya. He wouldn't quit!

At last he caught a train to Sokul. He was careful to sneak into the ghetto when he got there, as he had done the previous time, and quickly found the man who had helped him with his father.

The cabinetmaker was surprised to see Meyer had returned.

"I don't know if you remember me," Meyer began. "You helped me with . . . you helped me bury my father."

"Yes, of course," the man replied. "What is it? Why have you returned?"

"I'm looking for my mother and sisters. Do you know if they have arrived? I'm sure they came here."

"I don't think so. Not yet anyway," the man responded, picking up Meyer's hopeful tone. "But we'll find out. Just like you, other people have sneaked into the ghetto."

"If they aren't here, may I wait a few days? I know they'll come."

"Of course you can. Come, let's see if we can't find them," the man answered, ushering Meyer out the door.

The rest of the day was spent searching, going from house to house, with no luck. For three days Meyer waited, fighting the reality of Salki's words, refusing to pass over the threshold of belief. At the end of the third day, he knew it was useless to wait any longer. They weren't coming. He returned to the cemetery. No one was there. He could talk to his father in private. He closed his eyes and brought his father's image to his mind.

"Papa, I can't find them. What should I do?"

There was no answer, only tears.

"I'm sorry, Papa, for everything I ever did that hurt you. I'll try to believe, for you. But it's very hard. You did good all your life. I'll try to do just as you taught me. I know you're being taken care of now. You are at peace with the world. Someday this will be over and I'll tell my children about you, what a wonderful man you were. I'll be strong . . . it's just that . . . Oh, Papa, I can't find

Mama and the girls and I don't know where to look! If they're with you, tell them I tried, Papa, tell them I tried!"

Looking to the sky, he whispered, "Please take care of him. He did everything you asked of him. Don't turn away from him now." He turned slowly and left.

It was a long way back to Hrubieszow and Manya.

"Gone?" Manya had exclaimed to John Salki.

The man had only nodded his affirmation.

"What do you mean, gone?" she asked. She had waited nearly two weeks to tell Meyer that Chaim had been taken. Now Manya tried to balance her loss against his. Sheer logic told her his was greater. She could still hold on to the hope of being reunited with her family. Meyer had no such hope.

For the three days he was gone, she leased Meyer's hurt and lived in it. Then finally Janek summoned Manya to the Salki house. Meyer was back.

It took a long time for them to weep the whole story, and longer still before either could draw a smooth breath. They lay on the floor, Meyer on his back with one arm bent across his face, Manya on her side, pressed against him.

"I feel like I'm dead," he sighed at last.

"I know," she answered in a hollow voice.

41

This time it was with a different eye that he observed the towns and villages along his route. Now he wasn't so intent on skimming the surface. He was looking deeper, trying to formulate a plan. Meyer leaned back in his train seat and crossed his legs, being careful not to disturb the sleeping man next to him.

What should he do? He felt fairly confident that he knew the answer, but it wouldn't hurt, he thought, to go over it all again. He considered appealing once more to Tomitzki and Achler to get a set of identification papers for Manya. Then he and she could ride the rails together. Having Manya beside him would make the traveling easier. But for how long? How many weeks before he would tire of running? And Manya? How long could she take the endless routine? No, he couldn't really entertain that idea. He'd had too many close calls already.

He shuddered to think what might have happened if Manya had been with him that time in Warsaw. There were so many Germans on the first train, he had passed it up. When the next train arrived, it too was filled with Nazis, and Meyer stayed behind. The policeman standing in the station became suspicious of Meyer's hesitation. Twice he had seen Meyer start to board, then change his mind. Meyer knew there was no choice but to take the third train that pulled in, no matter where it was headed. That in itself was part of the problem. He had been on a journey without destination, origin, or definite points in between. The direction he chose to travel on any given morning might be 90 or 180 degrees different by midday, all the result of his scrambled judgment, instincts—yes, even superstition. How could he ask Manya to share that? How could he explain why he chose one train over another, this coach over that one? And how would they ever get enough money to cover food and lodging for two?

Meyer shook his head and sighed. The conductor made a noisy entrance from an adjoining car and gave Meyer a friendly smile as he made his way down the aisle. Meyer couldn't help but think of another conductor. There had been no smile on that occasion. He was on the train from Lublin to Chelm. The conductor walked up to Meyer, took his ticket, punched it, and started to return it. As Meyer reached for the ticket, the conductor had held on. "You've traveled with me many times, haven't you?"

Meyer quickly responded, "I don't think so. I rarely ride the train."

But the conductor hadn't been convinced. Every time he walked down the aisle, he looked the young man over. It was all Meyer could do to stay seated and look calm. The next time the conductor came through the car, he stopped beside a German soldier to talk. Meyer knew he couldn't ride any farther on that train. At the next stop, while the conductor was occupied, he slipped out the opposite end of the car.

Just the thought of it made Meyer squirm even now, and he inadvertently bumped the sleeping man's leg with his knee. "Excuse me," Meyer said in his most apologetic tone. Heavy lids flickered open, then descended slowly over bleary eyes. Meyer was thankful for the man's fatigue, and rather envied him his nap. As many times as Meyer had dozed off on the train, he never awakened with anything but a sense of panic. As a matter of fact, in all these weeks, he couldn't remember having even one night of soothing rest. Well, no more, he thought. He was sick to death of the routine, trapped by its monotony, scared of the consequences. While no one had ever come after him or challenged his identity, he was unwilling to chance it anymore. Luck would last only so long, and Meyer could see his beginning to turn. Finding out about his mother and sisters pushed him to the brink. Gorski's confirmation sent him over the edge.

As chief of police in Hrubieszow under the German occupation, Gorski had a dual role which at times caused him to walk a very thin line. He was held accountable for the actions of the citizens of Hrubieszow, but also had a responsibility to protect and look out for their well-being. The Nazis were concerned only with his first duty, but would placate him as far as the second was concerned so long as they were not overly inconvenienced.

When Gorski received word about the deaths of four people from his town, he went to the Gestapo to investigate. Since he was certainly within the bounds of his responsibility, the Nazis were not suspicious and humored his inquiry. They had been led to believe that Gorski was cooperating with them one hundred percent and viewed him as a loyal and trusted ally.

With some annoyance, the Germans provided Gorski with information about the people who had been shot: one woman, they said, and three young girls. Gorski stood before them and listened as they continued, hoping he wouldn't recognize the descriptions, but he did. He wanted to be sure, so he pushed them for the names of the victims. The response had set his insides on fire, but he controlled himself as he heard the answer: "What does it matter? They were only Jews. It's of no concern to you."

Meyer winced when he thought of how difficult it must have been for Gorski to tell him about his mother and sisters. Seeing his friend's outrage and hurt and recognizing the helplessness of the situation, Meyer was convinced that he had to make some changes. No more running; no more trains. The underground— he wouldn't be talked out of it this time.

Meyer was gentle with Manya when he told her. She was so fragile and vulnerable. She had no Chaim in the ghetto to comfort her. She no longer looked for his return every two weeks. He remembered that night so well. The four of them were sitting in Salki's living room: John, Gorski, Manya, and himself. There was nothing to say after Gorski related his information about Malka and the girls. Meyer was holding Manya's hand. There was an eerie silence in the room, each person waiting for the other to speak first. The crying had long ago ceased.

Finally Meyer spoke, a bit more abruptly than he had planned. "Manya, I'm going to the underground. Nothing you or they can say will stop me." He expected her to explode and was prepared to understand when she did. But she didn't. She brought his hand to her lips and kissed it, then just stared out into the room, drained of any emotions.

"I don't want you to go, but I understand," she said finally. "You've lost your father, your mother, your sisters. You have no idea if your brothers are alive. You want to fight back, to lash out. Do you think I don't understand? Don't you think I feel the same way? I was fighting back by helping you. They've taken Chaim, I don't know where the rest of my family is. I only have you. If you leave, what have I got to fight for? You say you've made up your mind. So have I: where you go, I go. You must understand *that*."

And so it had been decided that Salki and Gorski would make contact with the underground. But it would take time, they warned—as long as two weeks—especially because of recent events. Only three days ago, six partisans were caught and executed right outside of town. Salki and Gorski themselves no longer knew whom they could trust. There was no alternative but for Meyer to get back on the train. Hopefully, by the time he returned they'd have everything set up. After establishing himself with the partisans, Meyer would send for Manya. Gorski would see what he could do about getting Manya forged papers. They still didn't want anyone to know the couple was Jewish.

Meyer felt relieved, but not triumphant. He had stuck with the decision, and in the end his friends had supported him.

Two weeks, John Salki had said, and two weeks it had been, Meyer thought as the train sped along. The whistle blew.

"Next stop, Mislavitch!"

He was through running.

42

"How long has Janek been gone?" Meyer asked.

Salki looked at his watch. "Not long, Meyer. Manya will be here shortly. I sent Janek to Gorski's first."

"But that means it will take longer for her to arrive. We need to spend as much time as possible together. Who knows when we'll be with each other again."

"I know, but it's important that we talk to you first. And it's better if Manya isn't around. She's already frightened enough about your leaving. There's no reason she has to sit here and listen to us discuss it."

"How is she, John? You've seen her during the past two weeks. Will she be all right?"

"She cried like a baby the first time she came here after you left. But she accepted your decision to go to the underground. And she's come over many times since then, just wanting to talk and be with someone who knows you—I think it gives her strength. Sitting here, she knows that she's with people who care what happens to you. We've talked about her family, how much she misses them, and what an agonizing decision it was for her to leave them. She still thinks about it constantly."

"Is she sorry she came with me?"

"Sad, yes. Regretful, no. She's been with the man she loves. Everything she's done was for you and Chaim. Now there is no Chaim, only you. But she won't give up hope. She will never believe they aren't alive and that she won't be reunited with them. I think her sheer willpower defies the odds. Her belief is so indomitable that even I am influenced by it. Beliefs can be lost, Meyer, but they are the most difficult things to conquer or destroy. She believes in you more than anything. You may not see it all the time, but she is strong, Meyer, very strong."

"I know, John. I love her so much. My parents loved her also. I think they saw, even before I did, how much she really cared for me. I won't shatter her beliefs. Promise me, John, that after I leave you'll do everything you can to watch over her."

"Of course we will. You don't have to worry about that."

There was a knock on the door. It was Gorski.

The older men explained to Meyer what had happened for the past two weeks. "I haven't been able to get papers for Manya yet," the police chief informed him. "But we're still working on them."

"It will take some time," Salki added.

"I'm afraid our greatest fears have been borne out, Meyer. The partisans in the area are very fearful of letting anyone they don't know into the group. As we told you before you left, there is strong suspicion it was someone from Hrubieszow who betrayed the others," Gorski continued.

"Don't they trust the two of you, even? You've helped them!"

"Of course we've helped, but these days trust is a word that few people have faith in. Too often in the past, people have seen it crumble before them."

"Do they know the Gestapo is looking for me?"

"Yes, they do, which makes them even more cautious. They may think the reason you're still alive is that you made a deal with them, or that you're being watched and might lead the Nazis right to them."

"What if I told them I was Jewish?"

The two men looked at each other, contemplating whether that might be a good idea.

"No, I don't think so, Meyer. That wouldn't be the safest thing to do. It might even make it more difficult," Salki finally answered. "We told you from the beginning there were no guarantees."

"Then what do I do?"

"The arrangements have been made. You'll go to the wooded area two miles north of here tomorrow evening. There, two people are supposed to meet you. They'll question you and look you over. Then they'll decide. But you must listen to them and abide by their decision. If they decide yes, you go with them. If they say no, you come back here. Do you agree?" Gorski asked him.

"Yes, but what will we do then—if they say no, I mean?" Meyer asked.

"We'll try again," Salki answered.

Meyer was sure both men hoped that he would be sent back. He was glad Manya had not been present to hear the discussion.

"I've got to get home. It seems as if a few of the SS like my neighborhood," Gorski said sarcastically. "They've decided to move in next door. It wouldn't be good for them to see me come in late at night. I won't say good-bye, my friend, only good luck. We'll see one another again. May God go with you and watch over you."

Manya arrived shortly after Gorski departed. There was so much to talk about, but words were hard to find. Most of the time was spent looking into each other's eyes, holding, caressing.

"Manya, it's getting late, you must get back to the ghetto," Meyer finally told her.

"No, I'm going to stay with you all night."

"You'll be missed at the count."

"I don't care, Meyer, I want to be with you."

"You have to go back," he implored.

Holding his face in her hands ever so lightly, she gazed into his eyes and gently asked, "Would you?"

He gave her the only answer he could. He took her in his arms and squeezed.

"How will you get into the ghetto when it's light out?" he finally asked, breaking the silence.

"I won't have to go to the ghetto," she answered. "I've been assigned to work on the farms. They aren't far from here—many times we've passed right by. I'll hide in the underbrush until the rest of the girls come past and then join them."

"Aren't there any guards with them?"

"There were the first couple of days, but not since. The Polish farmer would report immediately to the Gestapo if one of us were missing, so the Nazis needn't waste one of their men on that duty."

"I'm still worried about you. I don't want anything to—"

"Shh. I'm worried for you as well. But let's not think those thoughts. Let's just be together."

All too quickly the night turned to morning. Neither of them had slept. Each knew it might be months before Meyer could get back or send for her. Maybe longer. They had promised each other there would be no tears. That wasn't the way to remember each other.

"Manya, I promise you we'll be together again. You are what I have to live for—you're my life. I love you more than you'll ever know. It's because of you that I'll be able to go on. I'll think of you every minute we're apart," he promised her.

Then he said the words she so desperately needed to hear: "I believe, Manya, I really do. We'll all be together again. Your family is my family. We'll make it through this."

"Oh, yes, Meyer, yes we will," she exclaimed, throwing her arms around his neck. "I know we will. I love you so much. I'll be waiting for you, I promise. God will watch over all of us. He's kept us alive through all this horror. And my family—we'll find them once we're together again."

"Listen to me, Manya. I've talked to John, and if you need any help, you know that he's here for you. He'll watch out for you while I'm gone."

Then it was time for her to leave. He watched her until she was almost out of sight. She turned around to give him a final little wave. Some promises were just impossible to keep—the tears ran down his cheeks.

Manya didn't have to wait long for her work group to pass. Checking to make sure there was no guard, she quickly joined them. A few asked where she'd been and accepted her made-up story. They all knew it was sometimes better not to know the truth.

There was something different in their mood, though. Manya sensed it right away. It wasn't that they were happy, just different—more spirited, almost perky.

"Why's everyone in such a good mood?" Manya finally asked.

"Haven't you heard the news?" one girl responded.

Just then the farmer came out and began giving instructions. Manya could hardly contain herself. Why doesn't he hurry?

As soon as he was out of earshot, Manya grabbed the girl. "What news? I haven't heard anything."

"Those butchers are gone," she answered.

Manya didn't understand. "What are you talking about? What butchers? Who?" she demanded.

"The Gestapo. Damone, Alex, and Wagner. They've all been transferred," she responded with a smile. "They're gone from Hrubieszow."

Open your ears, Manya. You heard wrong. "Gone?" Manya repeated.

"Yes, now you know why we're in such a good mood!"

"Damone—gone? Alex—gone? Wagner—gone?" Manya could not ask it enough. "They're gone?" Then it became, "They're gone! They're gone!"

She was crying and laughing simultaneously. Meyer wouldn't have to leave! He could stay! They could be together! She had to tell him before he left. But she couldn't leave now. What if the farmer came back? At lunch! Yes, that was it. She'd sneak away at the break.

Time went ever so slowly. She tried not to think about it, but one thought kept popping into her head. What if he left before she arrived? No, he just couldn't. She picked vegetables as fast as she could, convincing herself that the quicker she worked, the more rapidly time would pass.

"Manya, don't work so hard, we have all day," one of the girls said to her.

They didn't understand. She had to hurry. To her chagrin, the only thing her pace had accomplished was to make her more tired. Finally the interlude arrived. Walking casually until she was out of sight of the farm, she took off like a shot, her short, exhausted legs carrying her as fast as they could.

Throwing caution to the wind, she didn't even attempt to sneak into Salki's. She came bursting through the back door, scaring Mrs. Salki half to death.

"Manya! What are you doing here?" she asked with a face as white as a sheet.

"Where's John?" she gasped.

"He hasn't come home yet."

"Has Meyer left?" Manya panted.

"No, he's still in the attic."

"Tell him . . . not to . . . leave." She continued panting, putting her hand on her chest, trying desperately to catch her breath. "They've been . . . transferred! He can stay."

"Manya, slow down. What are you talking about?" the startled Mrs. Salki asked.

"I can't explain now. I have to go back to work. Just tell Meyer not to leave. The Gestapo has been transferred!"

Before the astonished woman could say another word, Manya vanished. Looking through the window, Salki's wife knew she'd have to relay to Meyer what she'd just seen. She could swear that Manya was half-running, half-dancing her way through the fields.

43

They were in a different house now. The Nazis had moved them out of the first one under the guise of regrouping the dwindling number of ghetto inhabitants. Previously full houses had been emptied by the deportations or were so lacking in residents that they wanted to double up and be closer to each other. So when Meyer returned to the ghetto after three months of running, it was to another location.

Manya shut out the room and guided her waking dreams into a fantasy of being Meyer's wife, of a morning spent shopping in the old marketplace, of planning a big family dinner that would include the best of food his flour-mill profits could provide.

She let the dream dissipate and opened her eyes. At least Meyer was real, lying there next to her. She snuggled closer.

"Hmmmph?" he mumbled in his sleep, and turned over. She looked at the blanket they had strung across the room for privacy, and heard noisy yawns from Sam and Leon on the other side. In a way, she wished the two had been lodged elsewhere this time. Their presence seemed to magnify Chaim's absence. Innocent conversation cloaked hidden meanings; rare laughs were cut short by guilty feelings.

It was time to get up. They were nearing completion of the available work in Hrubieszow, and could make it last only a few more months. They continued to hope that the Nazis would come up with more projects before the present ones were exhausted. The food supplies were less generous and even more repetitious. More and more of the goods they collected were being traded to Poles for basic necessities. They considered that a bad sign. Attitudes were degenerating. Circles of friends tightened, people turning inward to insulate themselves against each other—an even worse omen. And most chilling of all, as the need for workers had diminished, their expendability had grown, and once again the old pattern of beatings and killings had begun. They had to reach deeper and deeper to find the will that stoked their determination to go on.

After work one day Sam seized an opportunity to speak to

Meyer alone. "I'm leaving," he announced nervously. "I want to go back to my hometown."

"Alone?" Meyer asked.

"No," Sam answered. "Another fellow is going with me."

Meyer could see that he wasn't about to identify his companion. "Leon?"

"No, someone else—but that's not important. I need information from you, Meyer. You spent a long time running, even had a set of papers. You know someone who can help. I was thinking you could tell me who."

The moment Meyer had dreaded so long was here. His friend needed help. Should he hand over his own means of escape? Sam might as well have asked for his passport. He was sweating, his thoughts racing, to think of another solution. There was none. Salki was the key. He had helped others besides Meyer; why not Sam, too? Sam and his friend. But Meyer didn't know whom Sam was planning to take along. Meyer thought he could rely on Sam's judgment, but what about this other person? Suddenly Meyer realized that he was thinking as Salki had tried to explain the leaders of the underground would think. No wonder the commissioner had been so cautious!

"Will you tell me, Meyer?" Sam prodded, a little louder. "If you won't, just say so. I'll understand and I'll find another way," the man went on.

Meyer raised a hand and patted the air to calm his friend. "I'll tell you," he said very slowly. "But you must promise to tell no one—including your friend—where you are going, do you understand? Just get your friend and lead the way. I'll tell you how to go. Do you swear?"

Sam gave Meyer a sober look. "I swear," he repeated. Meyer stared at him a long time before he was satisfied.

"I can't promise you anything," he began, "but he might be willing to help. I haven't seen him for a while, but tell him I sent you. He may not be able to get papers for you, but he might find a way to put you in touch with the underground."

"What's his name, Meyer?"

"Salki—John Salki," Meyer answered, chewing on the words.

"Yes," Sam replied with the look of someone who has just confirmed a long-held suspicion. "I thought so—I heard rumors."

Meyer remained aloof from the temptation to reveal too much. He used his hands to map out a safe route to Salki's house. The precious information electrified the air between the two men. Sam seemed about to offer awkward thanks when Meyer spoke again.

"There's something else I must ask you, Sam, something very difficult." He cleared his throat. "You can ask Salki to help you, but you must abide by his advice. Don't ask for one favor too many. If he says he can't help, you must accept it and be responsible for yourself. Can you do that, Sam?"

Sam's look got wiser as Meyer's words sank in. "I will, Meyer—I swear," Sam assured him.

A few clumsy minutes ticked by.

"When are you leaving?" Meyer finally asked.

"Tonight. I'd better get some things together." Sam rose to leave the room, changed his mind, and came close to Meyer. He hooked a muscular arm around Meyer's neck and shoulders. "I want you to know I tried to think of another way—I didn't want to ask you," he said sadly. "I know you're worried, but I don't know what to say." He fidgeted. "There's no way to thank you—"

"Keep quiet and take care of yourself," Meyer said in a double entendre.

"I promise," came the faithful pledge as Sam left the room.

"Good luck," Meyer called in a combined supplication and farewell.

Word came down a few days later, chilling bits of secondhand rumor and hideous innuendo. Cotton-mouthed and stiff-legged, Meyer headed for the Jewish Center after the evening count. The undertone of conversation within stopped when he opened the door, then, as they saw he was one of them, hummed anew.

"Did you hear?" one asked. "A tragedy," someone answered. "You say he was hiding Jews?" a third inquired. "Two," came the reply. "And he was shot?" "In front of his wife and children." "God help them!" the chorus grieved. "Such a brave man—a savior," they cried. "And the Jews?" "Shot too." Where would it all end?

Meyer was still trying to stay calm and make sense of the fragments of conversation, but the facts assailed him like sticky summer flies. His spirit waved them away furiously, but they rallied and set upon him again and again. The voices continued.

"An official?" one asked. Garbled words; then: "Roads." "Nazis," someone supplied. "Commissioner . . ." one person began. "John Salki," another finished.

The errant pieces flopped into order and pulsed their message in Meyer's head: Commissioner of Roads John Salki, shot dead outside his house; wife and children watching; two Jews shot trying to escape.

Meyer and Manya were on their own.

44

The couple grew closer still in the four weeks after Salki's death, whispering to each other till all hours, fingering the meager stockpile of valuables that would somehow finance an escape. Nothing would deter them, no one would prevent—or help— their plan. Over and over Meyer repeated the steps they would take to reach the underground together. Time after time they laid it out and looked at it, worrying over the weak spots, selecting rest stops and hideouts along the way. Meyer forced every detail of his three months on the run to the surface, spewing it by rote, as a child recites a multiplication exercise.

They reviewed it all, squeezed out possibilities, weighed probabilities, and set their course. They let go of the past and moved mechanically through the present, ever more dependent on what was ahead.

More than one conversation trailed off because of an accidental reference to John Salki. They tiptoed around the pain of his death, no more able to bear it now than they had been when it occurred. In their hearts they knew that the plans they devoted themselves to every hour of every day were still attributable to their friend's earlier support, and, yes, love. Even the memory of Salki's disapproval visited its warning in Meyer's mind each time he handled the gun he would tuck in his belt when they left for good. Salki's words hauntingly pulsated through Meyer's ears: "Do you think I'm not scared every time I let a Jew into my house, knowing what would happen if we were caught? Someday my luck or Gorski's may run out, Meyer, but it's the right thing to do . . . the right thing to do . . . the right thing to do . . ."

Meyer had no contact with Gorski during the last month. He wondered if Salki's death would deter Gorski from continuing his fight against the Nazis. It might slow him down, Meyer decided, but he doubted that Gorski would ever give up his battle. There was one thing that Meyer had pledged to himself: he would not approach Gorski for any more help. He had asked enough of him already. Besides, the plan he and Manya worked out was looking good, based as it was on the machinery Salki and Gorski had put in place weeks ago. All Meyer had to do was follow the steps they had outlined. Manya still had no papers, but he was relying on his to vouch for both of them.

Their heads were full of tomorrow when they presented themselves for the dreary morning lineup. But what was this? Shrieking voices, gunning engines, and the cadence of fast-marching military filled their ears. Meyer and Manya scanned the action before them. Her practiced eyes swept the crowd to choose a line, any line that wouldn't be led to the trucks. But there were no lines, no organized formations, no fought-for silence, no passive stares. The people were swimming before her, swaying one way, then the other, as rifles held sideways kneaded them into groups and herded them to the trucks. Manya felt herself swept from Meyer's side in a sudden surge, then saw him, face contorted, reaching, straining over shoulders, between linked arms, around another desperate hand. His fingers finally closed around her arm and she thought it would pull from its socket. Then he was behind her, his other arm across her front.

Still they were shoved on, the pool of humanity creating its own waves as some pressed ahead to avoid a blow and others pulled back in hopes of staying behind. Then they were climbing the ramp. Meyer was nearly carrying her now. It was dark inside the truck as they collapsed on the wooden seat that ran the length of both sides. The ramp crashed to their feet. The vehicle lurched roughly ahead, jostling the riders against each other. As it negotiated a sharp right turn, they were pressed still tighter together. Then a corner to the left sent them sliding the other way.

In a few minutes they came to a noisy halt. Guards holding jauntily to the rearview mirrors at the front and to the spine of the canvas support at the rear jumped to the ground and hustled into position. No ramps this time, as the soldiers ordered the Jews to leave the truck in leaps. When their turn came, Meyer went first, reaching up to steady Manya's descent. He captured her to him again and moved out of the way to await the next command. Gone was the precious plan for escape.

Manya pulled Meyer's arms tighter. The trucks belched their cargo at the train station. Her father had spent weeks and months at the depot doing the Nazis' bidding. There was hardly anything in her view that hadn't been touched by his hands. The thought was not comforting. Had this, too, been Chaim's last glimpse of Hrubieszow?

More shouts and echoing cries as the crowd was moved toward the track. Soldiers used their fists to knock loose the steel pinions that fastened the doors of railroad cars, then hauled them open along rusty grooves. They brandished weapons and hounded reluctant figures into the cavernous cars. Meyer and Manya tumbled to the floor of the cattle carrier. Again metal grated on metal as the sliding ponderous door swallowed up the daylight. They heard a loud clang as the iron arm slammed into its locked position. When their eyes adjusted to the darkness, they saw, in the corner at the top, a small window. A few people formed a human ladder to look out. Meyer and Manya didn't join them.

Manya tried not to hear the whimpering that enveloped the enclosure, and buried her face in Meyer's chest to muffle her own. So this was what all those thousands of her neighbors and friends had gone through the five previous times Jews had been driven from the city. This was what her own family must have experienced ten months ago, and Chaim only three months ago. This was what it was like to be deported.

45

Deportation! The word rang in Manya's ears. What did it mean? Death? Was this the end of all the hopes and dreams Meyer and she had dared plan? But maybe Wagner had been telling the truth, and all those people taken before them *had* been sent to work and not to die. She wanted desperately to believe that was the case. The only thread of optimism that wove its way through her mind was that maybe all the Jews deported from Hrubieszow were sent to the same destination. That would mean she might be seeing her family. But as strong as the thought was, she refused to pin her hopes on that speculation.

They had been divided into two cars. Tovah was sitting next to Manya with a glassy stare in her eyes. She stared, but Manya knew there was nothing to see. The crying had ceased, substituted by whispers so low that whole sentences couldn't be detected.

"Where . . . ?" "How long . . . ?" "Will . . . ?" "Is this . . . ?" "Why . . . ?" Manya didn't need to hear the complete questions to know what was being asked. She could finish them herself.

Minutes turned into hours, and still the train didn't move. They heard occasional banging or someone yelling an order outside, but other than that, it was quiet. Even the inside of the car was silent. All movement and whispering seemed to halt at the same time; people huddled together just waiting for what would come next.

As quickly as the stillness had engulfed them, a noise interrupted it. The engine spat out its message: they were leaving. The car lurched forward, then gradually accelerated. They were on their way. No one knew if that was good or bad, only that it was happening.

Meyer pulled Manya's trembling form still closer to his own. Neither spoke, but others began to talk. For about thirty minutes it went on like this, with Meyer's attention drifting in and out of the various conversations. Then he nudged Manya. "If that works, we'll try it also."

"If what works?" she asked.

He pointed to the corner of the car where the small window was. A number of people had gathered and were helping a young man climb up.

"What's he doing, Meyer?"

"He's going to crawl through and jump off the train."

"It's too small, he can't get through it. And even if he does, the jump will probably kill him. It feels like the train is going pretty fast."

"Maybe, Manya, but it's worth a try."

All eyes were riveted to the tiny opening that teased them with ideas of escape. Each move the man made was felt by each individual. When he slipped, they all slipped. As he pulled himself up with straining arms, their bodies tightened as if to transfer their strength to him. Would he fit through the small opening? Their eyes measured him, then the window. It looked doubtful. First his arms went out, then his head. Only his wriggling behind and legs were left; then they too disappeared. He was out. Someone quickly climbed up to see what had happened. The young man had made it to the top of the car. The train wasn't going at full speed, but it would still be a very dangerous jump. Nothing more could be seen.

Only a moment passed before a shot rang out. The train began to slow, finally came to a complete halt. The Germans must have seen the man get out. No one said a word. Suddenly the door was heaved open.

Bright sunshine flooded the car, causing them to shade their eyes with arms and hands. Outside, the SS were lined up, guns pointed at the occupants of the boxcar. One of the Germans began to yell. "Stupid Jews! We should shoot you right here. If anyone tries that again, we'll kill you all on the spot!"

The closing door plunged them into darkness; then they heard the clang of the lock falling back into position. Again they had to be responsible for each other. No action would be taken by one that might jeopardize another. Meyer and Manya resumed their position as the train picked up speed, arms entwined.

"Manya, did you notice? Two things which may be good."

She had no idea what he was talking about.

"What do you mean?"

"First of all, they didn't mention if they had killed the young man. And second, they must really have orders to deliver us someplace. Otherwise, they would have killed us for helping him to escape." The first part didn't sound as convincing when he said it as when he had thought it, but he preferred to picture the escaped prisoner running briskly toward freedom through the fields that flanked the track. He wished him luck.

Most of the people had something with them to eat, since they had taken their lunches in anticipation of going to work that day. Those who did shared with the few who didn't. The worst thing was having no water, and it was getting hotter and stuffier inside the car.

The train sped on. Some people went to sleep, others conversed, but most just sat quietly in their own thoughts. It wasn't long, however, before the locomotive was making stops. No one came to their car. They heard no talking, no yelling outside. The only sound was a big crash at the end of their car, with a simultaneous jerk that caused them to fall roughly against one another. They sat for a while before and after the crash, then felt the lurch again as the journey continued. The balance of the trip was full of stops and starts.

It seemed like days since they were rounded up and put on the train in Hrubieszow, but only one had passed. Through the small window they had seen the sun set, the moon come and go, and the sun rise again. Manya was asleep on Meyer's arm when the train braked a sixth time, or an eighth—they had lost track. Would this never end? Meyer thought.

There was the same quiet outside that had been evident before, but it lasted only a moment. Meyer heard a lot of noise and commotion. People were yelling. He shook Manya awake. She opened her eyes and looked up.

"What is it, Meyer?"

"I don't know, but something's happening."

Now everyone was awake, staring at the door. They heard the familiar clank of the metal lock as it was disengaged. The door yawned open. "Raus! Raus!"

At first no one followed the order to get out.

"Raus! Raus!" the command was barked again.

Slowly they got up and moved toward the door. There was no ramp to walk down, and they had to jump. What they saw when they got out frightened them.

Many more cars had been coupled to the train. Each of them spewed people. There was no way Meyer could count them all, they multiplied so fast, but by the time the train was empty, there were over a thousand people standing next to the track, maybe twice that many.

"That's why we kept stopping," Meyer whispered to Manya. "To pick up more people."

In front of them, in rows with guns ready, were the SS. Some were holding snarling dogs on leashes. Occasionally a soldier would pretend he was going to release the strap and let his vicious animal attack. But then he yanked back the leash, after getting the response he wanted from the prisoner he goaded.

They were ordered into rows of five. Meyer held Manya's hand and pulled her toward a line; she in turn grabbed Tovah's hand. With the SS on either side of the group, another command was shouted: "March!"

Meyer gripped Manya's hand tighter. Where were they going? There was only open land to the right and left. In the distance, in front of them, he could see buildings, lots of buildings. On they walked, getting closer and closer. Then he spotted a fence, stretching as far as he could see.

"Look, Manya, there are people inside the fence."

The closer they got, the more people there were. Now they were crowding against the fence. The panorama was horrifying to the incoming group. Manya took hold of Meyer's arm with her other hand. "Are they alive?"

Meyer didn't know whether to say yes or no. The inmates he saw were standing, but he didn't know how. They were like sticks. He could see the outline of bones through their identical striped clothes. Their skin was almost white—no, not white, gray. He had never seen a human being that color before.

"My God, what have they done to these people?" Meyer asked into the air. He saw them shove each other aside to get a closer look at the incoming group. Then they all started yelling at once. A word begun by one seemed to be finished by another, suffixed again by a third. There were "Co . . ." and ". . . berg," "Gott . . ." and ". . . wald," peppered with "do you know . . . is there a . . . where are you from? . . ." The fragments of words that assailed the ears of the arriving contingent collided with one another crazily.

"Meyer, they're calling out names," Manya exclaimed.

The SS shot their guns into the air and screamed at them to shut up, to move away from the fence.

Meyer, Manya, and the rest of their group stood in front of the entrance. It had been a bright day when they emerged from the train, but as the towering gates swung slowly open, a sudden darkness came over the camp. Perhaps it was his imagination or maybe just a cloud hiding the sun. Meyer considered it a sign.

"Meyer, where are we?" Manya begged.

"In hell," he mumbled. "In hell."

46

"Men line up to the right and women on the left. I don't want to say it again," the SS officer yelled, pulling his gun from his holster.

Separate! No, Manya wanted to go with Meyer. She wouldn't leave him, no matter where he was sent.

Very quickly the black uniforms on either side of the prisoners jumped into the group and began shoving men to one side and women to the other. Some of the Nazis dragged women away and threw them to the ground. Manya's screams joined those of other women and men who were torn from spouses and loved ones. Outstretched hands strained to touch other outstretched hands. The gunfire in the air neither drowned out nor quieted the desperate cries of anguish. If Manya was to die, she wanted it to be with Meyer; but her protests, like the others', were in vain.

With their segregation accomplished, the SS marched the newcomers into camp. The eyes of the old prisoners showed sympathy, fear, and expectation.

Once the last Jew was inside, the gates were closed behind them, sealing their fate. The two lines were led in different directions. Manya scoured the departing group of men for Meyer, her thoughts pleading with God to give her another glimpse of him. Within seconds, neither group was visible to the other.

When the men finally stopped, they stood in front of a large building. They were ordered inside and told to remove all their clothes. Meyer quickly ripped the lining of his jacket and removed a Russian gold piece that had been hidden there for some time. He couldn't risk putting it in his mouth, so he pushed it up his rear end for safekeeping. The impulse was ridiculous. If he was to be killed, he'd have no use for gold, but at least his captors wouldn't get it. He stood there naked, his clothes at his feet, thinking this was the end. His life was to be taken away in this godforsaken place with hundreds of other men, standing nude, with only the Nazi bastards to witness their last breath on earth.

"You will go into the showers and clean your filthy Jew bodies," one of the guards yelled. "You will be quick. We have no time for slow people."

They were ushered into the shower stalls. No one's shower lasted over a minute, if that. Even if the guards would have allowed them to stay longer, Meyer soon learned why no one would linger—the water was ice cold. He jumped out as quickly as he could and joined the others who were drip-drying. After the last person finished, they were ordered into another room, still shivering and damp. Each was handed a set of clothes: striped shirt and pants, a pair of wooden shoes. No man could put on the paper-thin garments quickly enough, but the material absorbed the water and stuck to their skin, prolonging the discomfort instead of ending it. The clothing was mismatched. On some the shirt was too big and the pants too short; on others, the reverse was true. The wooden clogs were narrower or shorter than the feet that poked into them.

They were led into still another room, with chairs sitting in a row. The first to enter were ordered to sit while the rest watched their hair being cut. No, Meyer thought, "cut" was the wrong word. The bewildered Jews' heads were being shaved. The falling hair began to pile on the floor. He fingered his own, trying to imagine why this was done. Wasn't it enough that they were treated like animals? Did they have to be made to look like freaks?

They were taken out of the building and marched to their living quarters. Each person was assigned to a barracks and ordered in. Even though it was daytime, there was very little light inside. The floor of the barracks was dirt, and rows of wooden bunks, three tiers high, crowded the walls from one end to the other. Loose straw served as the mattress, sprinkled unevenly across the wooden slats. As more and more people entered the barracks, it was evident to Meyer that he wouldn't enjoy the luxury of a bed to himself. At the same time, he couldn't see how two people were supposed to fit in one bunk. He quickly claimed a middle berth away from the door and proceeded to extract the gold coin from its hiding place, thankful it was out and still in his possession.

Soon he was joined by an unfamiliar face. "Do you mind if I share this bunk with you?"

"No, not at all. My name is Meyer Korenblit."

"I'm Adam Herling. Where are you from?" the newfound friend asked.

For the next hour they exchanged stories about what had happened to each during the past four years. The whispers that wafted through the barracks gave evidence that similar conversations were going on all around them.

"Why do you think they brought us here, Adam?" Meyer asked the older boy.

"I'm not sure, but I don't think they're going to kill us. Otherwise they would probably have done it when we first arrived."

"Do you think the same is true of the women? My girl . . . uh, fiancée . . . came in with me. I'm worried about her. I . . . I . . ."

"She must be all right. We haven't heard any shooting."

"Yes, yes, that's true. She must be all right. If only I could see her for just a minute."

But Meyer's thoughts of Manya soon vanished when the door to the barracks was flung open and everyone was ordered to line up outside.

"You will be issued a cup and a spoon for your food. You had better take care of them—you will not be given another if you lose them."

They were allowed to stay outside as a kitchen crew took food from barracks to barracks. Some of the new arrivals began to mingle with those who'd been there for a while.

Meyer grabbed Adam's arm and pulled him toward a small group standing nearby. "My name is Meyer and this is Adam," he announced.

"I'm Sol and this is Felix," a man said, then proceeded to introduce the rest, but Meyer didn't remember all their names. He had too many questions he wanted to ask.

"Where are we?" was the first thing Meyer wanted to know.

"A place called Budzyn," Sol answered him.

"I've never heard of such a place. Is it in Poland?"

"Yes, we are in Poland. There's a city not far from here called Krasnik."

"Why are we here? And why does everyone look so terrible?"

"You were brought here to work—either in the factories or on the roads. We have to work twelve or thirteen hours a day, sometimes more. They give us very little to eat and not much sleep. You've seen the conditions here. The place is filthy and overrun with lice. You're only able to clean yourself maybe once a week, if you can call it that," Sol answered him.

"But if they want us to work, why do they treat us like this?"

"Because they really don't care if you live or die. There are many more to take your place," someone else responded.

"How long have you been here?" Adam asked.

"Most of us have been here close to a year. No one knows for sure—you lose track of the days, weeks, and months," Felix answered.

"Does that mean we'll go to work tomorrow?" Meyer asked.

"Probably not, since you're new. They'll make you go through hell first. You all came in looking fresh and healthy. The bastards don't like that."

The conversation was cut off as the food buckets came to them.

"A word of advice to both of you," Felix said as they hurried toward the meal. "Don't eat your bread now, save it for the morning. I promise you, you'll need it worse tomorrow than you do now. In the morning you'll get only coffee."

While Meyer hadn't expected to get much food for dinner, he wasn't prepared for what he did receive. He'd eaten only once in the last twenty-four hours, and he was ravenous. He held out his cup and watched as it was submerged in the bucket and handed back to him. He spooned through the liquid for something solid that would satisfy the ache in his stomach, but the spoon came up empty. He dipped it in again. Nothing. On the third try he scraped the utensil along the bottom and swished it around. He was finally rewarded with a couple of small pieces of vegetable. The broth was like water. Meyer was tempted to go ahead and eat the thin slice of bread, but heeded Felix's words. He hoped Manya received the same advice. Immediately after dinner, they were ordered to their bunks for the night.

The shrill wake-up siren cut into Meyer's dreams, and for a moment he didn't know where he was. The others in his barracks were similarly unsure of what to expect as they pulled themselves from bunks and made their way outside. It was still dark as they lined up to get their instructions. They would have thirty minutes to wash, get breakfast, and eat before lining up to be counted. There was a rush for the latrine. Meyer quickly saw that it would be difficult to get clean. They were all going to the same place to wash and use the toilet—not just the new arrivals, but everyone, thousands of people. It didn't take long to realize he'd have to throw away his manners if he was to be one of the few who got access to the bath house. Meyer wasn't lucky that first day; maybe Manya had been.

They were given coffee for breakfast. Meyer carefully removed his bread from his pocket. Within seconds, both were gone.

Soon they were standing with the others to be counted. It was a painstakingly slow process because of the number of people. He stood there, and stood, and stood. At last it was over and they were released to their work, all but the new arrivals. Felix's words about a day of hell came true.

The guards ignored the leftover prisoners, leaving them in line for hours. Then the Nazis paced up and down the rows, staring the prisoners down and cuffing them about the head, until the desired servility was established. For variety the prisoners were ordered to do sit-ups—10, 20, 30, 40, 50, 100. The guards kicked them as their torsos rose and fell. Another command was barked, and the inmates rolled over on their fronts for push-ups—10, 20, 30, 40, 50, 100—and were squashed to the ground by the Nazis, who walked on their backs. But the prisoners suffered more than physical abuse. For hours nothing but obscenities and filthy names were directed at them. And so it continued through most of the day: standing at attention, sit-ups, push-ups, standing again, and so on. When it finally came to an end, the prisoners lined up yet another time and were given their work assignments for the following day. They returned to their barracks, only to be called out a few minutes later to join the old-timers, who were just returning from work, to be counted.

After their water-soup dinner, they were given a little free time. Someone told Meyer that if he had a wife or girlfriend, now was the time to find her.

"They don't give us this opportunity every day," the man had said.

It took Meyer most of the interval to find Manya. At last he spotted her in a crowd of women.

Thank God they didn't cut her hair, he whispered to himself.

"Manya! Manya!"

For half a second she didn't recognize the figure moving toward her. Then she went running into his arms. "Oh, Meyer, what have they done to you?"

"I'm all right, Manya. How are you?"

"It's all so horrible, Meyer. Hold me, please, touch me. Show me something is still real," she begged.

He did hold her and touch her soft face. "We'll get out of here some way, my love. I promise you."

They exchanged stories of what had happened since their separation. Meyer told her he'd be working outside the camp on road construction. She also had a job outside the camp—in the fields picking vegetables. But Tovah had been assigned to the kitchen. She and Tovah were together in the same barracks, and like him, had met some new people to be close to.

All too quickly their time was up.

"Manya, I'll find a way to come and see you. I love you."

"I love you, Meyer, but please don't take any chances. I want you to stay alive."

As Meyer walked away, he heard Manya call after him: "I'll love you forever."

47

It couldn't be much more than seven-thirty or so, Meyer judged as he lay on the loose straw that covered his bunk, using his arm for a pillow. He'd have to wait quite a while before it was dark enough for him to sneak to Manya's barracks. He'd gone the night before, also, and ordinarily wouldn't have risked it two nights in a row, but today he had decided they would put their plan of escape into action. He had to let Manya know that in two days they'd be out of Budzyn—free.

He poked his fingers under the thin layer of straw to check for his morning slice of bread. It was still there, growing hard and dry, but he would dunk it in the tepid brew that served as coffee in the morning. Next to the thin slice were his wooden shoes. He rolled over on his back and tucked them under his head. He tried not to notice the sharp edges that pressed against his bristly scalp.

Meyer had been jarred by the size of Budzyn, sickened by the lice and their insidious onslaught against the thousands and thousands of identically garbed skin-headed men who occupied the rows of one-story barracks. No wonder they shaved our heads,

Meyer had thought, remembering how Manya had cried when she saw him, then shuddered to think what she, with her long dark blond hair intact, must be going through. The idea sent him into a frenzy of scratching, and brought a sleepy complaint from his bunkmate, Adam Herling. Meyer willed the itching to stop and Adam to go back to sleep. He didn't want his friend to know he planned to go to Manya again so soon. Adam and two other men were ready to cover for Meyer last night, but wouldn't approve of this second trip, and there was no way Meyer would try to convince them by divulging his plan to escape. No, tonight Meyer was on his own. When the wake-up siren sounded at four-thirty the next morning, he would be back in his own bunk. He'd file out with the others to the latrine, then queue for some coffee. It hadn't taken long for Meyer to adopt the eating style of the hungry prisoners. He learned to hold his bread in one hand and cup the other underneath, ready to catch the smallest crumb that might fall. With coffee, he held his cup just under his chin to capture errant drops.

Before they were led away to work, they were counted, then marched out the gates—the women to farms and the men to do road and factory work. The Ukrainian guards insisted that they sing as they marched, going and coming. When work was far from camp, they brought their cups and spoons along. Forgetting them meant no lunch. The food was brought to the work site and was, of course, cold by the time it arrived. During the midday break, they were lined up again, counted, and given the same thin soup. They felt lucky to find a piece of vegetable in the cloudy liquid.

Meyer's watchful eye had noticed exchanges being made during the workday between some of the prisoners and Poles, and a few old-timers at the camp had confirmed that it was possible to get food and other extras in this fashion—for a price. It amazed Meyer that the Poles always kept their part of the bargains they made; they could just as easily have stolen the valuables that the Jews gave them. But a few helped without asking something in return, and Manya had chanced to come across one of them. Having nothing to trade, she convinced a Polish farmer to give her some paper and a pencil. When Manya told Meyer that she intended to use the materials to keep a diary, he wasn't impressed, would rather she put her persuasion toward a more practical goal. But that was her affair. He did worry that the diary might be discovered, but she assured him she had torn the paper into small squares and rolled it around the pencil, sometimes hiding it in the straw of her bunk and other times knotting her long hair around it.

Meyer's gold coin was still hidden in his bunk, ready to buy his wishes. But it wouldn't be bartered too cheaply or too quickly, he decided, even though his growling stomach debated the issue. He wasn't alone in having a gold piece. Once he saw another prisoner cut such a coin in four pieces to stretch its purchasing power. It was just as valuable to the Poles in quarters as it was whole.

So in the ensuing weeks he fingered the coin, knowing it was the only thing he had left that could be of value to someone else. Finally Meyer decided that he would trade it not for food, but for implements of escape—a far more important commodity. The camp diet would sustain him, supplemented as it was by an extra chunk of bread or a few potato peelings that Manya got from Tovah, who worked in the kitchen.

But finally, with trembling fingers Meyer handed his gold piece to a Polish man in exchange for a pair of rubber gloves and wire-cutters. Then, the following Saturday, during the routine barracks and grounds cleaning, Meyer was able to hide the tools beneath some rocks outside his barracks. On the appointed night, four of them—he, Manya, and another couple—would retrieve the tools, snip the wires of the electric fence, and make a run for it. The plan dissipated there, for they had only the striped clothes they wore, no further valuables to trade either for help or for food, no way to camouflage the telltale bristly heads of the men, no idea where they would go, indeed, unsure of where they were. All that, they agreed, would be handled somehow when the time came. First they wanted freedom.

His neck tingled from the pressure of the clogs, so he moved the shoes to his side, then curled around them protectively, resting his head on his arm. It was very dark now, and very quiet except for a snore here and there and a moan or two. If he lived to be a hundred, he would never forget the smells that permeated the building, surrounded him at work, seasoned even his food: smells of humans overworked and underwashed, clothing stained with urine and diarrhea, bodies on fire with fever and disease, sliced with lash marks, swollen with infection, and flesh chewed raw by the lice—made rawer still by the host's frantic fingernails.

Meyer had suffered in the ghetto, but this—he had to get Manya out of here before they looked too much like the hollow-cheeked, sunken-eyed group that greeted them when they arrived. He didn't feel secure with the vagueness of their plan, but he quelled the doubt with assurances that it was the only thing to do. He was worried about the fence, had seen careless, desperate inmates jolted by the wires. He almost wished he had decided to escape while they were at work outside the camp. But he wanted darkness to hide in. Besides, he had the gloves and tools—those would get them through the fence safely.

Meyer eased himself to a half-sitting position under the overhead bunk and looked around. Adam lay fast asleep, undisturbed by Meyer's movement. Meyer crawled to the barracks door and slipped out into the cool October night. Staying clear of the floodlight's beam, he scurried through slender shadows from building to building, then crouched low at the edge of the clearing that separated the men's side from the women's side.

God, how he hated that empty expanse! It was about forty yards across, in direct view of a watchtower, and cut through the middle by a barbed-wire fence. For minutes Meyer scanned the perimeter of the open area, once around, then again, perhaps a third time to be sure—interrupting the sweep of his eyes only to glance periodically at the tower and to time the revolutions of the searchlight.

He dashed across, teeth clenched, body doubled over atop legs and feet that moved with accustomed stealth. At the fence he dived to the ground and slid under, then rolled to his feet again and streaked for a patch of darkness that could hide him. Weaving his way among the buildings, he reached Manya's barracks, slipped through the door, and crept down the length of the room, counting off the bunks. He climbed in with Manya, thankful that the next time he did this would be the last time. It was not something he would miss.

48

Manya lay in her bunk the next night, still shaking. She had untangled her diary papers from her hair a moment ago while the waning shafts of light from the setting sun would permit her to write a phrase or two, summarizing daily events. But she was unable to capture the terror of this day. How would she put it all down? She thought about the last twenty-four hours:

Dear Diary:
    Meyer came to see me again last night. It was such a thrill to open my eyes and see his face close to mine. He says we are going to escape tomorrow night—the four of us. I can't believe this is my last night here. It scares me, especially the part about meeting Meyer on the men's side, because I've never done that before, but he says the best place to go through the fence is over there. We talked and talked and ended up waking some of the other girls, but, God bless them, they didn't mind. A couple of them doubled up so Meyer and I could share my bunk. I kept thinking about the first time Meyer sneaked over. We were so afraid that the other women would report us if they found out he was there. But no one bothered us; in fact, those who saw him said they were happy for us, glad to know we had each other. Then I thought about the time Meyer was in my bunk with me and the guards came in unexpectedly. We lay very still and close. If there was ever a time when the other women could have reported us, that was it, for that would have saved them from being punished the same as Meyer and me. Nothing happened, though; the guards just stood there, shone a flashlight around, and left. Yes, I've made some good friends here. I'll miss them when I go. When the war is over, I'll look for them.
    I lay there a long time, it seemed, wide-awake, and nearly jumped out of my skin when the wake-up siren went off. There was a lot of shouting, then pounding on the barracks door. We all rushed to get outside. Of course it was still dark

and quite cold as we lined up. Across the compound behind the fence, I could see the male prisoners in formation, facing us. We stood there and stood there, and still no dismissal to go to the toilet. I couldn't understand what was going on. It was daylight before we got an explanation. The Ukrainian sergeant appeared on his horse and trotted back and forth in front of us, staring. I never saw such hatred in anyone's eyes. Any moment I expected him to capture one of us with the rope he always carries. Many times I've seen him lasso one of the prisoners and then drag his victim around as an example of his power over us. Whether for punishment or for fun, he takes great pleasure in his sadistic work. But today he didn't use his rope—for that.

He looked over the entire camp of prisoners with despising eyes, then said he was going to teach us a lesson once and for all. He said none of us would ever leave Budzyn, that we'd never outsmart him. Then he gave a signal to some of the guards and they led out some prisoners with their hands tied behind their backs. The sergeant pointed at them and explained their futile attempt at escape. Now they would pay the price for their stupid behavior. He said we were to watch them die so that we'd know what happens to Jewish pigs who try to run away. It was as if his words were directed right at me. I tried to find Meyer among the thousands of men standing across from us, but I couldn't see him. Off to the side, ropes were being tightened around the feet of the Jewish men. My skin was crawling; I wanted to run, hide, anything to get away. But the sergeant screamed a command for everyone to watch, saying he had plenty of ropes for the rest of us. The next instant the men were swinging upside down in the air. Their faces bulged with the rush of blood to their heads. A quick death wasn't good enough for the Nazi bastards. They wanted them, and us, to suffer. They left the bodies hanging there all day and all night. We had to stand in line the entire time.

When those people died, so did our plan to get away. So many thoughts and feelings went through my mind as we stood there in that horror. Those people were murdered, my senses told me. Do something: scream, run, fight back. I wondered how many others standing near me felt the same way, but there was only fear and shock on their faces. How many others had been plotting their own schemes for survival? So many of us standing in that clearing—surely we could overpower the guards. But who would be lost in the process? Me? The girl standing next to me? Meyer? I realized that as much as we tried to help each other in little ways—sharing food, tending each other's physical and mental wounds—we couldn't think and act as a group. At some point, I don't know when, we changed—I changed. There isn't one of us who isn't sickened by what we saw today, and there isn't one of us, including me, who isn't thankful to be alive instead of dead. We don't spend time worrying about those who die. I hear comments like, "One less," "Three less," "Their troubles are over," and we go on. Perhaps it's because there are no families to comfort, maybe we're just honestly relieved that it was someone else and not us. I wonder sometimes if I'll get my old ways back when all this is over. Perhaps that's one reason I wanted to keep this diary, to have a record of my feelings as well as of the events. I spend a lot of time trying not to think about what's going on here. Maybe one day I'll be able to read what I've written without this constant feeling that I can't believe what my eyes see or my ears hear. Oh, I don't know, maybe the diary is silly, after all. Maybe Meyer is right. I wish he understood, though; I wish I knew what he was thinking now. I wish he were here with me. Last night seems like a lifetime ago. So much has changed since then. The gloves and wire-cutters will have to stay put for now, but knowing they are handy gives me a little hope. We may not be free yet, but Meyer will think of a way. Until then I'll be patient and thankful. Thankful to catch a glimpse of him now and then, thankful to steal a few moments together when we can. Thankful we're still alive. I can feel good about that.

The exhausted young girl turned over on her side and curled up in a ball. The shaking had stopped, and she was very tired. Thinking about that day had been almost like living it again. If only she had the time to spend, the light to see, and enough paper to chronicle it all just as she had thought it . . . But she didn't. She could devote a few extra lines in this case, but God only knew what else was ahead. No, she'd have to stay with her habit of putting down only a few words. Tomorrow, as soon as she had the chance, she would write simply: "Jews hanged for attempted escape." It was all she wanted to remember of it anyway.

49

That day, Manya's group was taken to work in the fields. It was sometime after lunch, and she had just resumed her chore. She was on all fours, digging potatoes out of the hard ground, when another figure knelt down beside her and stuck his face into hers.

"Meyer!" she cried. "What are you doing here?"

"We're working on the road on the other side of that hill," he explained. "I thought I saw you marching along in front of my group, but I wasn't sure. I slipped away as soon as I could, and sure enough, here you are!"

Manya looked toward the farmhouse; no sign of the farmer or the guards—it should be safe to talk for a while. They sidled their way from furrow to furrow until they reached the edge of the field, then found a little hollow and sat down under a nearby tree. It was a raw day, but bright and clear, and it felt good to be shielded from the brisk wind that cut through the open field.

They huddled together, enjoying each other's warmth, talking and smiling, their hands busy with patting and stroking. Once or twice they peeked down at the kneeling figures in the field, but mostly they let themselves be transported away from the real world and were lost in togetherness. Meyer asked Manya about "the girls," as he called her close-knit group of friends, and she worried over how thin he was.

"How long do you think we'll be here, Meyer?"

"I don't know. Some of my friends have been in this place for a year. We just have to be careful and draw as little attention to ourselves as possible."

"I hope my family is in a better place than this—there must be a place where families are sent. But if the men and women are separated like you and I, it would be very hard on my mother. Do you think they're able to see each other?"

"Even if they can't, they still have the kids. Joshua would be with your father."

"Yes, and my sisters are with Mama. That will help her a lot."

"I'm sure they're taking care of themselves. We have to do the same, so we can be with them when this is over."

"Oh, I want so much for you to believe that as I do. I love you so much, Meyer."

"And I love you. Someday . . . well, someday we'll be together, all of us."

They continued talking about their future and the good times before the war. They weren't sure what brought them out of their reverie, but all of a sudden Meyer jumped up. He told Manya to wait, then disappeared behind the hill. In a few minutes he was back, breathing hard.

"They've gone!" he exclaimed, wiping his hand over his face.

"Who? What?"

"My group! They've gone back to the camp. Look, there, I think your group is getting ready to leave, too!"

They stared at each other. For a moment Meyer thought about escaping right then and there. But where would he go? He wasn't even sure where he was. Nothing but open land stood before him. The Jews were counted on the way back to the camp. He would be missed within minutes; he wouldn't have enough of a head start. And what about Manya? Could he leave her now?

"Come on!" Meyer yelled, grabbing her hand.

"Wait! What are we going to do?"

"I'll have to go back with you—there's no other way!"

"We could run . . . get away!"

"No!" he shouted. "That's suicide! Come on!"

They tumbled down the hillside and into the field. In a few moments the Ukrainian guards called everyone to line up. Manya and Meyer stayed as close to the others as they could. Meyer's mind raced to think of an explanation that would be acceptable if he were detected, weighed his chances of making it unnoticed. Some of the women had shaved heads, so his wouldn't give him away. He thought he could rely on the guards' usual attitude of ignoring the hapless crew they squired around. Maybe they would skip the count this time. They were just approaching the gate when one of the guards separated Meyer and Manya from the group. The others filed inside while the couple stood alone in the road.

"You!" one of the guards yelled to Meyer. "What are you doing here?" There was no time for an answer. Manya heard a whip whistle through the air and recoiled. She heard Meyer grunt from the blow and saw him fall.

A second guard took up the challenge. "I'll tell you what the filthy swine is doing here—he was trying to escape!" The whip zinged again and again. "You're too stupid to understand, aren't you? You won't believe that you can't escape! You were even dumb enough to come back to the camp! Do you think we can't count? You should have made a run for it, Jew-boy!" He punctuated each insult with another stroke from the whip; then the other guard joined in the assault, pummeling Meyer and kicking him. Over and over the lash cracked. Meyer writhed on the ground. Manya dropped to her knees at the sight, sobbing. The whip handle bashed into Meyer's head. Manya screamed.

"Get up!" the first guard bellowed. "Get up!"

Meyer groaned, but he hadn't heard the command. He lay in a heap, nearly unconscious.

"I said get up!" the guard repeated. "If you don't get up, you'll die right here!"

Manya crawled over to Meyer. Blood poured from his mouth and nose; his face was swollen and bruised. She tried to help him to his feet.

"Leave him alone!" spat the guard, waving his whip at Manya. "He is to get up by himself!" He shoved Manya aside.

Somehow Meyer dragged himself upright. The guards took them through the gates and in to an SS officer to explain themselves. Manya helped him along, wiped some of his blood away with her hand. He had a faraway look in his eyes, and he moved with great difficulty. They were in the officer's presence only briefly. It was apparent that the man was annoyed by the interruption and by the blood that dripped from Meyer's wounds. They were summarily dismissed and sent to their barracks without dinner.

For two weeks Meyer's friends did what they could to speed his healing. In the morning they pulled him out of bed when he begged to lie there. They shoved him to the front of the washroom line so that they could bathe his lash marks with cool water and rinse the blood and pus off his shirt. He leaned on them as they marched to work, and when they got there, they found a place for him to lie down while they worked. Then they helped him back to the camp at night.

When Manya told Tovah what had happened, she came to the rescue with extra bits of food from the camp kitchen. In the mornings before the count, in the usual commotion of getting to the latrine, Manya would move close to the fence between the men's and women's barracks. She made a pretense of dropping something or examining her shoe while she slid the food under the fence. Sometimes Adam was on the other side ready to scoop it up; sometimes it was Sol or Felix. A few times Meyer himself was there, especially when he had regained some strength. He had a different look about him, though. He had coped with death before, but this was as close as he had come to it himself. He was wrestling with an acknowledgment of his own mortality.

Before too long, however, he was sneaking to Manya's barracks again. It was a gradual process, starting with a hesitant "Maybe I'll come see you tonight." When Manya shook her head no, he seemed relieved and dropped the idea. Soon he didn't give up so easily when she told him it was too dangerous, and finally, as the lash marks faded, so did his reluctance to tempt fate.

The second time he picked his way across the compound to Manya, he appeared to be preoccupied and heard only half of what she was saying as they lay together.

"Meyer, something is bothering you. Tell me what it is—please!"

"It's nothing, really. It's just . . . There's something I want you to do for me—something I want you to promise."

"Of course—anything."

"I've been thinking," he continued, "if anything happens—I mean if we are ever separated—I want you to promise that you'll go back to Hrubieszow when all this is over. I'll meet you there. If for some reason you get there and don't find me, go to . . ." He paused, thinking of all the people who wouldn't be there: his family, Salki, maybe Gorski even. "Go to Josef. If I arrive before you, I'll leave word with him in case I cannot stay. You do the same. Do you promise?"

"To meet you in Hrubieszow?"

"Yes."

"I promise."

"And you'll remember to tell Josef where I can find you?"

"Yes, I'll tell Josef, but why—?"

Meyer waved off her question before she asked it. "Can you think of anyone else who will be there for sure?"

"No, I . . . I guess I can't," she replied, throwing her arms around him.

"We meet in Hrubieszow," he repeated.

"I promise," she whispered.

50

How many more people would she see die before it might be her turn? New faces, brought from overcrowded barracks to hers, replaced those who were killed or who simply never woke up. She was thankful that all her friends were still with her. She prayed to God every night to keep them alive and to watch over Meyer and his small group of friends. Her belief in God did not falter. No matter what else happened, she wouldn't give up her faith. Some of her friends couldn't understand it at times, especially when she picked a day to observe Yom Kippur. Tovah and Hannah tried to talk her out of it, told her it was foolish to fast, harmful to her health.

"God will understand," Tovah said.

It was true, God would forgive her if she let it pass, but she felt it was important, even though the time she picked to observe the Jewish Day of Atonement was a random choice. The Nazis could deny her almost everything else, but they couldn't stop this. Although it was a small thing that hurt only herself, it gave Manya control over something in her life. It reminded her she was still a human being.

So that day Manya had given her bread to Meyer, and her soup and coffee to her friends. She was glad to be able to give something back to Tovah, who so often risked her life by smuggling a little extra food from the kitchen to share with the girls. It was amazing how that tiny bit more made them feel so much better.

Time was a disorienting factor for the prisoners of Budzyn. Days flowed into weeks, weeks into months, under the rigid and endless routine, adding another dimension of futility to their existence. Each morning the siren growled its announcement of a new day. Manya opened her eyes.

She carefully tucked her diary into her thick hair, and wound a few locks around to hold it secure. For the past few months she had kept the precious pieces of paper with her at all times out of fear they might be discovered if she left them in her bunk. The Nazis had begun conducting surprise inspections, especially when the barracks were empty. Patting the knot of hair that hid the diary, she bent over and carefully picked up her bread, eating the small crumbs that fell off.

She walked outside with Tovah and the others to join the race for the latrine and to get their share of the muddy liquid for breakfast. But something was different. There was an extra contingent of guards outside. The count proceeded, but it took longer than usual. Manya kept looking for Meyer, hoping to see him before everyone went to work. But then something else caught her eye.

"Oh, my God! No! No! This can't be!" Manya croaked to Tovah. "Look!" she said, pointing to the front of the camp.

The gates were open and trucks were rumbling in.

"Please, God, not us," she pleaded.

Soldiers jumped from the back of each truck, taking their positions.

"Move to the trucks," an SS officer bellowed, motioning to the women's section.

The additional guards moved in and began pushing, shoving, and dragging women toward the waiting vehicles. People ran in every direction, but it was no good—they were surrounded. This time the gunshots were not just into the air. Manya saw someone fall. The trucks were filling; she was getting closer. Maybe there won't be enough room, Manya prayed. Still she got closer. Screaming and yelling saturated the air, husbands shouting to wives, sisters bawling for brothers, boyfriends yelling for girlfriends, and Manya crying out for Meyer. Arms flailed the air and bodies crunched together. Manya saw men being beaten by the Ukrainian guards. Finally she saw Meyer.

"Meyer! Meyer!" she screamed, throwing her arms out in a vain effort to feel him. "Please, God, *please!*"

She was thrown into the truck. She got up to look for him. He was still there, tears streaming down his face. She saw his lips moving, but she couldn't make out the words. With a jerk, the truck started forward. She leaned out, reaching, straining toward him, as a guard slapped her arms down again and again, and tried to stuff her back into the truck.

"I love you, Meyer. I'll meet you—"

The roar of the engine drowned out her final words.

The heat inside the cattle car was unbearable. They were packed in so tight they had to stand up or suffocate. Some were lucky enough to brace themselves against the sides of the car; the rest leaned heavily on each other. For hours and hours they were sealed up in this darkness with no food or water, little air to breathe, and no recourse but to relieve themselves where they stood.

Finally the train stopped and the door was hauled open. Pushing and clutching at the same time, their hands reached out to each other as they descended to the platform. A late February wind refreshed the sweltering prisoners with its first blast, then set them shivering as it turned their sweat-drenched uniforms to ice. They tried to circle around each other, backs to the wind, but orders barked them into lines and rifle butts cracked against ribs and heads to get them moving. Manya attached herself to Tovah and looked back to see that Hannah and Molly were following on their heels. The slush on the well-traveled road alongside the track was beginning to freeze as the temperature fell, but the tramping wooden shoes churned it to liquid again—liquid that spattered on the legs of those in front and into the faces of those behind.

They marched for several miles, slipping and sliding, splashing through chuckholes. They came to a farm and were prodded in its direction, then shoved headlong into a dark, drafty barn that offered little more room than the cattle cars they had just vacated. Manya and the girls curled up together, seeking warmth and comfort. They slid out of their shoes and rubbed some circulation back into their freezing feet. Each time they heard a sound outside, they looked toward the barn door, expecting at least a ration of water. But the door never opened, and no food or water appeared.

How long had they ridden? they asked each other. From sunup to sunset, someone replied. No, longer, insisted another woman, who had watched through the tiny window at the top of her car and had seen the daylight go to black, then dawn again. More than thirty-six hours it had taken them to get here, but where were they? In Poland? They weren't sure. Voices pushed through dry throats soon cracked, and it became too much of an effort to speak. They resorted to hoarse whispers, and finally fell silent.

Manya had never felt so alone in her life. At first she was ready to give up from the torture of being plucked from Meyer's side; then she was quickly consumed with fear. Stuffed tight into the cattle car, she had had no time or inclination to think. Now, in the crowded barn, Manya unleashed her thoughts of him. They warmed her numbness, poured into her emptiness, but stabbed at her ravenous emotions like heat on frostbitten skin.

She felt Tovah's arms tighten around her and heard her friend's gravelly voice. "Shhh, Manya, it's all right, don't cry. Just rest. There, that's better, rest now, shhh." There were no tears, no sound—just a body heaving violently as if it meant to vomit its heart.

They slept until they heard shouting and the barn doors swung wide. Water, they thought as they opened their eyes. "March!" the guards shouted, canceling their hope. The front of the line was on its way down the road before some of the barn's occupants were on their feet.

This time they trudged only a mile or two in the drizzly dawn. Manya could see the first rows of the column approaching a gate, watched a wave of uniformed prisoners surge toward the new-comers, heard the clamor of voices desperate to match a name. Ahead of her, Manya saw a chunk of the line break away and enter a barracks; then a second bunch peeled off toward another building.

"Where are we?" one of Manya's group called to an old-timer.

"Mielecz," the man yelled back.

"Mielecz," the woman repeated, "Mielecz . . . where?"

"Poland," came the reply.

Manya and her friends were herded toward a third one-story frame structure. There was a rush for bunks, but Manya and the girls were able to find room together. Manya was inspecting her bunk when she was seized with panic. The diary! Her hand shot to her matted coil of hair. The papers were still there, thank God! She hadn't given them a thought since leaving Budzyn. In a flash she wrenched them from her hair and slid them under the straw of the bunk.

A guard shouted for them to line up single file. They followed him to a large building and were handed, one by one, another striped dress, a cup, and a spoon. The shoes they had would not be replaced. They were ushered into a large room and told to strip off their ragged dresses and put on the new issue, as the Germans watched their humiliation. The guard pointed toward a door at the far end of the room. Again they were to assemble in a column in front of it. A few voices pleaded for water. The guard looked in their direction meaningfully, then turned his back on their request. Manya and her friends hurried into the clean garments. Perhaps it wouldn't be so bad here after all, she thought. They wouldn't be issued new clothes if they were going to die. Maybe, on the other side of that door, they would finally get something to drink and eat.

When Manya crossed the threshold, she peeked around one side, then the other, trying to see what was ahead. She got a glimpse of the corner of a table and the sleeve of a jacketed man sitting down. A few other officials bustled about behind him.

Even abreast of the table, she couldn't make out what was going on. A second man sat down and checked things off in a ledger. The man in the jacket appeared to be writing something very slowly, and each time he paused and raised his head, the line moved up one. Finally Manya was in front of him. Her eyes swept the equipment on the table. What was it?

"Hold out your hand," he growled.

Manya hesitated.

"Your hand, your hand," he said, pointing impatiently with an instrument.

She started to raise her right arm toward him, then changed her mind and held out her left.

"The other one," he instructed.

Her right hand moved toward him obediently.

He raised the instrument.

Manya looked away.

"Turn around," he said with a leer. "Watch!"

She met his eyes, then blinked to break his hold on her.

"Use your other hand to hold the skin," he instructed, demonstrating on his own arm. "Pull it tight."

With her left hand she pinched the skin together on the underside of her right wrist.

He pressed the instrument to her skin. A needle pierced the flesh and deposited a blob of blue.

She tried to hide her face in her chest.

"I said watch!" he yelled without looking up.

She obeyed, trying not to flinch as he used the needle like a sewing machine. Then it was over.

"Next!" he growled.

Manya cradled her hand as she moved away from the table toward another open door. Her arm throbbed and burned. Finally she held it up to look. In block letters she read the indelible mark: "KL."

Manya had been tattooed.

51

After eight or nine days, Meyer lost track of how long Manya had been gone. He knew it must be over a month, possibly closer to two. The image of her face and the arms she held out to him was vivid in his mind. She's strong. She can make it, he would say to himself. There was only one thing he must do: stay alive so he could be with her again.

Budzyn had gotten a hundred times more terrible since their arrival. The lice were everywhere. Not a day went by that they didn't have a sweeping of the lice. It was the first thing they did when they got out of bed. Each person would use his hands to brush the bugs off his arms and legs. Then they took turns with their bunkmates to sweep them off their backs. But there was no way to get rid of all them. Those brushed off in the morning attached themselves again at night.

The food had deteriorated, tasting more foul than ever. And beatings of prisoners had come more frequently and at the slightest justification. Deaths were no longer sporadic. But the Ukrainian guards were the worst, taking pleasure in the punishment they inflicted. Meyer couldn't understand this mad hatred the Ukrainians had for the Jews. Before the war, they had lived and worked in Hrubieszow with the Jews under tolerable conditions.

When the guards actually spoke to them, they would say things like, "This war is your fault. Now you're getting your just reward."

Or they would bait them with, "You should all go to Palestine, that's where you belong."

And someone would answer, "All right, let us out and we'll go."

But it was always the same sadistic response: "It's too late now. You're never leaving this place. You'll die here."

And so it went, day in and day out.

But not today. A large group was excluded from the count and led out to waiting trucks. Meyer looked to see if all his friends— Adam, Sol, Leon, Wolf, and Felix—had been chosen. For what, he didn't know. There was very little of the commotion that occurred when the women were taken. Their attitudes had changed and hardened over the months. They thought about themselves, staying alive, looking out for and helping those few people they were close to.

The ride on the trucks wasn't a long one. The canvas flaps at the rear were flipped up and the prisoners were ordered out. As soon as Meyer jumped down, there was a flashback to Hrubieszow. He saw the same train of boxcars, the same SS guards lined up along its length, Jews being forced in at gunpoint, packed like fish in a can. Was this what had happened to Manya?

Clang! Again the familiar sound of the lock securing its human cargo. They were being shipped somewhere else. They traveled on and on, standing shoulder to shoulder with no food or water. It was cold outside, but the temperature in the cattle car rose steadily until it was almost unbearable. For some it was too much and they either passed out or passed away. The train made numerous stops, but the doors were never opened.

Then it slowed again, slamming the occupants against each other as it came to a halt. The door slid open and the command of "Raus! Raus!" was screamed in front of each car. It was all too familiar: SS guards, pointed guns, snarling dogs, and "March! March!"

They were at another camp. The guards led them to barracks. This camp was much smaller than Budzyn, but inside, the environment was the same. Watchtowers, guards, electric fences, and identical bunks. Adam and Meyer again teamed up to share a bed. They waited in the barracks until the call for dinner came.

Meyer hoped for something different to eat and more of it, but he was disappointed. After his first taste he would have preferred even the slop they served at Budzyn.

Maybe Manya made a stop here, Meyer thought as he lay in bed. No, there were just too many other places she could have been sent. Wherever you are, Manya, I love you.

The siren sounded, rousing him from sleep. What would today be like? The new arrivals were led away to a large building, similar to the one at Budzyn. Once inside, they went through the same procedure: strip naked, take freezing shower, get issue of striped clothes, have head shaved. But this time there was an additional room. It was bare except for six small tables, each with a chair on either side. Half of the chairs were occupied by SS guards, each holding some kind of pencil instrument in his hand. Meyer and the others were ordered to make rows behind each vacant chair. He couldn't imagine what was going to happen. Everyone's eyes watched as the first six people took their places in the chairs.

"My God! They're tattooing us!" someone whispered.

Meyer couldn't believe his eyes or ears. Why are they doing this? If he hadn't been convinced before, this confirmed it. The bastards really do think we are animals. We're being branded like cattle.

It was Meyer's turn; he slowly sat down.

"Hold out your right hand, palm down. Now grab the skin underneath with your other hand and pull it as tight as you can," he was instructed.

The needle pierced his skin in rapid succession. It stung and burned. He watched as the blue ink began to form a letter.

Please hurry . . . get this over with, his mind screamed.

K

Meyer started to pull his wrist away.

"I'm not finished! Stick your wrist back out!"

Again the sharp stings and the burning feeling.

L

"Now I'm finished," he was told with a smile.

Meyer got up and rubbed his wrist in an effort to wipe it off before it dried. But it was on for good.

They were all taken back to the barracks, lined up, and counted; then an SS officer addressed them: "Tomorrow you will begin work. You'll be taken out of the camp to a factory, where you'll be instructed in how to make parts for airplanes. I advise you all to do the best you possibly can. If you don't, what happens to you will be your fault, not mine."

He turned and left. The prisoners were ordered into the barracks.

"Do you know where we are?" Meyer asked a group of people.

"A place called Mielecz," someone answered.

52

The Germans issued them light jackets during inclement months, but they offered little warmth. Many women succumbed to the weather. Manya didn't know how she escaped frostbite. They were given no gloves or socks. The most horrible part was the lineup every morning and night to be counted. They just stood there as the guards, dressed in gloves, boots, and heavy coats, slowly made their way up and down the rows. The Nazis would take their time, sometimes mess up the count on purpose so they had to start over.

The morning counts were always the worst. Although the barracks weren't heated, they at least gave protection from the biting wind. In addition, three, sometimes four girls would crawl into one bed together to generate as much heat as possible. But the small amount of warmth accumulated during the night soon dissipated with the first few steps on the snow-covered ground. There was nothing to prevent the slushy substance from entering their shoes. Starting with the bottoms of their feet as they walked, moving through the toes to the ankles, chills raced up their bodies and met shivers coming from the other end as the frigid wind traveled over fingers, wrists, and arms.

The lucky ones worked in unheated factories. Manya's group worked mostly outside. By the time they lined up for the evening count, their bodies were like icicles. They knew they had hands and feet because they could see them, but they couldn't feel them. When they finally got back to the barracks, they took turns rubbing each other's extremities to get the circulation going again. For some there was no strength left for the exercise, and it was over.

But the bitter winter days with piles of snow and freezing rain had come and gone. If she could get through that, Manya thought, she could survive anything. Every day she would think about Meyer's warm touch on her face, on her body. As each day passed, she was that much closer to being back in his arms. Like an assignment by a teacher to write a phrase on the blackboard so many times, Manya repeated over and over to herself: "I'll make it. Meyer will be waiting."

Manya tried to calculate how long she had been in the camps. She knew that they'd been taken from Hrubieszow in late August—no, it was September. They had seen the fall, winter, and some of the spring. It was warm outside when they jumped off the train at the next camp. The sun was bright and the ground along their path was green. It must be almost summer—how many months without Meyer? What difference did it make? There was only one thing that mattered—to make sure she survived this day so there would be a tomorrow.

As they neared the camp, Manya wondered if it would be any different here—better or worse.

"Manya, look how big this place is!" Tovah whispered to her.

It was enormous compared to Budzyn and Mielecz. There were buildings and fences as far as her eyes could see. The sheer size made Manya feel more insignificant and frightened than ever. And there were thousands and thousands of women. They all looked the same with their identical clothes, haggard and worn faces, and skeletonlike bodies.

Manya and her small group of friends stayed close together, not wanting to be separated when they were assigned to barracks. But this time when they walked in to choose bunks, there was a difference—people were already inside. They gathered around the new arrivals, throwing out questions and making introductions.

"Where did you come from?"

"Mielecz."

"How long were you there?"

"We have no idea. Maybe two months."

"What was it like there?"

"Horrible, but much smaller."

Manya and the others who had just entered reciprocated with their own questions and names.

"What's it like here?"

"The worst possible thing you can imagine."

"How long have you been here?"

"Over a year."

"Where are we?"

"In Plaszow."

"Where's that?"

"In Poland."

Some of the women showed the new ones where the empty bunks were, but most stayed together, passing on what information they knew. It was very dimly lit inside, but Manya noticed a tiny girl standing in the very back with a small round face and beautiful eyes that begged to be talked to.

"Oh, my God!" Manya screamed, the tears pouring from her eyes. "Make it be true, God! Yes! Yes!"

She ran to the little girl, her arms opened wide. "Oh Cyvia! Cyvia, you're alive!"

It was Meyer's youngest sister.

53

Wielczka. It was a name he was sure he'd heard before, most likely during his days as a fugitive. It was near Krakow, he thought—yes, he was sure it was near Krakow. He tried to think how long ago that had been. It was summertime when he'd given up running to return to the ghetto, and he'd been there only a couple of months before he was deported to Budzyn. There he had spent the winter, and just before spring was transferred to Mielecz. Now it was summer again and he had arrived in Wielczka less than a week ago. That would make it nearly a year inside these cursed fences.

It had been months since he had watched Manya reaching to

him from the truck that carried her away. He didn't think about her often anymore. Perhaps it was because he couldn't conjure up positive images about where she was and what was happening to her. Helpless to protect her, he rejected the idea of pasting her face on the skin-headed female figures he'd seen hauling rocks, favoring an untended broken bone or nursing the wounds from their latest beating. Given that alternative, he preferred to picture her face as he'd last seen it, anguished though it was. But mostly he kept the thought of her locked away, to be taken out and savored only when he doubted he could go on. On those occasions he breathed as deeply of her as he did the outside air when he left the dank salt mines he worked in ten hours a day.

There were about one thousand men on his shift; another thousand took up where his group left off. Other work details marched in a different direction. What chores they performed, he didn't know. It was a thirty-minute walk from the camp to the mines. Well, not a walk exactly; the pace was fast.

He felt lucky that his friends from Budzyn were still with him. Sol, Felix, Adam, Wolf, Leon, and he shared the same barracks and occupied neighboring bunks. They were friends, but not confidants; close, but not intimate. There was an unspoken but generally acknowledged barrier they erected around themselves, a fragile shell that encased their individuality and insulated each from the predictable loss of the other. But the pattern was not unique. There were hundreds of similarly guarded groups of friends in every barracks.

Meyer remembered the first time he entered the mines to work. The candles burning inside cast an eerie glow that flickered with the draft created by the passing workers. The walls of the cave glistened with sweat that ran to the floor and made shallow puddles. The abundance of moisture made it difficult for him to breathe, and he had to adopt a rhythm of working that would allow him to progress with his task but that wouldn't wear him out too soon.

Tools were distributed at the start of each shift and collected when it was time to return to camp. They were meticulously accounted for. Perhaps that was why the shifts lasted ten hours instead of twelve. It took a long time to equip and unequip the workers.

Meyer's job was to chip out blocks of salt; others sacked it, still others loaded it on little trams that carried it away. A whistle blast announced the twenty-minute lunch break, then sounded again to repeal the freedom. The workers filed back to the cave as another prison crew loaded the empty soup kettles on a wagon. Meyer didn't know any of those men, had no way to garner extra food. But he never saw those soup kettles without thinking of Tovah. He hoped she was still with Manya, taking care of her and somehow continuing to supplement the diet that barely sustained life. The soup was wet, sometimes spoiled; the bread was dry, sometimes moldy. But it was something to swallow.

Meyer's three transfers to camps had all been conducted in the same manner: a truck ride to the train, hours or days in a boxcar, then disembarkation on a siding, and a march to the gates of the camp. As they entered, it was always the same, too: wild-eyed shadows of humanity pressed against the barbed wire of inner enclosures, shouting or croaking names of loved ones. By the time he reached the gates of Wielczka, he knew the routine.

"Korenblit!" he yelled. "Korenblit!" His eyes scanned the crowd; his ears tuned in the chorus that answered him.

"Korenblit!" he tried again.

A voice screeched "Kor . . ." and he stiffened. But it finished with ". . . man!" He wrapped another layer of rationalization around himself. Then he let a precious corner of his mind come to life. He searched the faces again. Hands reached through the wires. Of course—he'd know them anywhere! He panned the length of the fence. There were so many.

Then he said it, softly at first, powerfully the second time, as the dose of Manya took hold.

"Nagelsztajn! *Nagelsztajn!*"

There was no answer.

54

Cyvia's face danced with delight when she recognized Manya. The two girls fell into each other's arms. She dug her fingers into Manya's shoulders, clamping on for dear life. The tears of joy didn't escape the others, and they joined the happy reunion.

Manya looked at the diminutive figure whose tiny hands clutched her like a vise. There was no hair, only scabs over her entire head. The Nazis had obviously shaved her in an attempt to get rid of the lice. Poor Cyvia had scratched and clawed herself raw. There were bites all over her skinny body as well. Manya had seen starving dogs who looked better than Cyvia. That she could still be alive was a miracle.

The happiness of finding Cyvia had long since expired. How many weeks had elapsed was a lost memory. That first night, Manya told Cyvia the whole story of what had happened to Meyer, Chaim, and herself after they left the haystack. The story conjured up sad and horrible memories for the older girl, but just the mention of Meyer's name had given Cyvia more energy and more hope. She wanted to hear about Meyer over and over again. If there was one thing that hadn't changed about Meyer's sister, it was her inquisitiveness.

As Cyvia lay sleeping next to her, Manya fumbled through the straw for the diary. A soft glow sifted through the windows from the floodlamp outside the barracks, and gave her barely enough light to read and write. As she looked over the words on the torn pieces of paper, she started her mental monologue.

Dear Diary:

Cyvia is much better, but what a painful experience to go through. Thank goodness my friends were here to help. Every night I cleaned her scalp. At first I tore little bits of my dress or Cyvia's, and then others donated scraps, and we managed to get a small amount of water. Very gently I dabbed the sores with a piece of wet cloth. The most difficult thing physically and the hardest emotionally was to keep her from scratching after it was clean. I would hold on to those hands that so desperately wanted to attack the unbearable itching. Then I listened to her moans turn to whimpers and whimpers to cries at being unable to relieve the pain from her throbbing head, and finally she fell asleep, exhausted from the struggle.

Cyvia hasn't said anything about what happened to her mother and sisters. She probably just blanked it out of her mind. I can't bear to think of her living with all that darkness inside, but I can't bring myself to ask her about it. Maybe she'll tell me in time.

For the first few weeks the extra food Tovah sneaked into

the barracks was given to Cyvia in an attempt to get her strength back. Yes, somehow Tovah was again assigned to kitchen detail. Now Cyvia's hair is growing out and I can see the tiniest touch of color returning to her face.

I met a new friend, Marie Gaitler. She is a wonderful person and we have become close. She has a boyfriend here and occasionally I sneak off with her to see him. Now I know how the other girls at Budzyn felt about Meyer and me—happy we had one another, but a bit envious. I long for Meyer's touch, his closeness, his companionship. The feeling grows even stronger when I see Marie and Herman together—just as others must have felt when they saw Meyer and me.

Manya moved her head to a different position on the wooden clogs. Yes, she wouldn't want to leave that out of her diary.

One morning I woke up to find that someone had stolen my right shoe. I was so mad—mad to have to walk to the fields with one foot bare, and mad to think that one of us would do such a thing to another. But then I calmed down. We have to take care of ourselves, and that's what that person was doing. The other girls urged me to do the same.

"You have to, Manya. You can't walk around like that. What if you get cut?" Hannah said.

"I can't, it's not right!" I argued.

"Was it right for someone to take yours?"

So I gave in and that night took—no, stole—one for myself. Unfortunately, things have a way of getting even with you. I now have two left shoes.

There are two very sick girls in our barracks. They have no strength to go on. They told us to just let them die. But instead my friends and I helped them up for roll call, then sneaked them back to the barracks. Tovah stole food from the kitchen and we shared our own rations with the pair. It has been a couple of days, and they're getting better. I think they want to live now.

One thing that's different at Plaszow is Sunday—at least they tell us it's Sunday. We're allowed to wash our dresses. There's not enough water for ourselves, just for our clothes. They tell us we have our chance to wash in the mornings. So they stand there and watch to make sure no water is used for any other purpose. Even if we could get away with it, we'd be denying the person next in line the water to wash her dress. They don't add to or change the water very often. We take our dresses off and rinse them in the basin, then wring them out and put them back on wet. The first time, it was so degrading standing there naked. The next time, I didn't think about it so much. I just told myself everyone is doing it. At least my dress is clean. The summer heat dries it quickly, but for a few minutes the cool cloth refreshes my body.

That's what she would have written about her time in this camp if there had been ample paper, but instead were the words: "Cyvia, joy, horrible condition, no hair, Cyvia better, new friend, replaced shoe, washed dress, farmwork."

Manya rolled the paper around the pencil and carefully tucked it into her hair, slowly closed her eyes, and drifted off to sleep.

The next morning, she was standing in line for the count, Marie on one side and Cyvia on the other, with the rest of her friends close by. The count was over, but no order was given for their release to work. The SS officers walked along the lines. They looked at each person, pointing to some and passing others.

"What are they doing, Marie?" Manya whispered to her friend.

"They're searching for the most unhealthy to send away."

"Send where?"

"We don't know. But we never see them again."

Manya eyed all the women around her. Did any of them really look any better or worse than anyone else? she thought to herself.

"Listen to me, Manya. When they get closer to us, I want you to pinch your cheeks as hard as you can. No matter how much it hurts," Marie instructed.

"But why?"

"To get as much color into them as you can. If you have any color they'll just pass by. I'll tell the others on my side, and you do the same on yours."

When the SS in the row in front of them turned their backs, Manya and the others grabbed their cheeks and pinched hard. Manya squeezed with such force that she almost cried out, but she had to do it. The self-inflicted pain could mean her survival.

"Please, God, make the color stay, please," Manya begged.

The SS inspector stood in front of her, his steel-like eyes examining every inch of her body. She waited for his hand to point at her, to select her as one of the unhealthy. Then it would be over once and for all.

Slowly he moved to the next in line.

55

The trip had taken four days this time, or so he thought. How could he judge for sure, cooped up like that? But the patchy stubble on his eighteen-year-old face had pushed out of his pores a little farther, and his body clock was becoming more and more reliable, so he guessed he was close to right anyway. He'd try to catch a glimpse of the moon tonight—it would be another clue.

They'd been given food for the journey before they were loaded into the cars. That told Meyer one thing for sure: the Germans meant to keep their prisoners alive—perhaps only barely, but alive nevertheless.

Events along the way had followed the predictable pattern, but as Meyer marched down the road and looked at the camp up ahead, he saw something he'd never seen before: smoke. Thick columns of it grew in the distant air. He couldn't imagine why fires were necessary on such a hot day.

Crossing the compound, Meyer was eventually able to question an inmate and was told that the camp was called Flossenburg. The verbal exchange was cut short by an impatient guard, preventing Meyer from asking the location of Flossenburg. It wasn't a Polish name, so it couldn't be in Poland. That and the long trip meant that it had to be in another country. It was at dinner that someone told him he was in Germany.

He was startled by the condition of the camp. The grounds were tended and very clean. In the barracks the bunks were covered with straw-filled mattresses instead of loose hay. The inmates were still assigned two to a bunk, but Meyer felt the promise of more comfort. It looked like a large camp, but how large, he couldn't tell. The boundaries of the fences were hidden for the most part by groves of trees, which in turn were ringed by mountains.

They queued for an inspection, a shower, a new set of clothes. Heads and faces were shaved; a tin cup and a spoon completed the routine. The morning air was crisp and clean despite the season. As the day got older, though, the sun beat down on them and the temperature soared; they sweltered.

On the second morning they rose, fought for the latrine, were counted, and then set off for work with the usual, unvarying procedure.

They walked a great distance, and Meyer looked from side to side, trying to get oriented. They should have reached the main gate by now; surely he couldn't have missed it. Yet still they trudged on in the cold morning, and still there was no fence to give him his bearings. My God, he thought finally, we must still be *inside*! There were watchtowers and checkpoints sprinkled along the way. Wherever he looked, he saw buildings. This place was enormous!

The dirt road they followed went into an incline and began to curve around, and back, then around again. They were on the slope of a mountain. A short time later they stopped. The group was circled and given instructions. As the guard spoke, Meyer surveyed the area. The trees were abundant below him, farther apart on his level, thinner and skinnier above the clearing where he stood. There were piles of rock everywhere and one or two low-lying buildings several hundred yards to his right. As he looked up, the mountain was bare and concave, its white face misshapen and jagged. He saw some soldiers busy at one side of the gutted area. They appeared to be making holes in the rock. Spools of wire lay at their feet.

". . . the stone quarry for buildings and roads," Meyer heard an officer say. He should have been listening more carefully.

". . . explosives, and loosen the rock," the officer continued. Damn, he had missed it again! If he didn't pull himself together, he wouldn't know what to do.

". . . over there," the officer finished.

Where? Meyer yelled in his head, waiting for someone in his group to lead the way. But no one moved in a constructive direction; in fact, they tightened the circle and retreated a few steps. What the hell was going on? Meyer's darting eyes asked. He saw the soldiers pick up the wire and attach it to the mountain. They jogged backward on the slope, unraveling the wire as they went.

Meyer saw a kneeled conference behind a fortified area, then heard an "all-clear" shout. The group of prisoners again shied away.

An explosion shattered the air and a chunk of the mountain collapsed; rocks and debris showered the unprotected prisoners. An order put them into action. Meyer took his cue from the others. Some scooped up canvas bags and bent over to fill them with broken rock; some stooped to hoist the larger slabs.

"Schnell! Schnell!" the guards screamed at the struggling workers. Whips cracked in the air.

"Do it yourselves if you can go faster," Meyer muttered. Already his shirt was drenched with sweat, and the sun was barely an hour old.

It seemed forever before the whistles blew and they staggered away from the mountain. As they got closer, Meyer again saw smoke climbing into the darkening sky. Later, in the barracks, Meyer talked to Felix: "So, I've told you about me—what kind of work did you do today?"

"The same, Meyer, everywhere I've been, it's the same," Felix replied.

"Planes?" Meyer asked incredulously. "There's a plane factory here?"

"Oh, yes."

"But where?"

"In a mountain."

"The factory is *in* the mountain?"

"That's right. There's a long tunnel, and the factory is at the end of it. We're making parts for airplanes, drilling holes for the rivets, *you* know. It's a pretty big place, too, and they're making it bigger every day. Another crew digs it out and loads the dirt in a string of tram cars that carry it to the outside."

"Do you realize how big this camp is?" asked Meyer, changing the subject. "It's huge!"

"I'll tell you something else—the prisoners here aren't only Jews. Some of them are here because they were caught helping Jews. There are Polish and Russian prisoners of war, Germans and Austrians who were labeled as traitors."

They continued to compare notes, but Meyer was still preoccupied with Felix's announcement about the plane factory. Not only was the stone quarry within the limits of the camp, but so was a plane factory—and both were in the mountains. He wondered if every mountain in his view housed its own industry. The size of the operation was staggering and depressing.

Some weeks later, Meyer's group felt the impact of death. It had hovered all around them for months, but for the first time it reached out and snatched one of Meyer's friends—Leon, who was led away to be executed. His death forced them to recognize that their circle was not impenetrable after all. But Meyer grieved for more than a cherished friend. Leon and Meyer had been together since the ghetto. He was a link with Manya. When Meyer lost Leon, he lost a little of Manya, too.

About a month later, Meyer was given a new work assignment. He knew, not because it was explained to him, but because he was steered to a different route—one that led past the barracks area to the other side of the main compound. Again he saw the smoke; his nose picked up an odor, a hint of which had hung in the air since his arrival. They got closer, and the smell intensified. He was finally going to see what the fires were for.

He looked at the crew that marched with him. Some were as curious as he, but most stared blankly ahead. Meyer's eyes moved to the trail of reeking vapor and tracked it downward. There, on his left, he saw naked bodies in a huge pile. They were on fire.

56

Death and deportation had become as routine as the roll calls, the tasteless, miserly amounts of food, the long hours of hard work, the short time of restful sleep. They awoke to the next day thankful only to be living rather than dead. Manya's hope of survival didn't diminish, but frequently it faltered. Then her thoughts would turn to Meyer, to the day she would meet him at home in Hrubieszow. How happy he would be to see her standing there, hand in hand with little Cyvia. If only there were a way she could let him know that his youngest sister was alive. She prayed to God to give him a sign. The smallest bit of information gave a person the added incentive to make it through another twenty-four hours. Manya knew Meyer would never give up, but his impulsiveness frightened her. She wasn't near him to act as a stabilizing force.

With Cyvia near, Manya felt especially close to Meyer. Every time she looked at his sister, she saw him. Cyvia was a link with the past who could talk about and listen with affection to stories of the wonderful days before the war. It was almost like talking to Meyer.

Manya stood for roll call. The count had been completed but the usual selection of the unhealthy seemed to be delayed. The SS officers weren't taking their daily walk along the lines. The girls pinched their cheeks just as they had done every time they expected a selection. The longer they waited, the more they pinched. Tovah had done it so hard and so often that there was a spidery blotch on her cheek from an injured vein.

Still they stood, and the Nazis continued to watch over them. More guards arrived.

"Manya, something is terribly wrong," Marie said.

"Maybe they're going to kill us all," Hannah exclaimed.

"Shh! They can't kill everyone. There are over twenty thousand people here," Tovah tried to reassure her.

But Manya wasn't sure. The Nazis had proved over and over again that they were capable of anything. Was killing twenty thousand people any different to these butchers from murdering a single person or one hundred?

"Maybe they're just going to send us away," Manya said, trying to convince herself as much as Hannah and the others.

The thought of another camp terrified her. Here she was familiar with the procedures. She knew what to avoid and how to get away with little things that kept the spirit if not the body going. Here Tovah was able to supply the much-needed extra bits of food. What if she wasn't assigned to kitchen duty the next time? They all depended upon and helped each other. Each of them had times when she was ready to give up. But the prodding and encouragement of the others would pull that person through. What if one of them was left behind?

The noise they all feared, the roar of engines, could now be heard. Apparently the Nazis intended to take a lot of people out this time. As the guards began to move in, Manya reached down and grabbed Cyvia's hand.

"When they start, we're going to run, Cyvia. Just follow me," Manya instructed.

The gunfire and screams started at the same time. Other people took off. Manya turned, jerked Cyvia by the hand, and ran. Tovah and the others were close behind. People scattered in every direction. More shots rang out. Manya let go of Cyvia's hand to help maneuver them through the scrambling people. Manya and Tovah were side by side. Their hearts pounded, their legs churned. Neither looked back. More shooting. They could hear bullets fly over their heads and saw their impact on the ground around them. The barracks were just ahead. They could hide there until it was over. They got closer. The screams were louder. Manya tried to block them out. She didn't want to hear them. They meant death. Don't look back.

"We're almost there, Cyvia! Hurry!"

Only a few more steps. Manya's chest was ready to burst open. The barracks were directly in front of them. They made it. Manya got down on her stomach and crawled under. "Hurry or they'll see us!" she yelled.

There was just enough room between the ground and the building for their bodies to squeeze through. Had anyone seen them? The gunfire continued. Manya breathed in sporadic gulps, and she could hear the others trying to get their wind back. They were all there. Tovah, Hannah, Cyvia . . .

"Cyvia, where are you?" Manya whispered.

There was no answer. "Cyvia!" Manya yelled.

"Manya, not so loud, someone will hear you!"

"But where's Cyvia? She was right behind me!"

They scooted themselves farther back under the building and waited. Time passed very slowly as Manya wrestled with the impulse to get out and find Cyvia. How could she have left her out there? But Manya had been so sure that Cyvia was right behind her.

"Oh, my God, please keep her safe," Manya implored.

She tried to look for Meyer's sister in the chaos they had just escaped. There was no sign of her. She had slipped through Manya's fingers and disappeared. Why hadn't she looked back? her conscience asked. Because you don't look back, she answered, you just run.

Suddenly she saw black boots run by, then heard heavy footsteps pound the wooden floor above her head. The Nazis were searching the barracks. Would they look under the building? The girls held their collective breath. The guards came out empty-handed. Manya could tell there was still a lot of commotion in the camp. They waited about an hour, then heard more footsteps. These didn't sound like heavy boots; instead, they heard the familiar scuffling of wooden clogs.

"I think it's over. They've let some come back to the barracks," Tovah said.

"Maybe we should go out," Hannah added.

But no one wanted to be the first to go. Finally they crawled out together and quietly stole their way inside. The girls in the barracks warned them to go back to their own building.

"What happened out there?" Hannah asked.

"They took thousands away. It was terrible!"

"Was anyone killed?" Manya asked.

"Yes, some were, when everyone started running."

Manya's heart sank. She felt sick. Tovah put her arm around Manya and led her out the door. "Maybe Cyvia's back at our barracks."

But when they returned, there was no Cyvia.

"She was probably taken with the others, Manya. She'll be all right," Tovah said, trying to console her.

Manya hoped her friend was right. There was no way she would ever know. Even if Cyvia wasn't killed, Manya knew one thing to be true: she had lost Meyer's sister, just as she had lost her own brother, Chaim.

Manya now prayed that God would spare Meyer the knowledge that he had lost his little Cyvia again.

57

When Meyer was transferred from the stone quarry, he was taken to the mountain Felix had described to him a few weeks before. Not only was his assignment changed, but his shift was also, and now Meyer worked nights.

At about the same time, word had gone out that the SS wanted volunteers for kitchen duty. Meyer was in the right place at the right time and was one of a few who landed the job. Even though it would mean a double shift of work, he considered himself lucky to have the chance. He decided it was well worth the loss of sleep. He would make do with four or five hours.

The camp kitchen was hot, the Jewish workers were kept busy chunking vegetables and tending kettles under the watchful eyes of the Nazi guards who directed them. The mandated procedure didn't allow for removing dirt caked on beets and carrots, but the Jews rubbed it off on their clothes when the Nazis glanced away. Nor did it provide for paring away rotten sections of potatoes and turnips—as often as possible the prisoners hid the spoiled pieces when the collection buckets were passed.

Meyer's job was to fill the huge kettles with water and hoist them to the surface of the wood-burning stove, ready to receive the scanty cubes that would do no more than cloud its clarity. If they could have managed it, the inmates would have salted the pots with extra ingredients, but the supply for each meal was allotted grudgingly by the guards who held the key to the storehouse.

The kitchen workers didn't take their meals at work. They lined up the same as the rest of the striped crowd. But somehow handling the food was a step toward satisfying their hunger, and the morsels they popped secretly into their mouths and pockets helped, too.

Meyer went directly from his eight-hour shift in the kitchen to dinner, then assembled with another work group for his night shift at the plane factory. At first Meyer worked at making parts for Messerschmitts. Then he was put to enlarging the underground area to allow for expansion of the factory. Sometimes he wielded a pickax for twelve hours; other times he shoveled dirt and rock into the tram cars. When the whistle announced the end of the shift the next morning, Meyer dragged back to camp. The only thing that kept him going was the thought of the lone slice of carrot he might be lucky enough to purloin in the kitchen after his four-hour nap.

One night, as his group stood ready to enter the tunnel, the SS asked if anyone knew how to drive—they needed someone to operate the tram. Meyer's hand went up and caught the attention of the officer in charge. What are you doing? asked Meyer's conscience. You don't know how to drive! The officer took a few steps in Meyer's direction. I can figure it out, Meyer countered to himself. It looks a lot easier than hollowing out the whole damn mountain. The SS beckoned to Meyer. You're really in for it now, the conscience predicted. They'll see immediately that you don't know the first thing about driving! Meyer stepped away from the group. I can do it, he said, silencing the voice in his head and following the uniform to the head of the string of cars.

The explanation of the controls was confusing and peppered with "of courses" and "you knows." Meyer didn't know, of course, but he nodded and muttered a few "of courses" of his own to be convincing, while his eyes and ears drank in the steps of operation. The officer gestured toward the driver's seat. Meyer climbed aboard clumsily, if a bit uncertainly. The instructor eyed him. There was a false start or two—a matter of reverse and forward—but in a moment Meyer had it figured out and was waved inside the tunnel. Whining along one of the two tracks, Meyer averted his eyes from those whose task he'd no longer share, but refrained from looking too pleased with himself. He knew very well that the next week, the next day, even the next hour could find him back swinging a pick.

Meyer thought that the less-strenuous job of manning the tram would make it easier for him to continue working a double shift. But as attractive as the motorman's position was, it proved tedious and lonely. Back and forth, in and out he went, twelve hours a night, waiting inside for the cars to be loaded, and outside for them to be emptied. And when he chugged out of the continuously lengthening tunnel, there was no glare of sunlight to snap him out of his dreamy state. It was a job that exaggerated his fatigue.

It was probably his twelfth trip out of the tunnel one night when it happened. Everything had been routine: the humming of the tram's motor, the far-off grinding of drills biting into metal down another cavern, the chunk-chunk-chunk of the excavators deep within the shaft muting as the car moved away. But in a flash, a different set of sounds bombarded his ears. First a crash, then shouts, then a whirring of free-spinning wheels, a revving engine, and more shouts. He opened his eyes. He was lying on the ground. He looked at the tram. It had derailed. He reached to the controls and pulled the throttle to neutral. The revving stopped, the wheels slowed, the shouting got louder. He was frantic for an explanation. There was only one: he had fallen asleep and failed to apply the brakes at the unloading dock. The tram had run right off the end of the track.

An SS pulled Meyer to his feet and punched him viciously. He called the foreman, who slapped Meyer around some more and screamed at him to explain the accident. Meyer threw up his arms to fend off the blows, but the rhythm of his defensive maneuvers was off, and he failed to anticipate where the fists would land next. Finally the man shook Meyer from side to side, again demanding to know the boy's excuse.

"The brakes," Meyer stammered, "they didn't work."

"This is the first time all night that you used the brakes?" the man asked sarcastically.

"No, but they didn't work this time."

The foreman made no comment as he shoved Meyer to the ground and bent over to inspect the tram. Just as interested, an SS major had watched Meyer's beating. Two SS latched onto Meyer and hauled him to the foreman's office. Two more came in, and the four of them set upon Meyer again. They called him a son-of-a-bitch Jew and a swine. They said he had sabotaged the operation and they were going to shoot him like a dog, but first they were going to beat him so badly he would pray to die. They left him to bleed on the floor and walked out.

A few minutes passed and another SS entered the room. He told Meyer to take his clothes off. Meyer pulled himself over to a wall and used it as support while he painfully got out of his shirt. Apparently he took too long to undress, for the German raised his whip before Meyer could pull off his pants. Meyer rolled on the floor as thirty lashes were delivered, his fingers clawing the walls, his feet executing a slippery crawl away from the singing whip. He raised up only to be cut down again. His head crashed against a wall as he fell. He was ready to die as the bastards had predicted. Then, seeing the boy was nearly senseless, the officer slammed him in the face with his leather gloves and stomped out of the room.

Meyer was in a heap in the corner. Manya . . . His mind called to her. Manya. But she wasn't there to help him get up this time. Yet it seemed . . . yes, he could see her face—perhaps she was with him after all. He tried to look around, but the room was spinning. She appeared, was lost, appeared again, then faded away. He leaned on the thought of her, but couldn't get up.

The major entered the room and sat down at the desk. He swung his squeaky chair around to stare at Meyer. Meyer looked back at him through foggy eyes, waiting for the German to speak.

"You lied to the foreman," he said in a low voice. "There was nothing wrong with the brakes—I checked them myself."

Meyer's eyes dropped to the jagged SS insignia on the man's collar. He didn't know what to say if he could speak at all. "The brakes . . ." he managed to mumble.

"No, not the brakes—there's nothing wrong with the brakes. Why don't you tell me what really happened?"

The major's voice was calm, sympathetic even. It invited Meyer's confidence. Could he trust the officer? Probably not.

The hesitation brought another question from the major: "What do you do when you leave here in the morning? Do you go back and clean up and go to sleep like you're supposed to?"

Meyer eyed the questioner.

"Well?"

"Yes—mostly."

"Either you do or you don't—give me a straight answer. Do you return to your barracks and sleep until it's time to go to work again?"

What the hell difference would it make for Meyer to tell him? Could they kill him twice?

"No."

"No! What do you do, then? You can't work if you don't sleep!"

"I take a nap, but . . . well, I work in the kitchen during the day."

"But why? Don't you work hard enough already?"

"The food," Meyer explained. "I . . . The food."

The major was quiet; then he sighed. "So what really happened tonight?"

"I fell asleep," Meyer began weakly. "I've been working two shifts for quite a while now. I guess it was too much."

"You lied to me when I asked you the first time."

Meyer didn't respond.

"You lied to me, and I lied for you. I told my staff that the brakes were faulty. I'm going to save your life—or what's left of it."

There was another awkward silence as Meyer tried to believe his ears. The major looked at him expectantly.

"Danke schön, Herr Oberführer, danke schön," Meyer whispered in the fragile air.

"You can thank me by not letting it happen again."

"Yes, Herr Oberführer, thank you."

"I won't be able to help you again," he warned. "I shouldn't this time. You'd better give up the kitchen work."

"Yes, Herr Oberführer."

"No more kitchen," he repeated to be sure.

"Yes, Herr Oberführer."

"The shift is almost over. I'll see you tomorrow night, if you don't die on me. Get out of here now," he said, swinging his chair around to his desk.

Meyer got to his knees and picked up his shirt. He pulled himself up the wall and limped toward the door. As he opened it, the major spoke again. "You forgot your shoes."

58

Which would happen first—no more paper to write on, the war would come to an end, or she would . . . ? Manya didn't complete the thought. Many of the torn sheets had been filled. Each sentence fragment, every word, had meaning. She wouldn't forget the interpretation of a single one when she explained them to Meyer. His name rarely appeared. If there was anything she didn't need to write down, it was his name. Not a day went by when her thoughts didn't turn to him. It was his image that kept her going from day to day.

The conditions at Plaszow were deteriorating rapidly. Food had become worse and less, if that was possible, the work harder, the hours longer. More and more people were sent out, endless others brought in to replace them.

She unrolled the diary and read the words: "chosen, not taken." Manya and her friends had been lucky that day. All of them had been picked for the deportation. There was nowhere to run this time, the Nazis had surrounded them. Truck after truck was packed. Step by step, inch by inch, they moved closer to the vehicles that would take them to an unknown destination—death at worst, another hellhole at best. But they were all together—all but Cyvia, who had preceded them to one of the possible solutions.

They stood behind the final truck. It was half-loaded. They moved closer. There were five women in front of Tovah, who was the first of Manya's friends to approach the vehicle.

"Stop!" the guard yelled.

The truck was completely full; not one more person could be squeezed in. They had received a reprieve. With relieved sighs they were ordered back to the barracks. Manya knew it was only a matter of time before the trucks would have room for her.

That had happened a few weeks ago. Now Manya's departure day had arrived. Of all her friends, only Molly wouldn't make the trip. Instead of going to the roll call, they were led directly to the gate where vehicles waited. There was little commotion this time.

Manya knew what to expect when they got off the trucks. First they were packed into the boxcars; the doors were shut and the train sat; the temperature rose, the car became stuffy and smelly, and the weakest soon left them. They received no food or water for the journey. The collective obsession of the trapped women was to get out of this container. They prayed the ride would be a short one. It didn't matter what they found at the other end.

But the trip took most of the day, and it was dusk when the train came to a rest.

The doors slid open. They jumped down expecting a walk of some distance to the camp, but the first glance told them that that was not the case. The train had actually pulled inside the camp itself. They were standing on a platform. Manya looked around. There were fences on either side, running along in back of her and intersecting with a long brick building with watchtowers perched on top. The wings of the building were one floor high, but in the center, the structure grew to three stories, except where heavy metal gates spanned the ground-level entrance. The train had entered the camp through those gates.

Dark clouds filled the sky and there was a foul odor in the air. She felt a chill, but it wasn't cold. There were rows of buildings as far as she could see, and behind the fence on the right were men with the same hollow faces as people she'd seen before. Their striped pants and jackets and shaved heads made them all look the same. They were yelling out names.

"Is there a Chaim Nagelsztajn?" Manya screamed.

No one responded.

She moved closer to the fence. "Is there a Chaim Nagelsztajn here?" she repeated at the top of her lungs.

"Yes!" she heard from somewhere in the middle of the group. Was that yes for her or someone else?

"Chaim Nagelsztajn!" she screamed again.

"Yes, Nagelsztajn!"

Oh, my God, someone was saying her name! A voice was telling her her little brother was here! But it was only a voice. Why couldn't she see him?

"Chaim! Where are you? *Chaim!*" Please, God, let me see him!

"Where are you, Chaim?"

She saw a hand wave in the air, and followed it down the arm to—she lost it in the crowd. Again she screamed his name. There . . . that was it! She saw the face. It looked terrible—no hair, sunken eyes, drained cheeks. No! Those were not Chaim's eyes or his round cheeks. This wasn't her Chaim Nagelsztajn. This ghost-of-a-person was not her brother. She must have followed the wrong hand.

"Chaim Nagelsztajn from Hrubieszow!" Where was the voice screaming out to her?

"I knew Chaim Nagelsztajn." It was the same person who had responded to her before. It wasn't Chaim, but at least . . .

"You know Chaim? Where is he?"

"They took him yesterday to—"

The guards rushed in, yelling and screaming at the prisoners. She was pushed and shoved from the fence, and fought to stand her ground. But she never heard the last of the man's message about her little brother.

The Plaszow women stood in a row along the length of the platform. The door of a small one-story building close by opened, and three men stepped out. Seeing a selection coming, the Jewish women pulled themselves a little straighter, tried to smooth matted hair, licked their dry lips with drier tongues, and pinched their cheeks pink. They were ordered to form several lines.

The SS officers faced the women at the head of each line. Appraising eyes evaluated the female prisoners one by one. A hand signal communicated the judgment to guards who carried out the sentence. The lines shrank as people were shunted off in two directions.

Manya neared the front of her line and pinched her cheeks again. She was next. The SS officer looked her up and down, then gestured his decision, and Manya was shooed to a path on her left that led through some gates and inside a fence. She had seen most of the women being led in a different direction. She was going with the fewest number. Her experience told her it was a negative sign, but she took heart when Marie and Tovah caught up with her. At least they were together to face what was ahead.

Manya looked around as she walked, and gasped at the vastness of the grounds within the barbed wire. As Tovah had said, Plaszow had seemed enormous to them, but this—this was impossible to describe. Every bend in the road they followed gave a new and more overwhelming perspective of the gigantic enclosure. Off in the distance, Manya watched the smoke that oozed across the darkening horizon. It would be night soon, and she hoped they hadn't missed dinner.

They had walked for about ten minutes and were delivered in bunches to several barracks.

In the back of her building, Manya heard a woman's voice. She seemed to be explaining the camp to the newcomers. Manya was curious, but she had something more important to do. She reached into her hair and removed the tattered roll of diary papers and buried them in the straw of her bunk, then edged her way to join the rapt audience.

Seeing more faces draw up to the group, the girl started over. "This camp is called Auschwitz," she began. "It is a very bad place—a death camp. The path you took from the train was the path to life—at least for tonight. The other road went to the gas chambers and crematoriums. Tomorrow you'll be inspected again, and some of you may not come back to this barracks. But even if you do, that isn't the end of it. Every day they make selections— every day."

The girl's voice continued, but Manya had heard enough. Had she listened, she would have gotten a description of the size of the camp and the daily routine, and possibly the kind of work there was to do. But it was all drowned out by the fourth sentence the girl had uttered. It rang in her ears with a clarity that she couldn't deny. Now she realized what the man who knew Chaim was going to say when he began, "They took him out yesterday to—" In this place there was only one way that sentence would have ended: "—the gas chamber." She retreated from the group and pulled herself along the bunks, then fell into her middle berth. She covered her face with bent arms and let racking sobs engulf her. When they passed, she used numb fingers to draw out her diary and unroll the paper. Her hands shook as she wrote: "Auschwitz—Chaim dead." Then she collapsed against the straw and slept.

Manya woke with the first whine of the siren and stumbled outside with the others. Thirty minutes later, they were led to another building. Gun-toting SS lined both sides of the huge hall inside; a staccato voice shouted instructions over the wails of panic that filled the air.

"Strip and line up!" the shrill voice directed, bringing a new chorus of cries from the women, but no compliance with the order.

"Achtung!" the voice screamed, but they paid no attention. Then another command was heard and shots were fired into the ceiling. There were screams, and wild eyes searched for safety, desperate hands flailed, bodies circled the room, colliding with each other like ants in a stirred-up nest.

"Strip and line up!" the voice directed again.

The crew of inspectors pushed into the throng and looked the naked women over. There were signals of thumbs up or down. Manya saw a thumb point to the floor when they came to her. She was muscled toward one of two groups forming in the chaos.

She looked at the faces around her. Some were old, some young. But they were all strangers. Her friends were on the other side of the room. She had to get over there—she wanted to be with them. But she was trapped in a tight circle of females; more were added every second. A string of guards snaked through the middle of the room, trying to cordon off one group from the other. She didn't have much time. Dropping to her knees, she used her arms to wedge her way through the frenzied crowd. Sometimes she was able to crawl a few steps; more often she resorted to clawing her way across the floor and between pairs of legs. Any instant she expected to be lifted upright and captured by a uniformed arm. But the Germans didn't notice her escape in all the confusion. She stood up, only a few people away from her friends.

Manya's adopted group was taken into another room, where they received the usual camp issue. At the next inspection station, an SS officer eyed her hair, turning her around to get a better look. Tovah and Marie were brushed on down the process. A guard herded Manya and a few others into a third room. When she came out, there wasn't a hair on her head. She walked, staring at the ground, trying to hide her baldness with her hands. Her fingers fanned protectively over her bare scalp, incredulously stroking the smooth skin. She patted the top, then the sides, then the back of her head, fascinated by the strangeness. The shame that came from the barbarity was matched only by her fear that the action was a prelude to death.

The next time Manya looked up, she was at her barracks door. She rushed in and threw herself onto her bunk. Relieved that Manya was back among them, the girls formed a circle of comfort around their friend. They had been spared the barber's razor, but their hair was already short. Manya's had been long—long enough to hide her precious diary. What would she do now? The friends gathered closer to the weeping girl and promised positive solutions, reassured her about her appearance.

About forty-five minutes later, a bucket of soup was carried into the barracks. After they drank their lunch, they were called outside. Line after line of women stood facing a bank of tables. The columns inched forward in the autumn afternoon. Manya's knees buckled when she saw the tattoo equipment. She turned dreading eyes to Tovah, who stared back, then nodded her confirmation.

It was Manya's turn. The arm she held out this time was absent of fatty tissue, the muscles atrophied from starvation. The needle made its first inky puncture, then continued. Manya read an upside-down A, then 2, 7, 3, 2, 7.

As she walked away, her throbbing arm pulsed a message to her brain. She was prisoner A27327 of Auschwitz. They wouldn't go to all this trouble if she was going to die.

59

As Meyer stood in line for the lunchtime count, he thought about his near-encounter with death. It had been two weeks, and he was still in bad shape. There were marks all over his body, and the pain in his ribs was a nagging reminder of the countless kicks the Nazis had inflicted upon him. He was unable to turn over, get up, or lie down without help, and at work he used his arm to support his aching sides whenever he could.

He could never have imagined a worse beating than the one he got in Budzyn, but this one *had* been worse. As they had on that occasion, Adam and Wolf and the others shared their food with him and again nursed him back to something that approached living. But other than an extra bit of food that Sol and Felix came up with—how, Meyer didn't know—they had nothing but encouragement to give their friend to aid in his recovery. Meyer knew for himself the consequence of not getting up for work two mornings in a row: his body would join the others at the ever-burning fire.

Meyer spooned through his soup hopefully, found nothing but a few shavings of vegetable. One time they actually had had meat in their soup. Airplanes dropping bombs in an attempt to hit the plane factory and adjacent Nazi facilities had killed some horses. The Germans ate their fill, then allowed the leftover meat to be given to the inmates.

The men who worked in the quarry were in horrendous condition. Meyer was grateful that the Germans let him keep the job of driving the tram. If he had been reassigned to that hell pit, there would be little chance of survival.

While he ate his solitary lunch, he felt someone staring at him. Cautiously, without moving his head, Meyer glanced to his left. He *was* being watched. With nervous hands he continued to eat, never taking his eyes off the cup. He wanted to look over again, but forced his face down. One of the first things he had learned in the camps was not to draw attention to himself. He couldn't shake the penetrating gaze.

Meyer started to walk away, then heard a command: "Halt!"

He stopped, but didn't turn around, preferring not to see the blows this time. The guard approached and stepped in front of the frightened boy. Meyer was trembling. He hoped the man wouldn't notice.

"Tell me, what is your name?"

"Meyer," he answered. "Meyer Korenblit."

"Meyer . . . hmmm, that's Polish, isn't it?" the guard inquired.

"Yes, it is."

"Well, I'll call you Max. Yes, in German that would be Max," he said in a friendly voice. "My name is Hans-Wagner Gerber. Tell me, Max, how old are you?"

"Eighteen or nineteen, I'm not sure."

"You don't know how old you are?" the man asked.

"I have no idea how many months I've been in the camps."

"I see," he responded with a look of understanding on his face.

The inquisitive guard pursued his questioning. He seemed to want to learn as much about the boy as he could. "Where are you working? What shift? Where is your hometown?" With each question, the man became more friendly, but Meyer was wary of his intentions. This Nazi was treating him like a human being. It must be some kind of trick. Meyer offered no more information than was necessary, but then something happened to change his mind.

"Where is the rest of your family?"

"They were murd . . . killed by the . . . near my town."

The man's face showed a sign of deep dismay. "I'm sorry," he responded sympathetically, quickly changing the topic. "Do you get enough to eat?"

"The only time I've had anything substantial was when the bombs killed those horses. They put meat into our soup," Meyer answered.

Hans reached into his pocket and pulled out a package. "Here, take this," he said, handing it to Meyer.

Meyer hesitated, not sure what to do.

"Take it, it's all right," the man insisted.

Meyer's slightly shaking hand reached out to the mysterious package. He unfolded the paper. Inside were a few small hunks of sausage. Meyer's eyes darted back to the man.

"Go ahead, eat it."

Meyer didn't need further urging. He downed the scrumptious meat. "Thank you, Herr Gerber."

"Call me Hans, or Hans-Wagner," the man instructed.

"Thank you very much, Hans-Wagner."

"How did you get all those nasty marks on your body?" he asked.

Meyer explained the accident with the tram and being accused of sabotage.

"And you're still alive? You don't know how lucky you are. Even a hint of sabotage means death."

Meyer nodded his acknowledgment, then finally questioned the German. "Why are you doing this for me?"

"Doing what?"

"Well . . . being nice to me, giving me food, treating me as though I wasn't some kind of animal."

The man paused for a moment, as if he wanted to choose each word carefully. A faraway look came into his eyes. "Because you look like my son," he answered sadly.

Meyer was dumbfounded. "Like your son!" he repeated. "Look at me—you see the condition I'm in." Does your son look like a dead person? Meyer thought to himself.

"When I first saw you, it was from the side," he explained. "Your profile. But then I saw his eyes in your eyes, his face in your face." He sighed and went on. "He is fighting on the Russian front. He is only twenty-two years old. I haven't heard from him for a long time. If . . . if he is shot or captured, I just hope someone will do for him what I'm doing for you."

It was difficult for Meyer to imagine trusting this man, but for the next few days Hans-Wagner searched Meyer out to give him more food and to further their conversations. Meyer began to drop his distrustful barrier, and even went so far as to mention his friends in the barracks.

Then one day Hans didn't find Meyer at work as usual, so he went to his barracks. He located Adam and gave him two small packages. One was for Meyer's friends, the other for Meyer himself. Inside each parcel was bread and meat. At first Adam and the others were suspicious of the man's motives, but Hans-Wagner's generosity had now convinced Meyer that the man was a friend, and he soon laid their fears to rest.

The two men had frequent dialogues. They discussed everything.

"Germany is a beautiful and good country," said Hans, "with many fine people."

Meyer couldn't hide his horror. "Hans-Wagner, do you know what the Germans are doing to people right here? They are burning them! Many of those people are still alive!"

"Not everyone does such things—I don't—but there is nothing I can do to stop it," he responded, his voice rising.

Meyer had not intended for his accusation to extend to Hans. He didn't want to lose the man's friendship. He had never heard Hans-Wagner insult or blame the Jews for the war. The man looked angry, and Meyer hoped that Hans was showing his rejection of the Nazis and was only afraid to voice it, so he changed the subject. "Hans, I've noticed that you limp. Is there something the matter with your ankles?"

"It's my leg. I was wounded fighting the Russians. That's why I'm here. I didn't want to come to this horrible place like so many others did, but this is where they sent me to serve my country," he answered.

"Do you think this war should be going on?" Meyer asked.

"No! No! It's terrible, especially what they are doing here. We should never have started it. Hitler did many good things for Germany. Before he came to power, there were millions of Germans out of work. People couldn't buy enough food to live. He changed that. He made jobs, and people had plenty to eat. But this war is no good. If we don't stop, there will be no more Germany. When it began, everyone thought it was all right, especially when we were winning, but we are no longer winning."

Meyer tried to contain his happiness. For months they heard rumors, but there was never any way to check them out. Now a German was actually saying that the Nazis were losing the war. Meyer didn't know which to be more grateful for—the fact that his friend was supplying him with extra food or passing on news that could lift their hopes of getting out. He wondered if Hans's friendship was based partially on the fact that Germany was losing the war. But if he was caught helping to keep a Jew alive, he'd be severely punished. Meyer felt that the overriding reason Hans helped was because it was the humane thing to do. Hans's sense of right obviously outweighed his personal safety.

To be able to tell his friends the wonderful news made Meyer feel good. Anything that gave them encouragement was a most valued asset.

As the weeks wore on, there were times when either Hans-Wagner or Meyer would be assigned to different shifts. By pre-arrangement Hans would hide the food at a designated site. Meyer was glad it didn't happen often. He didn't want to be caught retrieving the food, and he didn't want to miss an opportunity for discussion with the older man.

"I long for this to be over, Max. I want to go home to see my wife. It's been quite some time since I've seen her. What about you, do you have a wife? Oh, no, of course not, you're too young," he said with a smile.

Manya's face flashed before Meyer's eyes. "Yes . . . well, no, not really my wife. We were never actually married. Her name is Manya Nagelsztajn. We've been together for many years. Even before the war. She is such a beautiful woman, with long dark blond hair that's soft, just like her skin. We were separated after the first camp. I have no idea what has happened to her or if she's still . . ." He stopped, refusing to finish the sentence. "From everything I've seen, it's very difficult to survive. Maybe someone is also helping her. In Budzyn, her good friend worked in the kitchen and was able to sneak out some food. Maybe she was assigned there again, wherever they went."

"Listen to me, Max. You must hold on. The war will be over soon. You'll be free to go back to your hometown, to find your Manya."

Meyer didn't know whether Hans-Wagner was telling him the truth or saying it to make him feel better. He wanted to believe it was true, that he had made it through this horror, that he would be free and hold Manya in his arms.

The weeks turned into months. Meyer couldn't help but wonder what "soon" meant to Hans. Again and again he repeated the words to Meyer: "Hold on, Max. It will be over soon."

As circumstance or maybe luck would have it, Hans did even more to help Meyer and his friends "hold on." He was reassigned to march Meyer's group to the plane factory. As they went, Meyer noticed an apple orchard on the way. After a couple of days with Hans-Wagner Gerber as their guard, Meyer finally asked him, "Do you think we might . . . ?" He pointed to the trees.

"Max, there are lots of people with us. If we're caught, it would be bad for all of us."

"No one will tell, and we could do it quickly while no other guards were around," Meyer begged his friend.

Somehow, Hans-Wagner arranged for the group to be last in line, and for a few minutes allowed the Jews to eat as much of the fruit as they could stuff into their skinny bodies. The agreement was that they wouldn't try to take any with them.

The food was a lifesaver to Meyer and the others. It, and Hans's insistence that the war was coming to an end, allowed Meyer to believe they would soon be free.

So it was a devastating shock to Meyer to be led again to waiting trucks. He didn't even see Hans before they were taken. Meyer knew why the man had befriended him—partially for his own reasons, but more importantly he tried to keep Jews alive because he disagreed with what the Nazis were doing. Meyer was sure of that. After all, the man could have helped Meyer alone, but instead he'd done what he could for many more, at great risk to himself. When this is over, Meyer thought, I'll try to find him and repay him. There was a difference between the two men, but as Meyer was packed into the train, he couldn't help but think he had just lost his "German John Salki."

60

For the third time in less than two months Meyer was on the train again. From Flossenburg he had entered Leitmeritz; then a three-day ride to Mauthausen; and after hardly more than two weeks, deportation to . . . He didn't know. He wondered if Manya's life had been the same since he'd last seen her. Alarms went off in his head when he thought of her. He had kept her safe in his dreams all these months. But now, weak and broken as he was, he had to admit to the possibility that she hadn't weathered the months as well as he.

He knew that he looked as bad as the living skeletons that greeted him in every camp. The question was whether he fell into the category of the worst of them, and whether his next destination would be his last. "Hold on," Hans-Wagner had told him, and he was trying. But the words that had been so encouraging ten weeks ago rang hollow now. Once every so often he would hear distant explosions. Maybe now, he'd think, reaffirming the potency of Hans-Wagner's words, but each time, no rescue came, and Meyer had dulled his hopes to match the tedium of the work he performed, the life he was forced to lead.

In Leitmeritz there had been another plane factory, modeled after the one in Flossenburg. Meyer was taken into the assembly area and handed a drill. As the parts came along the conveyor, it was his job to make holes for the rivets. He knew he might never have such an opportunity again, and he applied himself to the task with long-absent fervor. In Flossenburg, Felix and other drillers had waged an undercover battle against the Germans by making extra holes in the parts they handled. Meyer listened to his friends talk about their accomplishment, but he'd never had a chance to join the mutiny.

In Lietmeritz, drill in hand, it all came back to him. Here was his chance. Almost gleefully he picked up the first piece and saw twenty scored marks where the holes should go. He didn't know anything about planes, couldn't be sure his sabotage would be effective, but he didn't care. He drilled twenty-three holes. In the next one he made eighteen. If nothing else, his action would delay the eventual assembly of the fighter planes. He had liked that job very much, even though the noise was deafening and he was stiff with fatigue from holding himself so fearfully tense during each twelve-hour shift, as he thought up a new number to drill each time.

But the opportunity was short-lived. Only a month after arriving, he was selected to move on.

The feeling at Mauthausen was strange—trouble and death lurked everywhere. Meyer was assigned again to the back-breaking work of the stone quarry. It was a chore with no beginning, no end, and no sense of purpose. He spent every hour of every day lugging blocks of stone from the carved-out mountain to a pile that never seemed to change in size—due, no doubt, to another crew of workers who carried them from there to a new pile, and so on, ending with the hapless group that dragged them up 186 stone steps built by prisoners who had preceded him. As much as the dirt, sand, and exhaustion heaped on Meyer, he was thankful that he wasn't assigned to work on the steps. Perhaps that contributed to the air of diligence he tried to project as he performed his chore, back and forth, hour after hour, day after day.

Then it was over, and he was off to a new hell. The Germans couldn't seem to make up their minds where they wanted him. The doors of the cattle cars opened, and he stepped out. The familiar march toward the fences began. A new set of gates swung wide to entrap him once more. At the top of the gates, letters spanned the wire: "Arbeit Macht Frei." "Work sets you free," Meyer translated to himself, and tucked it away for later.

The grounds were clean; there were trees lining a fastidiously raked gravel road. The initial inspection of the newcomers was marked by a disarming attitude on the part of the Germans. The inspectors had been soft-spoken, almost considerate.

His old clothes and shoes were replaced, he was shaved, then fed—it was surprisingly good. Hans-Wagner's words surfaced again, mixed with "work sets you free." "Hang on, the war is ending." But the prediction conflicted with the conditions. It didn't make sense. If the war was ending, why did this place look so free from disaster? The only thing he could do was rely on his German friend's prediction and on what he considered to be a promise on the front gate of the camp. If there was a future for him, one beyond what he had known for so long now, he wanted to be alive to see it. He might not have Manya, but he'd do it for himself.

As Meyer was marched toward his new barracks, he called out to a passing group: "What place is this?"

"Dachau," was the answer shouted back at him.

Dachau, he muttered to himself. Where was that?

61

There was no need to record the tattoo in her diary. It was already permanently implanted on her arm. Had Chaim been numbered as well? "Yesterday," the man had said. "They took him out yesterday." That was so long ago. If only she could have seen Chaim, cradled him in her arms as she did while they were in the ghetto and when he was small. But maybe it was better that she hadn't. It wouldn't have been the Chaim she knew. The picture of him in her mind was of a shy, loving little boy whose eyes sparkled with excitement whenever he and Meyer played together, whose cheeks dimpled with happiness at the affection she and Meyer bestowed upon him, who tried to mask his fear with courage when he acted as her watchman in the ghetto. Yes, that was the Chaim she would carry with her forever.

There were over a thousand women in her barracks. The bunks held not two or four, but six scrunched together on each level. Manya's was on the back wall, directly across from the door. It was a good location because there was no other bunk in front of her to obstruct the view if anything happened, and nothing to block their path when the food arrived. Manya always slept on the outside edge. She felt safer there, maybe because she could get out quickly.

What food they received was even more important, every single drop and crumb, for Tovah wasn't assigned to the kitchen this time. They got no stolen food here. Their luck was running out.

There wasn't just one latrine building, but a whole row. Each was as large as her barracks. A large concrete block stretched the entire length of the structure, with holes cut out for toilets. There was no dress laundering at Auschwitz as there had been at Plaszow. What little water went into the washbasins disappeared with the first wave of women to enter each morning. Even though the facilities were much bigger and more numerous than those of other camps, there were thousands more people desperately trying to get in. Seldom did Manya or her friends ever make it to the toilets. Most women resorted to relieving themselves outside on the ground.

When they were taken to work, the march from their barracks to the outside of the camp was very long. They passed building after building on either side of them. The first time they were led out, Hannah whispered, "If those barracks have as many people in them as ours, there are many, many thousands more people here than in Plaszow."

It was a frightening sight, but it was nothing compared to the terrified feeling they had about not going to work regularly. Here they were taken to a farm or factory only once or twice a week. Working meant they were still useful to the Nazis; without it, all they did was occupy space. The monotony of being in the barracks constantly was as bad as the work they had had to perform at the other camps. Manya sat waiting; minutes seemed like hours, hours seemed like days.

It was with mixed feelings that Manya would pull herself out to the three roll calls each day. She wondered that the Nazis had nothing better to do than count people. She spent at least three hours a day being counted. But the roll calls did serve a function in her life. They meant that somehow time had actually passed and she had managed to slip by a few more hours. Would they be her last? she would ask herself as she watched the unhealthiest waved out of line.

It always seemed to be wet and muddy, and there was a constant haze over the camp. It was as though even the light of the sun had given up on them. When she arrived and saw chimneys on top of the barracks, she thought of the warmth they would provide. But it had only been an illusion. There were no fireplaces inside, only coldness.

Manya's barracks was near a row of trees; an electric fence separated her from them. She could just make out buildings behind them. These buildings had chimneys, and they worked—she could see the smoke rising.

The words the girl had spoken when they arrived were shrouded in darkness: gas chamber, crematoriums. They were new words in Manya's vocabulary, alien terms with increasing significance.

"Death camp," the girl had said. More and more, survival was becoming a remote idea. She prayed to God to let her live; to let Meyer live; to let Tovah, Marie, Hannah, and the rest of them live. Make it be over, she begged Him. But the evidence before her was strong: Chaim . . . death . . . smoke. That would be her fate if she didn't get out soon.

62

Dachau, Meyer had been told, was a model camp, and subject to inspections by something called the Red Cross. He didn't know what that was, and never witnessed their visits, but the name of the organization was delivered with such assurance and respect that he knew he should be impressed and relieved.

On the one day of the week that he didn't go to the nearby factory to work, he summoned energy from somewhere to perform his camp cleanup duties. It wasn't a new task, he'd done it everywhere—but here he did it differently and to a greater extent. Relying again on the pledge spelled out on the gates of Dachau and as a matter of frank self-preservation, he used great care in the duties he performed: instead of sweeping dirt into a crack in the barracks floor, he made sure it was picked up; scattered gravel was rounded up carefully now. He got a feeling of satisfaction from a job done well; it boosted his self-esteem and kept him far from the crematoriums that smoked day and night on the other side of the camp.

The routine at Dachau was little different from the six other camps he'd been in; the workday was just as long, if a bit more civilized. But the faces in the group that marched off with him each morning changed constantly. Someone who was with him one day was gone the next, and so on.

In the bunks at night, while they waited for sleep to claim them, they talked. Some shared rumors about how the war was going; others doubted that the rumors were true. A few spoke anyway of what they would do when it was over. But always a cloud of doubt hung over them, and no one could deny the smoking chimneys that created the shadow.

Winter turned to spring while Meyer was there, and the constant rains of the season soaked him to the bone, often twice a day. It was a cool morning, with an overcast sky that would keep the sun from drying them out, and Meyer and his bunkmates had just assumed their positions in the lineup. Thunder sounded overhead and a preamble to rain misted the air. The count proceeded. Then there was a delay and a conference of uniforms. A higher-up joined the military huddle. They began the count again. Drops fell from the sky. Still they were counting. Ah, finished. Another military parley. The officer cursed and swung around to address the prisoners: "There is one missing," he yelled. "One missing. You'll stand here until we find him."

Now the rain was coming down in torrents. Puddles formed around the feet of the inmates. All but the lowest-ranking military sought cover. No reprieve, though, for the prisoners. Striped uniforms that had hung in folds took the form of the bony frames they covered. Slices of bread turned to paste in their pockets. Gravel washed into the grass beside the road. Still they stood—through lunch and dinner, and all night long. Only a change of guards altered the scene. Every so often there was a spongy thud as the weakest keeled over. They were left where they fell.

At dawn, soldiers with clipboards took their usual posts. The familiar count proceeded. No explanation was given, no announcement made. The whole incident was ignored. The lines were dismissed. Morning coffee was doled out and the work groups tramped off through the mud. A new detail was formed to collect those whose bodies had given up during the ordeal.

Meyer found out what had happened later that day. The missing man had been found in his bunk—dead.

63

The day started the same as all the others. Manya scraped away the straw from the crack between the boards where she kept her diary at night. Her hair had grown some, but wasn't long enough to conceal the roll of papers. Manya prayed the Nazis wouldn't cut it again, that Meyer would never see her with a shaved head.

She sighed and fumbled for the piece of thread she had pulled from the hem of her jacket to tie around the diary, then poked the end through two tiny holes she had made in her dress. She never left the precious paper in the barracks untended.

The roll call was over, and all around, Manya could see barracks of women released for their work assignments. Manya's group continued to stand in the bitter cold. The guards stood watch. A couple of SS officers walked toward the group of freezing women. They began to look them over, then slowly started to check them. Selections! Please, God, let us make it through.

But the Nazis weren't conducting this inspection as they had before. The Germans ordered the women to hold out their hands; each pair was carefully examined. The officers were in Manya's line. Hundreds of women had already been chosen. She clenched and unclenched her frigid fingers.

"Turn them over," an officer yelled at one of the girls. The Nazis gave her a withering look and moved on. They never touched a single hand, as though they would contract a disease even through the gloves they wore.

"You, out!" one of them shouted, pointing to a woman.

"You!" Another was gone.

"And you!" Oh, no, not Tovah, please, no, Manya's mind screamed.

Manya held her hands out. She could feel them quiver inside, but kept them as steady as possible.

"You! Join the others."

He said it so matter-of-factly. Her heart stopped, her entire body shook. She felt her knees give. With a simple point of a finger, her life would be over. Her selection had been determined by the condition of her hands!

Hannah and Marie soon followed. All her friends were there. They had gone through so much together; now they were to die with one another, the final act as a group.

After a few more selections the Germans had their desired number. Manya heard one of the officers say, "Three hundred!" They didn't even look at the rest of the women.

Manya and the others were led away. She knew it wouldn't be a long walk. They turned right. Manya's heart pounded against her chest. The trees, the gas chamber, the crematoriums were in the opposite direction. They were being led to the front of the camp. They were being taken to work.

The Germans gave each woman a slice of bread. "You'd better make it last!" they were told.

Last! For what? Then Manya saw the train. They weren't to die, not today anyway, and not at Auschwitz.

They were divided into three boxcars. When the door slammed shut, the whispers started.

"Where could they be sending us now?"

"Does it matter? We're out of that death camp!" Hannah responded.

"Maybe it's just a trick or they're sending us somewhere else to die."

"Don't you remember what we were told when we arrived?" Manya countered. "No one leaves there, it's a death camp!"

"Yes, they must be sending us to another camp. They even gave us bread," Tovah added.

"But it may be a place even worse!"

"What could be worse?" Marie threw out.

Worse or better, trick or truth was not at issue in Manya's mind. She was leaving this most horrible place. She would make it through this day to see another.

The bread lasted only for the first day of the trip. On the second day they were given water—a single bucket for about one hundred women, but they shared so each person got a little.

"We're slowing down," Marie announced. "Maybe this is where we'll get off."

"Or just another stop along the way," came a disenchanted voice.

The train screeched to a halt. The door slid open. "Raus! Raus!" came the command.

They jumped to the hard ground. Manya glanced around. They weren't far from the camp. Snow covered the ground wherever she looked. It was very quiet and peaceful. There was a serenity about the place. Compared to the camps she had come from, this was like heaven.

The three hundred women trudged along the road toward the gates. As Manya looked ahead, she was struck by something different. No endless fences this time; she could follow the perimeter of the enclosure with her eyes. But that wasn't the source of her uneasy feeling. There were fewer buildings inside the small compound, but that wasn't it either. Then it hit her: there were no prisoners inside, no clamored greeting for the newcomers. Their arrival was quiet—marked only by the sound of scuffling clogs on the rutted dirt road. She looked for smoke. There was none. She searched for a scaffold. Nothing in sight. Then how would they die? She didn't know. What was this place? There was no one to ask.

Our hands, she remembered. The Nazis examined our hands. What did they have to do with this solemn little place?

"This is Lichtenwerden!" a guard announced.

The processing began. With so few to handle, it was over quickly. Two large female guards led the women to empty barracks. Lack of food was obviously not a problem for them. Manya couldn't remember if she'd seen female guards at the other camps, but it really didn't matter. If they were Nazis, they could be as mean and vicious as their male counterparts.

Manya and her friends hurried to find bunks together. When they saw them, they gasped. Thousands and thousands of names were carved in the wooden frames—names collided and intersected, spaced out at first and crowded in at the end, crude letters shaped by flattened-out spoons.

Where were all those people now? The names that stared at them gave the barracks a haunted atmosphere and conquered her first impression of roomier quarters, cleaner and more peaceful surroundings. This camp was no different. It was full of despair. Her optimism disappeared, replaced by the day-to-day numbness of the previous camps.

They were called out for the evening count, but when it was finished, they were led to another building with long tables and benches. It was a dining hall. They sat down to eat, hoping but not expecting something better and more substantial. The same nothing soup was dished out as grudgingly as ever.

The two female guards were joined by male guards, who paced in and out of the rows of tables. Suddenly Manya felt Tovah's elbow in her rib.

"Look!" she whispered, pointing with her eyes and head.

"Oh, my God! Is it really him? Is that really Schnauzer?"

Soon all the girls from Budzyn were aware of his presence.

Manya smiled at Tovah. "Maybe he'll remember you!"

After dinner the women were allowed to walk around outside their barracks.

"Go ahead, Tovah, it can't hurt," Manya encouraged.

"Do you think I should?"

"Yes! He won't do anything. He liked you."

"Only if you come with me," Tovah said.

The two friends walked to where Schnauzer was standing. He was alone.

"Excuse me, sir," Tovah began. "I don't know if you remember me . . . us. You were in Budzyn while we were there."

He eyed them carefully, not in an unfriendly way, but with an uncomfortable look. "I have seen many thousands of people. Why should I remember you?" he finally asked.

"You assigned me to work in the kitchen," Tovah responded.

He stared at her some more. Then a faint glimmer of recognition crossed his face. "Oh, yes. I think I remember you. We used to talk, didn't we? The last time I saw you was well over a year ago, close to two. I see you've made it this long. I'm surprised. Not many people do," he exclaimed.

The conversation came to an abrupt halt when they were ordered into the barracks for the night.

"What did he say?" Hannah asked.

Tovah repeated the story to the others. They felt good about his being there.

"Why are you so happy he's here?" Marie asked.

"I don't really know. I guess it's because we started out with him and now he's with us again. Maybe it's a good sign," Manya said in a hopeful voice.

"But why do you call him Schnauzer? Is that his name?"

The girls from Budzyn began to laugh.

"Oh, no. It's because of his nose. We gave him that nickname at Budzyn," Tovah answered, still laughing.

"I think it's grown even longer since we last saw him," Manya added.

It was the first time they had laughed about anything in a very long while.

The next day, when work assignments were given out, Tovah was assigned to the kitchen again. Manya and the others found out why their hands had been checked. They were to work in a textile factory. The Germans wanted women with the smoothest hands, so work could be done quickly. Women with rough hands might snag the fabric they wove on the looms.

They had to march to the factory in freezing weather. Except for the lint-filled air they breathed, the work wasn't difficult, especially compared to what they had done before in Budzyn and Plaszow. But the hours were long and monotonous. It made little sense to Manya that the Germans had taken such care to choose women whose hands would be right for the job, then put them in a building with no heat. Their already cold fingers grew numb, making work difficult and the chance of mistakes greater.

Whether it was the conditions in the factory or her near-starved body, sickness finally caught up with Manya. Tovah and Marie helped her to the camp infirmary, a small building with a dozen cots. But one thing was evident very quickly: it was much warmer here than in the barracks or the factory. A Jewish inmate acted as a nurse and cared for those who became sick.

Manya had a very high temperature and kept throwing up what little she was given to eat. The nurse thought she might have the flu, pneumonia, or possibly even typhus. She needed rest, a warm place to sleep, and some good food. But the only thing available was the somewhat warmer place to sleep.

"People who are brought in here are allowed to stay for only twenty-four hours. The guards will come in and check. If you're still here after that, they'll send you to another camp," the nurse warned.

Manya knew what would happen if they took her out of the infirmary.

The nurse took care of Manya as best she could. She kept cold compresses on Manya's forehead throughout the day, but her temperature wouldn't fall. Her stomach and throat hurt from gagging, though there was nothing to come up. When she did eat, it was the same soup, but at least it was hot.

The next day, Manya was still too weak to work. But she knew she must or be sent to the other camp. She had no intention of coming so far only to die in this place. She struggled to get up. Another wave of nausea swept over her, and she fell back.

The nurse leaned over Manya and whispered in her ear. "Just rest, Manya, until the others go to the latrine. I have an idea."

She helped Manya to the washhouse to meet the other prisoners, then whispered again, "Manya, I want you to stay in here and hide until after roll call and after they've checked the infirmary. Then I'll come back for you."

"Hide? Hide where?" Manya said weakly.

"In there, Manya," she answered, pointing to the cut-out holes in the concrete slab that served as a toilet. "There's no choice."

The nurse assisted her patient into the hiding place. Manya gripped the inside edges of the concrete slab with her fingertips and braced her feet against each side of the hole. The smell was nauseating. She tried to hold her breath. She wanted to pass out; instead, she moved her head to the side and threw up the food she had eaten only a few minutes ago. She prayed to God not to let her fall. What if she couldn't get out? "Hold on," she kept repeating to herself. "Hold on tight!"

When she thought there was no way to hold on any longer, she heard a familiar voice: "Manya, I'm here!"

Two hands reached down into the dark hole, grabbed her arm, and helped her snake up through the narrow opening. When she returned to the infirmary, she passed out, from both exhaustion and sickness. The next day Manya had recovered enough to drag herself to the barracks and back to work.

64

This was a place that reflected a fallen army and a rotting system—as rotten as the food Meyer ate and as seamy as the dilapidated barracks that housed him. No proud, pristine Dachau was this. This was Kaufering, the next stop on his journey.

Even the greening of the far-off fields in this season of renewal couldn't compete with the stench of old death and the hideous leftovers of a master plan that was disintegrating into individual plots as the Nazis worked on their explanations, their excuses, their escapes.

The officers in charge here were pale and tight-lipped, their faces etched with too much death, furrowed with anxiety. They administered the basic routine of the deadly plan stringently, but there were sloppy lapses. The guards were in a hurry, dipping cups into scant bucketfuls of sour soup and ignoring the cries when the line of prisoners outlasted the supply. Or perhaps they skipped a meal altogether. While the work schedules were carried out faithfully, the tasks were random and disorganized—the workers might sit idle at factory assembly stations, but the mandatory number of hours was fulfilled no matter what. Something considered important one day was immaterial the next, in favor of a new, more pressing German dilemma.

The plan had gone haywire. The result was an even more erratic environment for the Jews, who tried to keep rhythm with the heinous beat, only to be thrown off by a new syncopation.

The guards were older, replacements for the younger blood needed elsewhere. But the older men were no less vicious than their predecessors had been, perhaps more so in that their camp assignment hardly represented a career advancement. They took out that disappointment—and the greater one of a crumbling regime—on the only people more miserable than they: the Jews.

Explosions in the vicinity were louder and more frequent, and sometimes Meyer heard gunfire. Once in a while he saw a plane in the sky. There was no doubt that the war was getting closer. Rumors of German losses swirled through the camp, but there was no way to confirm them. When the sounds of war erupted, Meyer looked at the guards for their reaction, anxious to read some sign, some affirmation that the bastards could see the end too. But the muscles that twitched in cheeks and the eyes that darted in exaggerated denial belied the steadfast constancy of their duty.

Meyer still had his friends; they had made every transfer with him. The warped life they shared for so long had created a bond that could never be broken. They spoke more and more of escape.

"It's the only thing to do," one would say.

"But where would we go?" asked another.

"That's right. We can hear the guns, but we don't know whose— or where—they are. What if we do manage to get out of the camp and then run right into a nest of German machine guns?"

"It's a chance we have to take," insisted the first.

"We would have to go at night, that's for sure. Even if we're lucky enough to avoid the German emplacements, there's no guarantee that the other side would hold their fire if they saw something moving toward them. But let's say they spot our uniforms. How can we be sure they know we're no threat to them? What if they assume we're Germans in disguise?"

"I tell you, it's no good. There are too many risks," someone would decide.

"Every hour we spend *here* is risky. We could be killed off next week, tomorrow, this afternoon. We don't know what the Nazis are planning. They are crazier than ever. Maybe the work is all a front. We've seen the shortages in materials; half the time we can't do what we're supposed to because we don't have the supplies. They're just marking time. One by one, we'll all go up the chimneys, I promise you. I say we make a run for it."

"And *I* don't want to be shot while escaping. I've made it this far, and I want to be here when those gates are opened for good. I can make it another day, another week, another month if I have to. What about you, Felix? Sol? Everyone?"

They all nodded, and no one added the obvious "if they let us," but it hung all around them nevertheless.

"Then I think we should stay."

Some opened their mouths to begin the debate again, but they were too tired. Besides, there were no new points to raise; they had rehashed it again and again. They wanted to stick together on this, piecing their ragged spirits into a montage of hope, fastening it with the conviction that freedom was just ahead, and using patience as the varnish that would protect it while they waited.

65

Word was passed along as Manya and her group returned from work in single file. One woman leaned forward to whisper the signal to the one in front of her, and so on. They had talked about it for days, feeling each other out, noting the importance of banding together. The food was vile, they agreed. It was like eating nothing, so what would they really miss if they refused to eat it? What could the guards do about it?

They let the idea sit for a while to be sure no one would change her mind. If some of them did, the rest would be on the spot. But it looked like everyone was willing, so tonight they weren't going to eat. Tonight there was going to be a food strike. Manya couldn't wait to write it in her diary. It made her forget how sick she'd been a few weeks ago.

They were ushered in to the tables and benches and the soup was cupped out. The room grew silent as the female prisoners stared at the food before them. It took a few minutes for the guards to notice. Manya glanced around her table to see if anyone had weakened. So far, no one had.

A female guard, riding crop tucked under her arm, paced slowly from table to table, eyeing the prisoners. Her footsteps echoed in the room. She looked over at another, similarly uncertain guard, who raised her eyebrows in puzzlement. They clomped around a few more tables. No one took a bite.

The first guard tried to look menacing as she accosted one of the prisoners. "What's the matter?"

The prisoner's body stiffened with the direct confrontation. She squirmed a little on her seat, then felt the shoulders of those beside her press their support. The prisoner shrugged. The guard wheeled around to another striped dress. This one spooned contemptuously through the liquid in the cup and stared confidently at the uniform.

The guard decided a more general address was in order. "Why aren't you eating?"

There was no answer.

"I order you to eat!"

No one touched it. Many crossed their arms in front, perhaps to show resistance, perhaps to stifle noisy stomachs, maybe to arrest the impulse to relent—but no one ate.

"Very well, then," the angry guard shouted. "Back to the barracks!"

The group rose and filed out without a backward glance. Reaching her bunk, Manya pulled out her diary and recorded the triumph, amid a chorus of jubilant whispers.

For the fourth time, Tovah had been assigned kitchen duties, and she told them as they lined up before dinner the next night that a few extra potatoes and a little meat had gone into the kettles for the evening meal. The food did seem a little better when it was served. They *had* done it and it *had* worked. That night, there was a lot of energized chatting and more than a few grins.

Every day the prisoners were marched through the snow to the unheated factory where they worked. Winter seeped through every crack in the building, prolonging the frigid condition of the fingers that operated the looms. As terrified as Manya had been when her hands were inspected at Auschwitz, she now thought of the action as a compliment, a sign that she was still useful. If the Nazis thought so, she should, too. It helped to answer a question that was ever more prevalent in her mind: Where do I stand?

The cold weather seemed to drag on. Manya doubted that spring would ever come. Trudging back to camp after work one day, she drew the cotton jacket she wore tighter around her and thought of suggesting that the girls triple up in the bunks tonight. Then they would stay warmer during the freezing night.

They reached the camp and lined up, but instead of heading for the dining hall, they were marched off to the barracks. The buxom female guard with the riding crop accompanied Manya's bunkmates inside. Running the crop along the bunks as she strode to the rear of the building, the guard let the prisoners wrestle with what was about to happen. Finally she turned around and pointed at one of the bunks with the whip. She surveyed the faces of the prisoners. "Whose bunk is this?"

The prisoners looked at the floor.

"I want to know who sleeps here," the guard repeated. The group shifted uneasily. The guard bent down and fished in the straw. Manya's eyes bugged. A roll of papers was held up for all to see.

"Whose is this? Who writes on paper here? Tell me now, or *everyone* will be punished."

Oh, my God, why had she chosen today to leave her diary behind? There was nothing for Manya to do but step forward.

The guard nodded. Her threat had worked. "This belongs to you?" she asked Manya.

"Yes . . . it's mine," Manya admitted.

"Come with me!" the guard commanded, and led the way. Marie reached to touch Manya's arm as she followed the uniform out and across the compound. The female SS entered a building; a guard at Manya's rear shoved her inside.

"What is written here, what language is this?" the guard demanded, waving the diary at Manya.

"It's Polish," Manya answered. "I—"

"What does it say?" the guard interrupted. "You'd better tell the truth. I can find out another way," she warned.

"It's nothing," Manya began, "just a few words . . . it's nothing important—only things that have happened to me since—"

"What were you planning to do with it?" the guard cut her short again.

"Nothing . . . truly . . . just a diary, just things I wanted to remember."

"I don't believe you," the guard screamed, throwing the papers in Manya's face. She raised the whip and wielded it, crisscrossing Manya's body with blows.

"You are not allowed to have such things," she went on, puffing with exertion. The leather loop bit into Manya everywhere—face, arms, back, legs, chest, neck. Manya tried to cover her head with her arms; then the whip would land again, and an involuntary flinch would lower her defense. Finally she collapsed on the floor. Another guard dragged her outside and threw her to the snowy ground.

"I promise you, no diary will be needed to remember this night, if you survive. Kneel!" the guard screamed, yanking Manya's arm upward. "Kneel!"

Manya clawed the ground for the traction to obey.

"You will kneel here all night," the guard yelled. "Both knees on the ground—no sitting, no use of hands. I will be watching—you'd better not cheat!" She turned on her heel and went back into the building.

It was terribly cold outside. Manya shook with pain and exposure. A gusty wind cut through her thin garments. She wrapped her arms around herself to fend it off. It got darker and icier; she couldn't feel her knees anymore.

She looked toward the barracks. The floodlight at the top of each door cast its illumination on routes of escape. A searchlight inched along in its sweep across the compound. She had to close her eyes when it came to her.

The shivers were violent now, coming in spasms that threw her off balance. She put a hand down to steady herself, then snatched it away in case the guard was watching. Again the wind, and another spasm. The hand touched the snow. This time it stayed longer; there was no cry of discovery from the guard. She shifted some weight to it. A touch of relief for her cramping thighs. The searchlight was making another pass. She assumed the required position. On it went. She might as well risk it again. She rocked to the side and lifted one knee. Ahh, better. Now the other side. The guard couldn't be watching. She leaned back and sat on her feet. Blessed relief! Wait—the searchlight! She raised back up again till it passed. She continued to alternate her position, timing the movements with the progress of the searchlight. Late into the night she tried something else. As the circling beam approached, lit her up, and went on, she got to her feet. At first her knees wouldn't unbend. She shook her legs and rubbed some blood into them. They tingled, then burned like fire. They were coming back to life. But that cursed beam was only a building away. Back on her knees she went. An incredible fatigue came over her. She couldn't keep this up.

Another kind of trembling took hold—the kind that comes from within, and starts with a howl. Her diary was gone. She had been stripped of the last vestige of herself, just as surely as the Germans had stolen a large chunk of her life. Now they had stolen it again, and beat her with it. Her will caved in. She was going to die—not by fire, or gas, or even beatings. She was going to freeze to death, kneeling in the snow of this place that had looked like heaven when she arrived.

"Oh, Meyer," she whimpered out loud. "There was so much to tell you. Now I'll never get a chance."

66

Desperation had set in. The Germans were edgy and unpredictable, but the realization that the end was near didn't stop most of the SS from pursuing the hatred they had for the Jews by the cruel treatment they continued to inflict. Even without the usual means of destruction, Kaufering had become a morgue. More and more men died from diseases. The Nazis did nothing to help the sick, letting them suffer a slow, agonizing death. Others fell from the starvation diet, and a few just no longer had the will to go on to the next day.

The prisoners lived in the most hideous conditions. The general filth and smell of decomposing bodies was an incentive to those who could still walk to go out for work—to fill their lungs with air that didn't bring them to the verge of vomiting every time they took a breath.

If Manya was in the same kind of camp under the same conditions, Meyer held little hope that he'd hold her in his arms again.

He and his friends continued to encourage each other. They silently cheered when they heard the gunfire and explosions in the distance, grew ever more hopeful as they read the news on the faces of the SS.

The morning wake-up came and Meyer pulled himself from the dilapidated bunk. The roll call was done in a hurry, almost too quickly. They were given their coffee, and after that they were handed additional food.

"You'd better ration it wisely," the SS officer told them. "You won't get any more for a while. We're leaving. Those who can't walk will be left behind."

There was a light drizzle falling when they walked through the gates. Men who could barely stand tried vainly to put one foot in front of the other. They all knew their fate if they didn't drag themselves out of the camp. But many just didn't have the strength to even attempt the journey. There were those who were too weak to travel far but forced themselves anyway, thinking they'd have to walk only a mile or two to meet the trucks or train bound for their next destination. But there were no trucks and no trains.

The drizzle turned to a cloudburst. They were ordered to march faster. Some couldn't go on, fell to the mud road, and were shot dead. There was no stopping to bury them, no slowing down to help the stumblers. The guards simply shot them as they staggered.

On they trudged. The rain never let up. The dirt road turned to mire. Meyer's feet got heavier and heavier as his clogs collected more mud with each step he took.

"Faster, you filthy Jews!" came the command.

At the end of the first day they stopped and were allowed a few minutes to eat their rations. The bread in their pockets was mush. Meyer ate all he had. If tomorrow was the same as today, he wanted every ounce of strength he could garner. They were then ordered to lie facedown on the wet ground. Guards perched in the trees to watch them.

"Don't look up! If you do, it will be the last time you ever see anything, I promise you that," the officer in charge screamed at them.

Meyer could hear the SS officer order the posted guards to shoot if anyone so much as moved his head.

The next day was the same, only there were fewer of them stumbling along the road. Those that succumbed in the night were left where they lay.

The rain reverted to a drizzle. Throughout the day they heard shooting and bombing. On they walked. The sounds of fighting got closer. More people fell. It was the end of the second day, and they were ordered to the ground. There was no more food to put into their gnawing stomachs. They were running out of life.

"Meyer, wake up." It was Sol whispering to him.

"What is it?"

"Adam and I think we can sneak away. Do you want to risk it?"

"Yes, of course!"

"Tell Felix. I'll tell Wolf."

There was no argument from anyone. The Nazis might kill them at any time. It was better to die trying to escape than to be shot as they walked.

One at a time they began to crawl through the wet grass. Slowly, inch by inch, they moved away from the grasp of the Nazis. There was no moon to show their escape, and the continuous rain concealed the noise of their thin frames slithering along the ground.

They had covered about a hundred yards when Adam sprang to his feet. "Come on," he whispered. "Let's make a run for it."

The body said no, but the mind said yes. They all jumped up

and took off. Legs that had been too weary to function a few minutes ago operated with precision.

Then Wolf spotted a barn and flagged them to the ground. "Should we hide there?" he asked.

All the men answered yes. It would soon be light. They made their way to the rickety structure. It was empty. They threw their corpselike bodies into the soft, dry hay, each one breathing hard.

Finally someone asked, "What now?"

"We should take turns at guard duty while the others sleep. After everyone has rested, we'll decide what to do," Felix recommended.

They knew they weren't safe. They were somewhere in Germany, with striped clothes. They had no food and looked like skeletons. The war wasn't over and they would surely be missed from the group.

"Everyone get up!" Wolf hissed, shaking each person. "Someone's coming."

"Bury yourselves in the hay!" Meyer ordered.

Everyone dived into the thick piles. The door creaked open. Meyer heard footsteps walk past his mound and held his breath, sure that his heaving chest was causing the hay to move up and down. He detected some kind of activity—a scrunch/swoosh, scrunch/swoosh. Something was being thrown through the air.

Suddenly there was a loud scream. All at once five piles of hay went flying. Five scared faces fixed on one just-as-scared farmer with a pitchfork in his hand. They all stared at each other. No one moved or spoke.

Wolf was holding his leg. There was a little blood oozing onto his shoe. The scream had come from him. The farmer had stuck him with the pitchfork.

"We've just escaped from the Nazis. We need a place to hide!" Meyer finally blurted.

The man looked at the five figures before him with sympathy in his eyes. "I know. The Nazis are on my farm now. They told me they're looking for escaped Jews. They have dogs sniffing out the whole area. You hide here for now. I'll try to lead them away," the farmer said. He turned and walked out.

"He could be going straight to the Nazis to turn us in!" Adam said.

"We don't have a choice. If the Germans are out there with dogs, there's no way we could get away from them," Sol responded.

"Did you see his face? He looked like he really cared," Felix added.

"Yes, I think you're right, he was horrified by our condition. We have to trust him. Besides, Wolf can't run with that leg," Meyer said.

They kept watch through cracks in the walls of the barn. Hours passed with no visible movement. It was late afternoon.

"I see someone!" Adam yelled to the others. "It's the farmer, and he's carrying something."

Everyone scooted over to look.

In minutes the farmer had joined his five barn guests. "You were worried I would turn you in, weren't you?" he asked them. "I can understand that, with all you must have gone through. It took me longer than I expected because I thought you might need this."

He held out a large basket. Inside were fruit, bread, eggs, and chicken. Ten eyes nearly popped out of their sockets as they drank in the food, then the farmer, then the food again. It took them only a second to recover. Within minutes they had devoured the entire contents.

"I don't think you should stay here," the man said. "It's too dangerous for you, too dangerous for my family. If the Nazis catch you here . . . well, you know better than I what they would do. You can rest here for a while; then you must leave. I'll check the area to make sure it is safe."

"How can we ever thank you?" Sol said.

"Yes, we'll never forget what you've done," Meyer added. "You hid us, fed us, saved our lives by not turning us in. We'll repay you someday."

"I am sorry I can't do more, but I don't want my family harmed. Rest now. I'll be back soon."

The fugitives nodded gratefully and settled in to wait.

It took him about an hour. "It's clear, but you must be careful. There are German patrols all around."

They thanked their new friend over and over.

"Good luck, and may God go with you."

The five men headed for the trees. Luckily Wolf hadn't been

stabbed too badly and was able to walk on his own. After the barn was out of sight, they stopped.

"I know we'd be putting the farmer in great danger if we went back, but I think that's the safest place to stay," Adam said.

"I think Adam is right," Meyer echoed. "The Germans have already looked in this area. It should probably be safe for a while. We'll keep an eye out for the farmer and be sure to hide in a place where he can't find us."

They took turns again keeping guard. It was a peaceful night. The five men woke to a beautiful day. A bright sun shone down on them. They were discussing their plan of action when they heard the sound of engines. Sol went to the door.

"What is it?" asked Felix.

No one else moved. Sol turned around, and the tears were streaming down his face. He opened his mouth but no words came.

Meyer went running to the door and peeked out; then it was his turn to face his friends. He too was crying, but his lips formed a smile. Words didn't fail him.

"It's the Americans. We're free!"

67

Manya blinked her eyes. The sky looked . . . My God, it was getting light! She was alive! No, she was dead. She couldn't have lived through the night. She closed her eyes and listened. It was quiet. She tried to hear, then feel her heart. It was beating—slowly. She looked at her hands and felt them. They were white and hard and felt like wood when she rubbed them together, so she tucked them under her arms. With great effort she raised back up on her knees. No sensation. It was so tempting to curl up on the ground. She was so tired. But she had to keep checking. If she was alive, she wanted to know how bad off she was.

The siren went off and she nearly fainted. Across the compound, a few guards came out of their quarters and readied their duty sheets. She heard noises from the building just behind her. The door opened, and leather boots strode into her view.

"Still alive, eh?" said the buxom female SS.

Manya looked down. The guard took it as a nod.

"Well, then," she continued with a ghoulish curl to her lip, "it's time to go to work." She lifted Manya's chin with the end of the riding crop. "Get going—unless, of course . . ." She let the threat trail off ominously.

Somehow Manya struggled to her feet. The riding crop was pointing toward the lineup area. The guard watched Manya's struggle with relish, wanting to punish the girl for surviving the night. She seemed to have trouble deciding whether to prolong the agony or end it. Manya read the challenge on the guard's face and limped toward the line.

It took some weeks for Manya to break the habit of reaching for her diary at night. Each time her hand came up empty, it brought the whole incident back to her with renewed loss. She tried to recall as many of the words she'd written as possible, to lock them in her mind. Many things she would remember no matter what—even if she wanted to forget, she couldn't. Chaim dead, Cyvia gone, Meyer separated.

Tovah comforted her every way she could, settling finally on humming songs to distract her. Little by little others joined in, and eventually Manya's voice took up the melody. It became a ritual for the women of her barracks. First a few familiar songs as a group, perhaps a duet or two from Manya and Tovah, then usually Tovah would be prevailed upon to end it with a solo. Sometimes the guards who checked the barracks every night at curfew were late and interrupted the program, but normally the women waited to begin until after the guards were gone.

Spring took hold at last, melting the ice and snow and bringing at least some cheer to the daylight hours as the songfests had uplifted the nights. With the change of weather, Manya could guess that Passover had come and gone, but she was too weak to give up her morning bread for the customary eight days. They were all weak and sick, but no systematic selections had reduced their ranks and no new contingent of prisoners was brought in, though the population of the camp had dwindled somewhat.

It was after dinner one night, and the women were lying in their bunks talking. The guards should have checked them already, but something must have delayed them. The women waited, preferring not to begin their songs too soon. Still the guards didn't come. It grew quiet in the barracks. Quite a few fell asleep.

Then all hell broke loose. There were planes, ear-splitting explosions, machine-gun fire. The women dived to the floor, crowding under lowest-level bunks. The gunfire went on and on; moans erupted into wails.

"They're going to kill us all," whispered one woman. They pushed closer to the walls, then, sensing that bullets might crash through, scrambled the other way. Rifle shots spat in the distance, joined by muffled shouts and racing motors.

"What's happening out there?" someone croaked.

"Look outside," another pleaded, but they were too frightened. Ten, fifteen minutes later, the guns were quiet, the shouts louder. One woman crawled up to the barracks door and peeked out a crack. "I can't see anything," she called to the others. A few more inched along the floor to join her.

"The searchlight is out," one discovered. They didn't know what to make of it. Then boots scrunched rhythmically across the dirt paths outside. Those at the door recoiled and dashed under nearby bunks. They lay there crowded together and trembling all night, listening to noises they couldn't explain, missing the silence of earlier nights, when at least they had known what to expect.

Finally morning came. They heard footsteps approach, then the squeaky hinges of their barracks door. A uniform stood sideways, using the door as a shield. A rifle barrel panned the interior. They crammed their fists into their mouths or buried their faces in the persons next to them, anything to keep from screaming.

The uniform moved to the doorpost and took another sideways stance; then the rifle was lowered and the soldier stepped in. "You're free!" he yelled. No one moved. "You're free!" Eyes squeezed shut now peeked open.

My God! Manya thought. He's speaking Russian! She scooted noiselessly to the center aisle until she could see the man's boots, then drew forward slowly. Her eyes moved from the boots up to his pants, his shirt, and reached his helmet. He *was* Russian! He was saying they were free!

"You're free," the soldier repeated. "You can come out!" He
turned and left the barracks. Everyone left inside was too frightened to move or follow the man out. They clutched one another
nervously and sobbed.

"You go first," they begged each other.

Finally they couldn't stand it any longer and crawled out of
their hiding places. What began with fearful and halting steps
ended in a stampede. But once out, like well-trained animals, the
women stood confused, waiting for directions in the lineup area
of the camp. They stared toward the main entrance as the gates
were swung open, but they didn't move.

"I don't believe it!" Tovah cried, throwing her arms around
Manya. "I don't believe it!" But still they didn't move.

A soldier yelled out instructions. "If you're hungry, take what
you want," he said, pointing toward the kitchen, where other uniforms were wrenching doors wide.

"If you want clothing, help yourselves." Now he pointed at the
building that had housed the German guards.

"Whatever you want, take. We'll go with you to town—it's not
far. There's plenty more there."

There was another moment of uncertainty, then absolute pan-
demonium. Some of the women ran to the dining hall. They took
bread, tearing off chunks and tossing the loaves back and forth to
each other; hands scooped sugar and salt out of bins. Another
few made for the guards' barracks. Drawers were upended on the
floor; underwear flew in all directions, slacks that had belonged to
heavyset guards were held up against emaciated waists; belts twice
too large were tied instead of buckled, and when the supply ran
out, strips of cloth were torn from anything handy and threaded
through loops or wound around to secure a skirt or to hitch up a
too-long dress. Insignias were ripped from uniform jackets; socks
were pulled over feet deformed by missing toes, bunions, and
knobby corns.

Most of the freed inmates were escorted into town by the Russian soldiers. As Manya and Tovah approached the gate, they
clutched each other, half-expecting their exit to be prevented by
the Russians on either side of them. But the inmates streamed
through the gate, and clusters of them headed in all directions.
Manya and Tovah followed the soldiers into town, and as the Rus-

sians stood with them, joined the women who were taking night-gowns, robes, slips, sweaters, boots, shoes; marveling over face powder, cologne, combs and brushes, soap, cigarettes, and fountain pens. They fondled fruit, cheese, sausage; someone held up a bar of chocolate; they downed mugs of milk, pressed their ears close to news-blaring radios, and asked civilians for directions home.

Manya tore off her striped dress and found a skirt and shirt to put on. Then she and Tovah stepped into the street.

"What are we going to do?" Manya asked her friend.

"We're going home," Tovah responded, wrapping Manya's arm tighter around her own.

"But where are we? Which way do we go?"

"We'll ask along the way."

Each step they took brought Manya closer to the memory of her pledge to Meyer: *". . . there's something I want you to promise. When all this is over, we meet in Hrubieszow. . . ."*

They were out! They were *free!* The nightmare was over. Manya was going home—home to Meyer, home to her family. She would walk into town and head for the marketplace, go past the baker, turn right, then past the shoemaker, the tailor, the dressmaker, all shops in the brick building that was her house, had belonged to her family for generations. She'd tiptoe up the flight of stairs from the street to their apartment. Yes, that was it, she'd surprise them. Of course, they'd all be there. Let's see, her mother would probably be in the kitchen, and her father home from work, unless Ely had a soccer game. Her brothers and sisters would be sitting around the table doing their studies. She'd just walk in casually. Imagine the look on their faces! She couldn't wait!

68

As he looked out the train window, Meyer couldn't help but reflect on the thousands of miles he had traveled the last three years: all over Poland as a fugitive from the ghetto, in cattle cars

as a prisoner, going from camp to camp and country to country—
Poland to Germany, Germany to Czechoslovakia, Czechoslovakia
to Austria, and finally Austria back to Germany. But now he
didn't have to worry about where the train would make its next
stop, didn't have to be concerned about who sat next to him or
whether the train was full or empty. He could stretch out his legs
and get in a comfortable position. And he could stare out the
window and enjoy the beauty and peace of the countryside as it
passed before his eyes, without concern for who was riding in the
next seat or the next car.

It had been ten weeks since that April day when Meyer and his
friends were liberated. Meyer, Sol, Felix, Wolf, and Adam rushed
out to greet their liberators. Their debilitated condition hadn't
kept them from cavorting in circles and dancing each other about,
or from pounding their glee on the backs of the Americans. The
soldiers gave them food and water and listened to their stories
about Kaufering and the march in hopes that the soldiers could
save as many of their fellow prisoners as possible.

Then the Americans had loaded them into a truck to take them
to an infirmary. But before they went, Meyer and his friends had
something to do. They explained how the German farmer had
hidden and saved them from the Nazis and that they wanted to
repay him.

While the soldiers were a little surprised by the request, they
agreed to help out, saying there was a shoe factory not far from
the German's farm. They went there, and with the assistance of
the Americans, had carried scores of shoes and boots to the
truck.

The farmer was very surprised when the American truck
pulled up and out jumped the five men he had hidden. He was
extremely happy they hadn't been caught, and most sincere in his
joy at seeing them again. Meyer wished they had a camera to
catch the farmer's expression when they started dumping all the
shoes at his feet.

"What are these for? What am I supposed to do with all these
shoes?" he asked.

"We said we'd repay you for your kindness and courage,"
Meyer answered.

"The shoes were the only things we could find," added Felix.

"There are probably lots of people who need them. You can sell or trade them," Sol suggested.

"It's the least we can do for you," piped in Adam.

"If there were something else we could do, we would," Meyer said.

They left the farmer, thanking him a hundred times over, and watched as he waved to them from the pile of new shoes and boots at his feet.

The Americans took Meyer and his friends to the German town of Eggenfelden, where they received medical attention. Hotels in the town had been turned into living quarters for the Jews who were being liberated in the area. They were given three hot meals a day. While they could eat as much as they wanted, they were warned against it. The doctors had seen many prisoners die because their bodies couldn't tolerate the sudden abundance of nourishment.

The Americans repeatedly told him how lucky he was to be among the few who had been liberated, who had survived this hell on earth. As many camps as Meyer had been in, as many people as he had seen imprisoned with him, he was staggered to realize that his own experience represented only a fraction of the horror that had taken place. Meyer held on to the hope that Manya would somehow live through it, but when he remembered the weeks, months, and years and heard the endless reports of slaughter, his hope shattered.

There were many nights when sleep refused to come as he thought of the missing pieces of his life. He could mourn his father, his mother and sisters, and John Salki. But there were so many others whose fate he could only guess—one moment convincing himself that they had to be dead, and the next instant persuading himself that one or even all of them still lived. There were Josef Wisniewski, Franiek Gorski, Isaac Achler, Antonio Tomitzki, his own brothers, Shuyl and Motl, Chaim, the rest of the Nagelsztajns, and his precious Manya. He was full of unadmitted and unexpressed grief, unfulfilled impulses to repay debts of gratitude, and an unrelenting ache for family and love.

Meyer recognized that he was alive due in large part to luck. He was lucky that he had known Poles who were willing to give their lives to save a Jew, lucky the Gestapo who were hunting him were transferred out of Hrubieszow, lucky that Hans-Wagner Gerber had singled him out, lucky he had made such good friends in the camps, and lucky that he had the promise of Manya as his ultimate incentive. But there was another factor that swirled around and through all the luck: Meyer credited his father, for through him Meyer had learned courage and will and self-reliance. As a boy he had imitated his father's example; later—perhaps out of necessity, perhaps because Avrum entrusted the Korenblit family to Meyer's willing legs—Meyer was able to inspire the qualities on his own, for himself and for others.

Again he tried to convince himself that Manya could be alive. He wanted desperately to believe, but the odds were overwhelmingly against it. The images of violence that flashed through his mind were too strong: Salki shot dead, burning bodies, his father dying before his eyes, babies being smashed against walls, his mother and sisters murdered, the ground of the buried Jews still moving, and Manya's outstretched arms reaching to touch him as she was yanked from his life at Budzyn.

He had to face reality, but something inside him wouldn't quite let go of the hope. Maybe in a while, when he was stronger, better able to accept the inevitable truth that he wouldn't be spending the rest of his life with Manya, he could go home. But not now. Maybe next— His thought was interrupted by the train whistle. They were pulling into Munich.

Meyer was trying to go forward with his life, and the first thing he wanted to do was establish himself with some type of work. It would help get his mind off the past and plant him firmly in the future. He had been given the name and address of someone who might be able to help him get started in business. As he walked down the street, he thought he heard his name called out, but no one knew him here, so he assumed he'd heard wrong. Then a hand grabbed his shoulder and spun him around.

"Meyer! Meyer Korenblit, it *is* you!" the man said.

A little bewildered, Meyer stared at him. He looked familiar. Meyer didn't recall his name, but remembered him from Hrubieszow as someone who had done business with Avrum. The man had left for Russia when the war began.

The two men grabbed each other.

"It's good to see you are alive, Meyer."

"I'm glad to see you, too," Meyer responded warmly.

"But what are you doing *here?*"

"I'm living in Eggenfelden, and I came to Munich on business."

"No, no! I don't mean that! Haven't you been back to Hrubieszow?"

"No, I've thought about returning many times, but there is nothing left for me there. Only bad memories."

The man took hold of Meyer's shoulders in a firm grasp. "But, Meyer, Manya Nagelsztajn is in Hrubieszow!"

It took only a second for the words to sink in.

"My Manya's alive? Manya Nagelsztajn is alive? in Hrubieszow?" he yelled.

Now Meyer was doing the squeezing, pummeling the man's arms, pumping his hand. Then, for the slightest of moments his mind traveled back to Budzyn.

"Promise me, Manya . . .

"When all this is over . . .

"We meet in Hrubieszow."

69

It took several days for Manya and Tovah to reach Hrubieszow. Much of the journey was made on foot; a truck driver gave them a lift; and finally they caught a train.

There was no family awaiting Manya in Hrubieszow—indeed no house to return to. There was no Josef Wisniewski, no Police Chief Gorski, and no Meyer. One by one the hopes that had nurtured her splintered away. She didn't belong in this town anymore; it had taken little notice of her return. There were no familiar arms to welcome her home, no wonder-filled eyes to cheer her survival. Her homecoming was marked by anonymity and coarse reality.

As much as she tried to convince herself that it was a dream, she couldn't. She stood in the marketplace; the streets were the same and the storefronts hadn't changed. But when she looked in the direction of her house, it wasn't there. They got funny looks from the townspeople, looks that said, "What are you doing here?" and saw whispers exchanged that seemed to say, "Did you see—they're Jews. Just look at them!" Manya knew she looked bad—she weighed only about sixty-five pounds.

She wandered through the streets, hand in hand with Tovah, looking in the shop windows. They noticed a man inside the butcher shop who looked familiar. Wanting to be sure, she stared at him another moment or two. Yes, it had to be him. They went inside.

At first the man didn't recognize Manya, but then his face broke into a wide grin and he grabbed her and hugged her. It may not have been her family, but it was close to the kind of greeting she had dreamed about all the way home.

The man explained to Manya that he hadn't been back long himself and that the people who had run the butcher shop under the German regime had given it back to him. He told her he'd been in a camp with Meyer, but that it had been long ago, and he had no idea where Meyer was now.

"What are you going to do?" he asked finally.

"I don't really know. I have no place to live. My friend Tovah and I would like to stay together, maybe find some sort of work to do."

"Why don't you come live at my house? There are two other men sharing it with me. You and Tovah could take care of it for us, you know, clean and do the laundry and cook. I'll give you money to buy food. It's a good arrangement, don't you think?"

"Oh, it's wonderful! You're very kind. We'll do it!"

And so the two girls moved in with the three men, and together they worked at putting their lives in order. Manya thought frequently of leaving, but had no money to travel and didn't know where to go anyway. Besides, there was no Josef to leave a message with, and she had to wait in case Meyer showed up.

It was a few weeks before Manya found out what had happened to the rest of the Nagelsztajn family. After they were discovered in their basement hideout, the Nazis had taken them to the fox-holes outside the city and murdered them. Her mother, father, three sisters, and brother were dead; six more pieces of hope were destroyed. She had to lay them to rest, bury them—but there was no grave but the one she created in her mind. Her hometown was a mausoleum of memories, reflecting happy times, sad times, and worst of all, the end of both. Everywhere she looked—the marketplace where her mother had shopped, the houses and buildings her father had built, the streets where her brothers and sisters had played—memories taunted her, stabbing through the battered shield she wielded in her defense.

"Maybe one of us will survive," her mother had said. Well, that had come true. Manya was the lone survivor. They were dead, but not gone. Their faces and the memories of them would live forever inside her. Their memorial would be the wonderful stories of the Nagelsztajn family she would pass on to her own children.

About three weeks later, Manya was out shopping for food, and the next thing she knew, she woke up in the hospital. She felt a hand on her shoulder.

"Meyer?"

"No, I'm a nurse. You're in the hospital."

"What's wrong . . . I can't see you . . . where are you?"

"Shhh . . . please don't get excited, you're all right. You collapsed in the street and were brought here."

"But I can't see! I'm blind!"

"Please, you must rest—you're going to be fine. Lie back, now. We're going to take good care of you."

Manya fell against the pillows. She was blind. That's how it would all end. She would spend the rest of her life feeling her way around rooms and being led down the street. It was a cruel trick. Now she would never see Meyer's face again.

Manya stayed in the hospital for one week. The doctors told her they could find no physical damage. They attributed her loss of sight to the terrible conditions she had lived through in the past two years, plus the recent trauma of learning of her family's death. The doctors gave her medication, but that was all they could do besides wait and hope, and they told her to do the same. She went back to the butcher's house. Tovah was there to care for her, but they all knew this was a struggle Manya would have to fight and win alone.

Every day she prayed, and though she lay in bed helpless to move about without assistance, unable to distinguish night from day, in her mind she walked through the park and the fields with Meyer; in her thoughts she strolled hand in hand with him under the stars; in her dreams she saw him walk through the door and take her in his arms. Tovah was her constant companion, helping in so many ways, even knowing when it was better for Manya to manage on her own, listening patiently as Manya related a jumble of memories and dreams, trying to break through the dark barrier.

The pattern continued for three weeks. Then one morning the occupants of the house were readying themselves for the day as Tovah clattered dishes in the kitchen.

Manya opened her eyes. The room seemed blurry. She saw light. "Tovah! Tovah! I can see! I can see!" she yelled.

The battle was over.

Manya went to the park that morning, despite Tovah's protests that she should stay in bed. But Manya had to go. For hours she walked and sat, drinking in the sights and watching couples here and there strolling, sitting, talking, and kissing, just as she and Meyer had done so long ago. She refused to believe it wouldn't happen again.

Gradually she took up her tasks in the house, cooking, cleaning, shopping—generally settling in to the rhythm of her new life. But every few days she made a point of walking in the park, for it was there that she felt closest to Meyer.

A few more weeks went by. It was a hot August day, and Manya spent the afternoon in the park. She didn't feel like cooking, was even less inclined to add to the sultry atmosphere by lighting the stove, but it wouldn't be long before she'd have five hungry people to feed. She sighed and picked up some matches.

A voice boomed on the floor below, and echoed in the hallway. She jumped when she heard it. It called again, and now there was a thundering of feet climbing steps by threes.

"Manya!"

The word rang in her head; there was no mistaking that voice. She ran to the other room as the door burst open.

They reached out their arms and advanced dreamily toward each other, as if one was afraid the other would vanish. But this was no dream; it was real. It was all over, and as they had promised, they were together again in Hrubieszow.

"Oh, Meyer, I knew you'd come back, I just knew it! Oh, hold me, hold me, I love you so . . ."

"I got you back," he cried. "Oh, God, I got you back. Don't let go, Manya, don't ever let go."

"I never did, Meyer, I never did!"

Epilogue

Manya Nagelsztajn and Meyer Korenblit were married in January 1946 in Eggenfelden, West Germany. Meyer's good friends, Sol, Felix, Adam, and Wolf were in attendance. The newlyweds took a small apartment in a hotel and worked at building a life for themselves. On July 18, 1947, their son Sammy (named after Manya's father) was born.

In 1948, through a lucky set of circumstances, Meyer was reunited with his brother Motl in Eggenfelden. Motl told Meyer that he and Shuyl had been forced to join the Russian Army. Shuyl was killed during the liberation of Berlin shortly before the war ended. Motl married and moved to Israel later in 1948. In 1956, with Meyer's help, he immigrated to Chicago, Illinois.

Little by little their friends left Eggenfelden, and there was much talk of immigrating to various countries, Australia and the United States among the choices. Meyer and Manya were on the verge of filing papers to go to Australia when they learned that no couples with babies would be admitted as émigrés. Meyer was reluctant to apply for immigration to the United States. He had seen others wait with no luck for almost five years after applying, and he didn't want to be disappointed.

Without telling Meyer, Manya went to the authorities and applied for immigration to the United States, thinking they would have at least a year to decide whether they wanted to make such a move. It was quite a surprise when they received word two months later that their application had been approved, and they were to report to the USNS *General W. C. Langfitt* in Bremerhaven, West Germany, where they would embark on their voyage. It was with some reluctance that Meyer accompanied Manya and Sammy to Bremerhaven. In the five years since the war had ended, he had settled into their life-style and was leery of facing a new start. He spoke no English and had never heard of the destination chosen for him by his sponsor, B'nai B'rith: Oklahoma.

Manya and Meyer settled in Ponca City, Oklahoma, in April 1950. On July 30, 1951, their second son, Michael (named after Manya's mother), was born. With a family to support and a small apartment to live in, Meyer devoted himself to learning English and to making a living, and more than once swore he would never set foot outside the United States again.

Eventually Meyer was able to put a down payment on a tiny drive-in restaurant called the Dixie Dog. For thirteen years he and Manya worked sixteen hours a day serving hamburgers, dixie dogs, and french fries to the people of Ponca City.

In 1968 Sammy married Susie Platt. They have two children— Kimberly, twelve, and Todd, three. Michael married Joan Bravo of Oklahoma City in 1974. In April 1979 Meyer and Manya became citizens of the United States.

In 1980 Michael talked to his parents about his desire to chronicle their experiences during the war. As he grew up, Michael had heard fragments of his parents' stories, but had never encouraged them to go into detail because it seemed to be such a sensitive subject. Because he didn't ask, they decided to protect him and didn't volunteer. But in 1980 they were ready to discuss it, and Mike was anxious to listen. He spoke to Kathie Janger, a longtime friend, and asked her to join him on the project. They worked on it in the evenings and on weekends for just over a year and laid out plans for research trips. Meyer was adamant about not leaving the United States, but finally acquiesced to Manya's and Michael's urging, though business considerations didn't permit him to make the first trip.

June 1981

The World Gathering of Jewish Holocaust Survivors was held in June 1981 in Jerusalem. Mike, Joan, and Manya attended the conference. It was also an opportunity for Manya to visit with some of her cousins on her father's side, who had moved to Palestine, as well as to see her good friends Tovah, Hannah, and Molly. Tovah had visited Manya in the United States in 1979. But it was the first time she had seen Hannah since being liberated from Lichtenwerden, or Molly, who had been left behind in Auschwitz.

August/September 1981

Manya, Joan, and Mike returned to the United States for a few weeks; then, in August 1981 they traveled to Poland and West Germany with Meyer. It was a very difficult decision for Meyer and Manya to make. They would be reliving the nightmare they had experienced thirty-nine years ago. Accompanied by Mike and Joan, they visited Hrubieszow and as many of the concentration camps as they could find. In Hrubieszow they found out that Josef Wisniewski had been killed in 1944 when he was hit by a train. They found Isaac Achler in Mislavitch. In an emotional reunion between Meyer and Isaac, both men cried as the Pole talked about the love and respect he had had for Meyer's father. And they found Henrik Gorski and his sister, children of the police chief. Henrik explained that his father's activities had been discovered and he had been sent to several concentration camps. He was killed by the Nazis in Gusen (a subcamp of Mauthausen) for helping the underground and for hiding Jews. Henrik is not sure if they are still alive, but on the day his father was taken away from the house, hidden away in the attic were three young Jewish girls.

As the Korenblits were leaving, Henrik said one last thing to Meyer. "I want you to know, Meyer, my father did the right thing. I have no regrets. Knowing the outcome would be no different, I would want him to do the same thing again."

Right after that, travel to Poland was sharply curtailed and they came home feeling fortunate to have made the trip when they did.

December 1981/January 1982

For the next two months Mike and Manya urged Meyer to make a trip to Israel to see his elderly aunt, who had immigrated there in the early 1930's. The trip would also allow him a long-

overdue opportunity to see some of his friends from the camps.
Meyer finally agreed, and he and Manya scheduled another visit
to Israel in December 1981. During the trip Manya became aware
that a cousin on her mother's side lived in Israel. She contacted
him, and in the course of the conversation, Manya made the state-
ment that she had lost all her immediate family during the war.
The cousin told her she was wrong—that he had received a letter
from her brother Chaim after the war, postmarked, he thought,
Scotland. Manya was stunned and confused, but changed her res-
ervations and came home the next day.

Thursday, January 21, 1982

Manya and Meyer called Mike with the information. Mike was
surprised by the phone call, since he knew his parents were not
due back until the next Sunday. Manya was having trouble finding the words to explain to her son what they had found out, so
Meyer finally blurted it: "Mama's brother may still be alive!"

Joan was on an extension taking down all the information.
When they finished explaining what they had learned, Mike could
tell they were happy but a bit reserved. It had been thirty-nine
years since that letter had been received. Anything could have
happened in that time.

"Maybe we should go to Scotland and search for him," Meyer
said.

"First, Joan and I will check with the British embassy. They may
be able to help," Mike answered.

They talked for another thirty minutes, going over the whole
story again and again. When they finally hung up, Joan rushed
into Mike's waiting arms. He nearly squeezed the life out of her.

"Oh, Joan, we're going to find Chaim!"

"I know, Mike, I know!"

Then, as though reading each other's minds, they both said,
"Kathie!"

They raced to the phone. They would give her one more birth-
day present—the news about Chaim.

Friday, January 22, 1982

Because of work and snow, neither Mike nor Joan was able to
go to the British embassy. Joan called and enlisted the aid of an

embassy employee, Neil Matthews. She explained the situation and he said he would be glad to help in any way he could. Joan asked if he could look in the telephone directories of the largest cities in Scotland.

Neil called back in the midafternoon to report that he'd had no luck, but said they had many Scottish phone directories at the embassy and he would make them available. Joan told him that Mike would be there first thing Monday morning.

Saturday, January 23/Sunday, January 24, 1982

It was a very long weekend with little sleep. Mike and Joan talked about what steps must be taken if they didn't find his name in any of the phone books. They knew if Chaim's name wasn't listed it would be a very difficult process to locate him. But there was no doubt in either of their minds that somehow they would find—they giggled nervously as they said—"their uncle!"

San Francisco had beaten Cincinnati in the Super Bowl, but for the first time in his life Mike cared little about the outcome of the game. His mind was in two different places—the British embassy at 3100 Massachusetts Avenue, and three thousand miles away in Scotland. Finally it was Monday.

Monday, January 25, 1982

After hours of searching through the phone books, with calls upstairs to Neil to look in the directories of large cities in England, Wales, and Northern Ireland, Mike was disappointed but refused to give in to the thought that Chaim Nagelsztajn didn't exist.

He walked to the phone and dialed Neil's extension. A few words Joan had written down from the phone conversation of January 21 came back to him. He was so excited by the news that the only thing he thought about was Scotland.

"Hello, Neil, this is Mike. I know this may be a long shot, but I just remembered something else. Is there a Newcastle in England?"

"Of course! Newcastle upon Tyne."

"Could you please look there?"

Within five minutes Neil had located a Nagelsztajn, C.

Mike raced back to his office. At 1:26 P.M. he placed the call, and twenty-two minutes later, after finally convincing Chaim that his eldest sister was alive and living in America, Mike hung up the phone. Neither Mike nor Kathie could or wanted to stop the tears as they hugged each other.

"Kathie, he's alive!"

"I know, Mike, I know! I still can't believe it. You have to call your mother."

With nervous fingers Mike picked up the telephone and dialed. He looked over at Kathie; her eyes were red from crying, just as he knew his must be. They were both smiling.

"Hello?"

"Hello, Mama, it's Mike. Is Daddy home?"

"No, he isn't. What is it? Have you heard something? Is anything wrong?"

"No, everything is fine, but if you're not sitting down, please sit. I have something to tell you."

"Oh, no!"

"No, it's all right, Mama. It's good news. I found Chaim! I just talked to him. He's living in Newcastle, England!"

"Oh, my God! No!"

"Yes, Mama, he's alive!"

Mike hung up the phone and called Joan. He didn't give Chaim's phone number to his mother, preferring to wait until his father got home. Besides, Chaim had told Mike to have Manya wait an hour before calling. Chaim was later to exclaim with some incredulity over this action, "Can you imagine? It had been thirty-nine years, and I told her to wait an hour!"

Mike asked Joan to call Manya and to stay on the phone until Meyer got home. Then Mike set about locating his father in Ponca City, which turned out to be nearly as much trouble as finding Chaim had been! Meyer got home fifty-six minutes later and Manya and Joan were still on the phone.

For the next four days the phone lines between Ponca City, Oklahoma, and Newcastle, England, were in constant use. With each phone call Chaim managed to sketch in the story of the last thirty-nine years for Manya.

When Chaim was deported from Hrubieszow, he was taken to Majdanek and from there went on a death march, ending up in Auschwitz, from where he was transferred to Ebensee concentration camp in Austria. He had been taken away, as the man had yelled to Manya, but he had been transferred to another section of the camp. A week or so later, he was moved out of Auschwitz. Throughout his two years in the camps, he worked in construction, building roads and landing strips.

When he was liberated from Ebensee, he went to Italy, where he was told he could find a way to immigrate to Palestine, but the refugee centers were so crowded and the wait so long that he joined the Polish Army in Italy and was able to immigrate to England. It was then that a faint memory surfaced and he wrote a letter to a cousin in Palestine—the same one Manya saw during her second trip to Israel. After some weeks, he was taken in by a family in Newcastle, the Abrahamses, whose daughter Sonia and her husband, Bernard Lewis, remain close friends today.

After the war, Chaim searched for Manya through the International Red Cross, but her name was not listed, since she had never registered in a displaced-persons camp. He went back to Hrubieszow in 1968, but when he found no information there, he was finally convinced that she indeed had been killed. Today he continues his father's trade, and runs a small construction business in Newcastle.

He married and raised four children with his wife, Cecilia: David, Michael, Pola, and Julia. They are all married: David and Marion Nagelsztajn have two daughters, Lianne and Gemma; Pola and David Charlton have a son, Paul, and a daughter, Sarah; Julia and Graeme Nicholson were married in 1981; and Michael and Judith Nagelsztajn have a son, Adam, born in April 1982.

Friday, January 29, 1982

At 7:20 P.M. Manya, Meyer, Mike, Joan, and Kathie took off from Dulles International Airport on Pan Am Flight 106 for the seven-hour trip to London.

Manya was on her way to see a brother who for all those years had only been a memory. Meyer was to see not only his brother-in-law but also his friend whom he had loved and played with as they were growing up. Mike and Joan were to meet their uncle, an uncle they had never known but whose image they loved, along with a new aunt and cousins who four days before had not existed for them. And Kathie was to meet a man she had come to know and care for through Manya's heart and tears.

It was a one-hour flight from London to Newcastle. The airplane was on time. At 11:01 A.M. Manya Nagelsztajn Korenblit descended from the British Airways plane. Chaim is waiting at the foot of the ramp. It has taken thirty-nine years, but they are finally together. The young man who had only been a picture in Manya's mind is real again.

October 1982

Neither Meyer nor Manya can explain how Cyvia Korenblit (Meyer's sister) could have appeared in Plaszow concentration camp when they thought she had died with her mother and sisters. From Plaszow, camp records indicate that Cyvia was transferred to Auschwitz and then to Stutthof, but the trail leaves off there, although further tracing is under way as of this writing.